MW01487969

ON THIS DAY
Heavenly Food for
Spiritual
Hunger

Vol. II:
For weekdays of Ordinary Time-cycle 1

FR. BENJAMIN A VIMA

Order this book online at www.trafford.com
or email orders@trafford.com

Most Trafford titles are also available at major online book retailers.

© Copyright 2024 Fr. Benjamin A Vima.
All rights reserved. No part of this publication may be reproduced,
stored in a retrieval system, or transmitted, in any form or by
any means, electronic, mechanical, photocopying, recording, or
otherwise, without the written prior permission of the author.

Print information available on the last page.

ISBN: 978-1-6987-1795-1 (sc)
ISBN: 978-1-6987-1794-4 (e)

Library of Congress Control Number: 2024921234

Because of the dynamic nature of the Internet, any web addresses or
links contained in this book may have changed since publication and
may no longer be valid. The views expressed in this work are solely those
of the author and do not necessarily reflect the views of the publisher,
and the publisher hereby disclaims any responsibility for them.

Any people depicted in stock imagery provided by Getty Images are models,
and such images are being used for illustrative purposes only.
Certain stock imagery © Getty Images.

Trafford rev. 10/08/2024

 www.trafford.com
North America & international
toll-free: 844-688-6899 (USA & Canada)
fax: 812 355 4082

CONTENTS

Introduction

At a church service, I heard the choir singing a hymn, titled 'Seek the Lord'. Its first verse was: *Today is the day and now the proper hour to forsake our sinful lives and turn to the Lord.* That inspired me to focus totally on 'today' and leave the rest of my lifetime in God's hands and in my journals.

I was convinced that 'today' is the only 'day' available in my hand, that is very important to me to work out for my salvation and for the salvation of my fellowhumans. Today is the best day to forsake my sinful life and turn to the Lord. Such thought pushed me hard to commune with God fervently and wholeheartedly in and through his words, especially his ultimate Word, Jesus Christ.

And that is how I started to pay more attention to the daily Scriptural readings, which the Church has prescribed for her daily Eucharistic celebration. For centuries, the liturgical year of Catholic Church is made up of many seasonal cycles such as: Advent, Christmas, Lent, Easter, and Ordinary Time-cycle 1 and Ordinary Time cycle 2. I began to pray with them daily and gathered so many divine messages for my daily walk of life. The Spirit's words such as 'if today you hear his voice, harden not your hearts' alerted me to walk cautiously in right path.

In Biblical and Church history, we come across so many holy men and women kept their faith, hope and charity firmly and flaringly in their heart by meditating these divine words, praying; *Nourish your people, Lord, for we hunger for your words, which are without blend, silver from the furnace, seven times refined. Direct us to salvation through your life-giving words. May we be saved by always embracing your words.* And they were satisfied their spiritual hunger and thirst by the divine food and drink by praying with God's words. I want you also, my readers, experience such passionate embrace of God ON THIS DAY, which in reality is the only day humans can avail.

I present to my readers, in three volumes, my reflections and prayers on the Scriptural readings, prescribed by the church for weekday-Masses. I have already published vol. I, to be used in days of Advent, Christmas, Lent, and Easter. In this Vol. II, you will find my prayerful meditations on Scriptural passages which are prescribed for the season of Ordinary Time-cycle 1, wherein, as the Church contends, 'we consider the fullness of Jesus' teachings and works among his people yesterday, today and every day.'

Before you enter into this book's content, my friends, let me quote for you Saint Anselm in his work 'Proslogion' exhorting us how to pray daily with Scriptural words: *Insignificant man, escape from your everyday business for a short while, hide for a moment from your restless thoughts. Break off from your cares and troubles and be less concerned about your tasks and labors. Make a little time for God and rest a while in him. Enter into your mind's inner chamber. Shut out everything but God and whatever helps you to seek him; and when you have shut the door, look for him. Speak now to God and say with your whole heart: I seek your face; your face, Lord, I desire.*

With those golden words in mind, friends, start using this book. If God wills, I earnestly pray, your daily spiritual hunger will be certainly satisfied.

Fr. Benjamin A Vima

WEEK - 1

Monday

Jesus can change our ordinary day to an extraordinary one
(Scriptural Passages: Heb. 1: 1-6; Ps. 97; Mk. 1: 14-20)

Though with humanity Church calls the longer portion of her Liturgical Time of the year as 'Ordinary', her inner Spirit, quoting Jesus' words from his first public address, directs us to esteem our daily life as 'Extraordinary'. We hear the Lord proclaiming in the Gospel: *This is the time of fulfillment. The kingdom of God is at hand. Repent, and believe in the gospel.* It was the shortest sermon Jesus ever preached but it covered, as the kernel of all that he said and done in his life.

In today's first reading we see that things are changing: *In times past, God spoke in partial and various ways to our ancestors through the prophets; in these last days, he spoke to us through the Son.* Every day is one of those last days the Letter refers to. ON THIS DAY, now that Jesus, the Son of God, is here, he acts as the new means of communication between God and ourselves; we are gifted with a new way of life. Everything around us has changed by his Godly Presence. Consequently, not only the period Jesus lived, died, rose

1

was indeed an epic time; but also because of his continuous Presence in his Spirit, the world we live today is and will be an extraordinary Age. All that God had promised and pronounced in today's Psalm about his kingdom of justice, love and glory has been fulfilled in Jesus. The only thing left is we need to change according to his move. This is the first message Jesus declares in the Gospel.

Such a breathtaking portrayal of Jesus' ramification-Effects was explained concisely by Jesus who told us that the realization of our dream of living in that amazing God's realm is within earshot. When Jesus preached about such mind-boggling goal, undoubtedly so many were shocked; many were excited; but when he invited them to be committed to his discipleship, many hesitated to accept it. That was because he straightforwardly included in his first proclamation the hardest requirement to attain God's Kingdom. He wanted them first to repent for their ugliest past life and dust off from their inner spirit the filth of sin completely; and then to start living a renewed life according to his Gospel Values.

Jesus, knowing their limited strength and weakness, included one more reward to encourage those who wavered in responding to his call. As Mark underscores, Jesus said to his hearers: *Come after me, and I will make you fishers of men.* And the first team of Apostles immediately left everything and followed him.

Prayer: *God, Father of the Living! Having been called by your Son at Baptism we have started our life in fellowship with him and are trying to live upto his discipleship-requirements. We are also grateful to him for his permanent staying with us in his Spirit and guiding us to achieve our ultimate goal. At our lifelong climbing up to your Hilltop, we beg you to make us fully conscious of your mercy and goodness and offer our daily life to you as a living sacrifice of praise and thanksgiving. Amen.*

Tuesday

Jesus' Perfect Humanness is our original personality
(Scriptural Passages: Heb. 2: 5-12; Ps. 8; (Mk. 1: 21-28)

One of the Psalms most of us cherish to recite in our personal prayer is Psalm 8, in which usually we feel God's Spirit moves us to go deeper into our supremely-elevated humanness, despite its limitation. We see in the First Reading its author using this Psalm for exclaiming our usual reflection with some more facts about it. Our God is so magnificent and glorious that his name is revered throughout the earth; above all, the same unparalleled One surprisingly is "mindful" of us, the human creatures. The main reason is because he 'created us little less than a god and crowned us with glory and honor'. In this vein, God thinks always about us; and he cares for us.

Interestingly, the same author in his reviewing this Psalm underscores there is a classic reference to Jesus Christ, whom God sent to us not only to expose what the genuine and perfect humanness is all about; but also to pave the way for attaining it. Even though he for a little while was made lower than the angels, he was crowned with glory and honor because he suffered death for the sake of entire humanity. The stunning thing found in Jesus was, though he had existed already in the Father, who created us and intended glory and honor for us, he died so that we might become the men and women we were created to be. In fact, even though we are sinners and living beneath our rightful glory and honor, he is not ashamed to call us brothers and sisters.

It is this Good News we hear often in the Gospels. Mark superbly portrays it in a concise and precise way He confirms, Jesus demonstrated this truth, not merely by his authoritative teaching but much more by his deeds of casting out the evil demons against whom his teachings targeted. Surprisingly, we see these demons possess certain devotee, who had gathered to pray and hear God's words in one of their synagogues. And Jesus who came to pray there, he cast out that demon. People were wonderstruck in hearing and seeing him. Indeed he spoke with the authority of God. He spoke in such a way that people found out his words and deeds effected change and transformations in people's lives.

Prayer: *Father, Creator of all that is good, we gratefully concede that you have made us little less than a god; moreover, you have called us to work in your world with Jesus' Spirit to better the condition of mankind. But we humbly confess we behave below to our awesome dignity and responsibility. Grant that we may always live and work together with Jesus to realize your 'mega-dream' in this world and the world to come. Amen.*

Wednesday

Jesus became like us so that we become like him
(Scriptural Passages: Heb. 2: 14-18; Ps. 105; Mk. 1: 29-39)

Jesus, being a chivalrous Jewish Man and yet, being truly the Son of God, lived through his short-lived earthly life, filled with uplifting dialogical human contacts and healing activities. We read in the beginning chapter of Mark's Gospel a kind of summary of what Jesus committed himself to throughout his public life. Healing the sick, driving out many demons, preaching God's Kingdom and simply being the attractive person he was, by drawing wide interest among the crowds and especially among his special friends, the disciples. *The whole town*

4

gathered at the door. Jesus deals with them as they need him to minister to their ills.

Jesus' daily life-schedule didn't finish with the above-mentioned activities. Gospel indicates that he arose and went to a deserted place where *he prayed.* By adding ceaseless prayer into his daily timetable he recognized the interplay between his gracious activity among those in need and the need himself to acknowledge the relationship with his Father God. That relationship was central to his work, his words, and especially to himself as God's Son.

Jesus came to live among us because it was the Masterplan of heavenly Father to redeem and renew the glorious humanness he had created through Jesus' bloodshed and brokenbody. Jesus' main purpose of becoming Emmanuel is to deliver us from all evils, especially the evil of being afraid of evils around us. He encourages us in words and actions not to be anxious about our lives. Like the Psalmist he expects us, holding on to Father God's promises, we should give thanks to the Father and call on his name. He assures us that God the Father remembers his covenant forever.

Besides, God desired his Son to be a pattern of how a renewed humanness should live and possess his Kingdom. Jesus obeyed his Father *to* become like humans and related himself to them as his brothers and sisters in every way that he might be and he himself was tested through what he suffered so that he can be not only a merciful and faithful high priest before God to expiate humans' sins but also to free all his human siblings from fear of death and from the slavery of fear.

Prayer: *Benevolent God! In Jesus we find your unprecedented love with which you dive to our core and does not settle for what we are. Wherever we go, in Jesus' Spirit you*

are already there. We are alive and grateful. Realizing our own
poverty of being blindfolded to your Presence of Emmanuel, we
entreat you to open our inner eyes to find you within us and
around us, especially in the needy. Amen.

Thursday

Hardheartedness spreads unclean virus among humans
(Scriptural Passages: Heb. 3: 7-14; Ps. 95; Mk. 1: 40-45)

When Jesus told us to be perfect just as the heavenly
Father, he was stating a positive goal of his disciples' life.
But from all Scriptural teachings and miraculous deeds
we discover the same recommendation contains a negative
aim of our life. In the Letter to the Hebrews the Author
repeats what God's Spirit urges us in today's Psalm: *If
today you would hear his voice, harden not your hearts as at the
rebellion in the day of testing in the desert.*

In Scriptures the term 'heart' indicates to an
intangible heart, which is a composition of all the
components of our soul-our mind, emotion and will,
plus the most important part of our spirit-our conscience.
Vatican Council II Constitution "The Church in the
Modern World (para 16) sums up the entire Scriptural
description of this heart concisely: *Man has in his heart
a law written by God. To obey it is the very dignity of man:
according to it he will be judged. Conscience is the most secret
core and sanctuary of man. There he is alone with God, whose
voice echoes in his depths.*

Our intangible inner spirit clamors for, as Jesus
pointed out, *where your treasure is, there also will your
heart be.* And as feeble as it is, our heart seeks worldly
treasures in any crooked way possible and as the Letter to

Hebrews enunciates, it makes errors that provoke God's goodness and love and becomes evil and unfaithful heart. Consequently, we are under the curse of the Almighty and lose entering into his restful life.

This evil-oriented heart leads us to being unclean and sick, and the Bible qualifies it as sort of leprosy of the soul. Jesus took this case of humans very seriously and by curing physical leprosy of his fellowhumans as a sign of his ability to cure our spiritual leprosy of the heart. He also testifies to the typical cause of humans' deadly leprosy of sins is the lust of transient fame and reputation. We find him completely negating that lust in his life through his order to the healed leper: *See that you tell no one anything about who and how of his healing.* To avoid popularity, he also remained outside in deserted places in prayer and solitude with his Father.

Prayer: *Jesus, meek and humble of heart! We have formed our human hearts, by wrapping them in lust of popularity, fame and pride; they have become dead but sheathing out only unclean and sinful odor. Grant us Lord a longing to be in solitude with our Father so that every good that comes out of us be life-giving and not life-destroying; and that we may not cooperate with hardhearted people by whom your beautiful world is desecrated and unclean. Amen.*

Friday

For all of us 'Rest in God's Peace' is the need of the day
(Scriptural Passages: Heb. 4: 1-11; Ps. 95; Mk. 2: 1-12)

In the light of Jesus, we are glad to profess that, 'every malady we encounter in earthly life is for demonstrating the glory of God'. Jesus insisted that any sufferings we undergo in this world, as he did, if we willingly bear them with him, would be the great sources of redemption to ourselves and the humanity. However, he was so sympathetic and concerned to the sick and the suffering that we find him from the start of his public ministry he went about doing good deeds of healing sick persons.

Surely through such miracles Jesus proved as God's Son, who possessed immense power of healing; at the same time, he too loudly declared his immense power to eradicate human sins which are truly the roots of all evil. In the event of healing a paralytic man, we hear him saying first to the onlookers: 'That you may know that the Son of Man has authority to forgive sins on earth', and then to the paralytic: 'I say to you, rise, pick up your mat, and go home.' In this way, he called us to be convinced of such mindblowing revelation of God's glory became visible.

By performing a miracle of healing the paralytic on the Sabbath Day and connecting it to his forgiving of human sins, Jesus expressed this eternal truth that our human rest-ritual or social is not staying inactive like the condition of a paralytic person, but moving around to perform good deeds of mercy, justice and peace as Jesus. It means to act totally in accordance with God's will and realize our earthly goal of God's Rest.

The Letter to the Hebrews emphasizes this goal of restful peace as God-given privilege to us. Quoting the Psalm again, the Author confirms that the Sabbath rest God entered in, after his creation-works and mandated us to celebrate the resting in God as the main goal of our earthly life. Whoever enters into God's rest, rests from his own works as God did from his.

Prayer: *Lord, thank you for revealing to us that you are the healing source that came down from heaven. You possess* *unthinkable power of bestowing us the most needed healing of our inner spirit, damaged, wounded and paralyzed by sin; and thus, we lose our true restfulness. We know you are welcoming us stating: 'Come to me all you labor and on burden; I will give you rest.' We humbly today surrender to your compassion and love. Amen.*

Saturday

It is worth to be hurt by the Word for our wholistic healing
(Scriptural Passages: Heb. 4: 12-16; Ps. 19; Mk. 2: 13-17)

As Letter to the Hebrews asserts, Jesus is a true sympathizer of every human being, not only because he was born and bred like us and underwent the exact consequences and challenges of earthly life but also mainly, he is the Word of God who possesses all power to penetrate into the deepest recesses of our thoughts and feelings, "sharper than any two-edged sword". He is "living and active". By his words our most inmost thoughts and intentions are evaluated and judged as we make our quest for that eternal "rest" in God's bosom.

The Psalmist also praises, the words that come from Triune God, in the form of law, or precept or decree, or command, or ordinance, are the sources of Spirit and Life; they are perfect; they refresh our soul; they are trustworthy; they offer wisdom; they are right and just; they make us rejoicing; they are clear and candid; they enlighten our inner eye; they are pure and true; and they endure forever.

Jesus, whom we believe as the High Priest in the abode of God, and God's Word of compassion and love, never missed inviting any human being because of their sinful background. Gospels deliberate this factual truth especially in narrating the event of Jesus calling Matthew, a public sinner to join his Apostolic Team. Jesus' entire mission has been one of redeeming and restoring us to wholeness; he never goes by stereotypes; nor does he judge us by our past behavior. He is only interested in what we can be now and in the future.

We find him also choosing to be mingling with us as Emmanuel and heavenly Physician. He portrayed us sick persons who are in need of healing and rehabilitation. Hence, he said plainly: *Those who are well do not need a physician, but the sick do. I did not come to call the righteous but sinners.* Indeed, Jesus' straightforward invitation to us sharply hurts, as the two-edged sword, our fake human prestige and self-esteem, reminding us that everyone of us is a sinner, whom Jesus has been associating.

Prayer: *Lord, you love all people with a deep and perfect love. You came, especially, for those whose lives were broken and sinful. One among them surely me. Help me to understand your merciful and forgiving behavior of living happily in my company, though I am sinful. Grant also to always seek out those who are sick and sinful in need and to love every one of them with an unwavering and non-judgmental love. Amen.*

WEEK - 2

Monday

A new life of true joy is the product of
obediently suffering with Christ
(Scriptural Passages: Heb. 5: 1-10; Ps. 110; Mk. 2:18-22)

In the Letter to the Hebrews today we hear about Jesus' unique High Priestly honor, granted by the heavenly Father, in line with God's pronouncement: *You are my son; this day I have begotten you.* The Letter also, under the guidance of the Spirit, spells out quoting the prophetical statement of the Psalmist that Jesus is priest forever according to the order of Melchizedek.

In addition, the same Letter ascertains that Jesus gained this Godly reward as he perfected himself by undergoing all his sufferings in obedience. Thus, he also became the source of eternal salvation for all who follow him. Sufferings and particularly death-moments, have always appeared to the human conscious mind as unnecessary, futile, a huge waste. But we, who firmly hold the enlightening and revealing words in Scriptures, believe that Jesus, though he was God's Son, *learned obedience from what he suffered; and when he was made perfect, he became the source of eternal salvation for all who obey him.*

Besides being a High Priest, Jesus reminds us in today's Gospel, that he is also our Bridegroom from the heavenly places; he indicates that truly his presence with us should be a reason for joy. *Can the wedding guests fast while the bridegroom is with them?* And, using the practical metaphors of clothing-repair and wine-storage, he explains, the joy, he promises, is a legitimate product of his role of High Priesthood through which he brought a new covenant, new law, new hope, and new life. He can make all things new.

This kind of faith and surrender to God and His Son, gives us restoration. It transforms our earthly life, being lived according to the Spirit, to a joyful way of taking part in the good life we can have with God in Christ and not as a burdensome obligation.

Prayer: *Heavenly God, We are grateful to you for not only sending your Son to us but also elevated and glorified him as the High Priest in your heavenly Sanctuary. In the light of your Son's encouraging words, we too are blessed with sharing his priesthood in our Baptism and with the efficacy of all our prayers presented to you through him. Hence, we present today all our needs confidently as we join with our High priest in offering our entire life as a sacrifice of praise and thanksgiving to you. Amen.*

Tuesday

We, the dust, are enabled in Jesus to be
lording over earthly matters
(Scriptural Passages: Heb. 6: 10-20; Ps. 110; Mk. 2: 23-28)

Whatever much we have reached high in our human development, when it comes to developing in the ways of God, we are all only learners. The Lord always has much to teach us. The Lord continues to speak to us and to teach and enlighten us in and through his word. That is why we approach the Scriptures in a spirit of openness and humility.

God's people in Jesus' time, were convinced, very firmly but thoughtlessly, about God's Laws and his directions, including their religious approach and interpretation of Sabbath observation. In fact, to their mind, meticulous observation of Sabbath regulations was more important than being truthful and compassionate toward fulfilling fellowhumans' basic needs.

To the wisdom of God all religious practices are only and primarily for his human children to glorify him by their love-deeds and not neglecting their duties to take care of their basic needs. Hence, today we hear Jesus stating in the Gospel: *The Sabbath was made for humankind, and not humankind for the Sabbath.* He included one more subtle message. Relating himself as the Son of man, he pointed out all human creatures, as sons and daughters of God, are not only coworkers in God's creating, providing and redeeming works, but above all, they are the masters of their destiny of Rest.

Letter to the Hebrews today affirms this factual truth of unfathomable interactions occurring between God and humans. The just God will not overlook our good works

13

of love done to our needy neighbors and our faithful performance of all religious rituals.

Besides, the same Letter instructs us that we should show the same carefulness to realize the full assurance of hope to the very end, so that we may not become sluggish, but imitators of those forebears like Abraham and others, who through faith and patience inherit the promises God has delivered; and in a very special manner, based on Jesus, our High Priest, we must hold relentless hope, a sure and steadfast anchor of the soul, a hope that we will enter the inner shrine of God, where Jesus, a forerunner on our behalf, has already entered.

Prayer: *Lord, with the Psalmist today we gratefully acknowledge that you eternally remember your covenant with us; we have encountered so many of your great deeds of justice, compassion and love. Now help us Father with your Spirit of wisdom so that we are worthy enough to our dignified status, as your Son declared, and prevail against all evils by our consecrated human intelligence and goodness. Amen.*

Wednesday

God is the Lord of life, not of death; of peace, not of violence
(Scriptural Passages: Heb. 7:1-3, 15-17; Ps. 110; Mk. 3:1-6)

Human life is overwhelmingly filled with conflicts and struggles between the good and the evil. The Spirit enlightens us today to reflect on some of his solutions to cope with such life's challenges. We read in the Letter to the Hebrews that a priest called Melchisedek, meaning 'king of righteousness and king of peace', met Abraham. To our surprise, the normally peace-loving person, Abraham, was on his way back from the warzone where he with his men had fought and won the local chiefs in order to rescue his relatives from those violent plundering terrorists. And for such righteous accomplishment, he was blessed by Melchisedek.

We hear from the Author of the Letter to the Hebrews and in addition the prophetic words of the Psalmist declaring that Jesus our Master is a priest forever, possessing a unique power not only of defeating evils and evildoers but also of bestowing blessings of peaceful and just life, like the peace-loving priest and king Melchisedek.

Jesus was seen in the short tenure of his life, confronting often with his opponents, and winning them by not violence but by sharing his love, and his very life. In one such conflict with his inimical religious leaders, which was purely on what is allowed on the Sabbath, we notice Jesus in today's Gospel being deeply grieved by his opponents' insistence that not even a work of healing should be allowed on the day of the Lord. But he made it clear that it is above all a day for life-giving activities. He proclaimed this truth, not merely by words but much more so with his compassionate deed of healing the withered hand of a human in the synagogue.

By such lovable action Jesus teaches us how to confront and even fight with the evils and evildoers. It is a strange paradox, but one that is often true to life, that good can sometimes provoke an evil response. The goodness of some brings out evil in others. Yet Jesus teaches us that goodness is its own reward. He stresses, indeed, that God is the Lord of life, not of death; of peace, not of violence; of justice, not of oppression.

Prayer: *Almighty God of Justice and compassion! Your Son Jesus has paved to us a paradoxical but an admirable way of life in which he persisted in the good work that you gave him to do, regardless of his hostile reception by fellowhumans. Help us* with your amazing grace to try to be faithful to what is right and just but never failing in our compassion toward others, so that through our good works your glory may be shining in the world and bringing healing and life to others, no matter what it may cost. Amen.

Thursday

Not joining the destructive mob, let us
gather around Jesus for healing
(Scriptural Passages: Heb. 7: 25-8: 6; Ps. 40; Mk. 3: 7-12)

It is our firm belief that Jesus, the Son of Mary, alone is worthy to be called Son of God. As the Author of the Letter to the Hebrews professes, *Jesus is able for all time to save those who approach God through him, since he always lives to make intercession for them...We have such a high priest, one who is seated at the right hand of the throne of the Majesty in the heavens, a minister in the sanctuary and the true tent that the Lord, and not any mortal, has set up.* In other words, Jesus alone is worthy to be our priest, even to enter the Heavenly Sanctuary where the Father sits in majesty. He did not enter empty handed; rather, he carried the sacrifice of his own body and blood.

According to the writer of the Letter, Jesus didn't enter only his physical body but his entire Mystical Body, in which every one of his disciples is included. Despite our fear and trembling of God's majesty and our own feelings of unworthiness, we go with Jesus because we cannot refuse anything to one who has given so much for us. This is why, we are intrigued and drawn irresistibly to him. Baptized into his Body, we bow with him before God the Father.

The verses from today's Responsorial Psalm have been quoted by the NT Writer as Jesus the High Priest uttering at his conception: *In the written scroll it is prescribed for me, to do your will, and to obey O my God, is my delight, and your law is within my heart!* Following Jesus' footsteps his followers, like us, if we are sincerely committed to his discipleship, continue to recite those verses as litany, especially: *Here am I Lord, I come to do your will.* We mean: Yes, here am I Lord, crowded with personal and social evils; here am I Lord, surrounded by infights and wars; here am I Lord, strangled by good and bad news of printed and electronic and digital social media.

But still we add: *I come to do your will.* It is because: Just to give our hearts, to surrender our lives, and to delight only in the Lord, is our salvation; nothing more is required of us than that we embrace the gift of salvation and rejoice in God loving us; we are filled with awe and wonder at this marvelous world, and we respond with humility and service.; the things we do or fail to do, be they small or great, be they ordinary or extraordinary, be they good or bad, get their importance and specialty only because of this dominant motive.

We everyday come to the Lord with the greatest urgency when we are struggling, when we are in some kind of distress. Most of us rush to him in our days of needs, as the crowds portrayed in today's Gospel, and reach out to touch the Lord in our brokenness, recognizing him as the source of healing and life. The Lord is as available to us as he was to the crowds of Galilee.

Prayer: *Lord Jesus, we pray for all of us who are suffering sickness and disease at this time, that you, the Heavenly Healer, may bring us health, peace and hope. Kindly do not abandon the poor of our time, but grace all people with that commitment to justice which will ensure dignity for everyone and at the end of*

this life, we may gather together as One Blessed Body of Christ
enter courageously to God's Holy of Holies. Amen.

Friday

A Christian is God's New Covenant's
product and proclaimer as well
(Scriptural Passages: Heb. 8: 6-13; Ps. 85; Mk. 3: 13-19)

The purpose of Jesus' entire life was, as the Writer
of Letter to the Hebrews says, to be a genuine mediator
of the New Covenant that God promised to make with
his people. This was the unique covenant through which,
as God proclaimed, *he will put his laws in his new people's*
minds, and will write them on their hearts, and he will be their
God, and they shall be his people. For he will be merciful toward
their iniquities, and he will remember their sins no more.

The endresult of this God's New Covenant
made through Jesus is, as we sing in today's Psalm, an
establishment of mercy, faithfulness, justice and peace,
through which not only God's glory will shine in our
dwelling, but also all our undertakings will prosper and
fruitful. The Psalm also points out that God's eternal
intentional dream has been that every human structure,
established in this world, is to be a welcoming place where
truth and kindness meet.

In the beginning of his public ministry, as we hear
in today's Gospel, Jesus' primary concern was to form a
special taskforce of his own, selecting twelve out of those
who demonstrated their openness and faithfulness to his
life's purpose of being mediator of the New Covenant.
In order to continue his mission of enhancing and
maintaining God's New Covenant of salvation, which

is blended by both liberation and elevation, he chose from his followers whom he wanted to be his primary witnesses, the Apostles. His dream of their future duties was: Primarily to be with him and secondarily to be sent forth to preach his Gospel of New Covenant and to have authority to drive out demons. And that taskforce of the Twelve branched out thousands and thousands and multiplied to billions of disciples as of today.

We are belonging to that crowd of those apostolic workers, sharing Jesus' work of restoring God's New Covenant; we are to be his eyes, his ears, his hands, his feet and his voice. He wants to work in and through us. Each of us has a role to play. We are reminded today about our duties to preach and perform the New Covenant-led life and ministries, not merely based on law and judgment, rather an enhanced covenant of love and forgiveness. Every step of our services must be focused on the one and only goal that all shall know the Lord in this covenant of forgiveness, not just those people who are just our relatives and friends, and not merely those whom we like, but everybody.

Prayer: *Amazing God of Love! What an admirable privilege we are blessed with! Being one with your Son in abiding to your New Covenant we conform our wills to your will; not as slaves but as children; not for seeking reward but to express love and gratitude; and not for external show but for inner peace. Help us Lord to be ardent, as Jesus, in our communion with you through our prayer efforts so that we may find strong motivation for living the new covenant; we may find our own security in you; and being fully aware of your presence in our lives, we may let you renew our outlook and help us to enjoy a new covenant, vibrant with Jesus. Amen.*

Saturday

Jesus' entrance to Heaven paved the
Way for our dreaming heavenly
(Scriptural Passages: Heb. 9: 2-3, 11-
14; Ps. 47; Mk. 3: 20-21)

With the Psalmist today, we envision and hear the celebration in the heavens: *God reigns over the nations, God sits upon his holy throne; the Lord, the Most High, the awesome, is the great king over all the earth; he mounts his throne amid shouts of joy; the Lord, amid trumpet blasts.* It is this adorable scene we want to be a part of; and this is the mighty God that we yearn to be one with.

As the Letter to the Hebrews indicates, we, the disciples of Jesus, are united with God through the blood of his Son. The blood-symbol refers to life rather than death, but we should note, it was by Jesus' death that the veil of the temple was rent in two and he entered into the Father's presence. His death on the cross became the supreme sign of loving dedication to us, to bring us to the Father.

If we pursue our earthly with this visionary backdrop of our mindset, undoubtedly, we will be entering into some unwanted territory as Jesus Christ got into. In today's Gospel we see a scene in which Jesus was viewed by his relatives as being crazy. Those relatives, whom Mark refers, must be people who were close to Jesus, who have heard his message on multiple occasions and in multiple ways and yet they did not get it.

Jesus was so dedicated to his healing ministry that sometimes he hardly had time to eat. His dealing with the crowds was often so hectic that his relatives thought him out of his mind. There seems to be such a contrast between Jesus on earth being called crazy, as he was beholding his Father in heaven amidst shouts of praise as King of the nations.

Prayer: *Glorious God! We are sorry, due to our littleness and timidity, we have been discontinuing our internal spiritual connections with you as Jesus persevered. We worry too much about what other people think or say about us. That concern has prevented us from speaking up when we knew that we should have taken a stand. Grant us Lord your strength to reflect on whose opinion really matters in our life with you, so that we may see the mystical presence of your Son within us and not feel alone in such adversarial circumstances but always prevail against it. Amen.*

WEEK - 3

Monday

Christian Privilege is nothing but surety
of prevailing against Beelzebul
(Scriptural Passages: Heb. 9: 15, 24-
28; Ps. 98; Mk. 3: 22-30)

Our Judeo-Christian religio-culture is never tired of proclaiming God's marvelous deeds to all of us and as the Psalmist invites us today *to sing to the Lord a new song, for his right hand has won victory for him; he has made his salvation known; he has revealed his justice; and he has remembered his kindness and his faithfulness toward all his people.*

However, we, as the members of the Church, which is the unique religion that follows Jesus Christ as her Founder, Leader and God-sent Redeemer, specially proclaim God's mindblowing deeds done to us through his Son, Jesus. There are two main Scriptural reasons for such exceptional assertion. According to the Author of the Letter to Hebrews, the God's new covenant of grace has been established when Jesus entered heaven following his earthly death, so as to appear before God on our behalf, to take away our sins and assure our salvation. *Christ did this only once, and for all, that we might have eternal life.*

Also, according to the Gospel of Mark, when the Jewish Scribes of Jesus' time, being afraid of Jesus' power and unwilling to ascribe his works to God, started accusing him of obtaining his power from Beelzebul, namely Satan, something that Jesus could readily disregard. Through his parable, he let his critics know that to blaspheme God by rejecting the work of the Holy Spirit is to commit an unforgivable grievance. He refuted them tooth and nail and defended his heavenly reality of being the Son of God, as the sole victor of the archenemy Satan.

Our uninterrupted proclamation of Jesus as the Son of God and the Redeemer of humanity emboldens us not only to be closely related to Jesus as our Saving Companion in this world but also to be enabled to enter into the splendid heavenly Sanctuary of profound peace and joy during our participation in Jesus' sacraments as a foretaste but also more realistically at the reaching of our ultimate eternal destiny.

Prayer: *Compassionate Father God! Thanks to your beloved Son Jesus, we are truly humbled and uplifted by becoming conscious of being held and loved by you. It is only because of Christ's love and sacrifice that any of us will one day know and understand the spectacular identity of you and your Son, when we enter heaven. Meanwhile we beg you to enlighten and strengthen us with your grace to long for seeing Christ in the 'real' sanctuary of heaven, and seeing through your works revealed in our life, we may be assured of that gift. Amen.*

Tuesday

*Will of God is the only mechanism to
unite us despite our differences*
(Scriptural Passages: Heb. 10:1-10; Ps. 40, Mk. 3: 31-35)

In today's Gospel Jesus assures us that *whoever does the will of God, is my brother and sister and mother.* Mother of Jesus, and the other family members had to learn to set aside their own plans for Jesus and surrender to God's will for him. It is perhaps reassuring to be reminded that even for our Blessed Lady it was a struggle to live out the implications of the prayer, "Thy will be done on earth as in heaven." It is a daily struggle for all of us to give priority to what God wants, but it is a worthwhile effort.

In fact, Jesus' entire life in this world was revolving around fulfilling the same God's will. The Letter to the Hebrews today verifies this truth. Quoting the Psalm, the Author writes, when Jesus came into this world, he said: "*Sacrifice and offering you did not desire, but a body you prepared for me; holocausts and sin offerings you took no delight in. Then I said, 'As is written of me in the scroll, behold, I come to do your will, O God.'* We also hear from the same Author that by this will, we, Christ's disciples, have been consecrated through the offering of the body of Jesus Christ once for all.

Fidelity to God's will makes the Church, as one family of all Christians. Jesus identifies the true disciple not by rank or position, special privileges of birth, talents and financial resources, but by fidelity in the routines of life. We are asked to undertake all we do in our social, religious and public life, as though in the context of family life, regarding others as our sisters or brothers, mothers or fathers to us. It is the Christian effort and in that struggle we are assured of the help of Jesus and Mary.

Prayer: *Dear God, Jesus through his word, brings us today into relationship with him, as close as his own earthly family. We entreat you that we may receive your word from your Son with grateful hearts and live its mystery day by day; and also that joining with our own family members, we may be blessed every day with peace and love, by doing your will because your Spirit has been given to us in Baptism and Confirmation. Amen.*

Wednesday

*Jesus sows his Word in us; church waters
it, and God makes it grow*
(Scriptural Passages: Heb. 10: 11-18; Ps. 110; Mk. 4: 1-20)

We heard in today's Gospel Jesus expounding the mystery of God's Kingdom which he came to reestablish and proclaim it. According to his Parable of the Sower, this amazing Kingdom is nothing but God's Word, which is sown by Christ as the Sower, and all who come to him will live forever. The Gospel assures us that such hope will blossom in its time; but it insists on the human factor too, the condition of the soil, dealing with the thorns, rocks and obstacles to growth.

We are not to stay passively doing nothing, and simply waiting for God to bring all to fulfilment. While life is often beyond our control and eventually we must leave all into the hands of God, still we are expected to be faithful through difficult times. Salvation is the interaction of God's mysterious grace and our cooperation. In this lifesituation, our religion always exhorts us to listen and receive humbly and sincerely the words of Jesus and his

Church; consequently our inner spirit would be cultivated as fertile land for God's word producing abundant fruits. In a very special manner, we are told that when we turn to God in prayer and sacraments, we should not separate ourselves from his Son Jesus.

This is because, as the Psalmist sings, God himself has prophetically sworn about Jesus, declaring: *"You are a priest forever, according to the order of Melchizedek."* Ascertaining such glorification, the Author of the Letter to the Hebrews underlines, *Jesus, being eternally priest, offered, in this world for the forgiveness of our sins, one sacrifice of Brokenbody and Bloodshed; besides he took his seat forever at the right hand of God; moreover, in that heavenly Sanctuary he continues to offer his prayer on behalf of us.*

Against this backdrop, whenever we participate in Church prayers, especially in her Liturgical services, Christ is always joining in partnership with himself his beloved Bride, the Church, which calls upon her Lord and through him gives worship to the eternal Father. At those moments, Christ prays for us: he is our priest; he prays in us: he is our head; we pray to him; because he is our God.

Prayer: *God of Power and holiness! We are so blessed to have Jesus Christ exercising his priestly office in all our spiritual and religious activities. Help us to participate in them consciously and faithfully so that each of these practices, made effective, may become sources of giving true honor and glory and getting our fuller sanctification as well. Amen.*

Thursday

Hiding or fleeing from shining can never be a Christian lifestyle
(Scriptural Passages: Heb. 10: 19-25; Ps. 24; Mk. 4: 21-25)

The Author of the Letter to the Hebrews in not tired of uplifting his readers by the conviction of Jesus' present status in heaven, by exhorting us to remember that *we have a Great Priest over the house of God, and that we should hold fast to our confession that gives us hope for he who made the promise is trustworthy.* At the same instance, knowing that it would be hard for those people living back then for they had not met him in person, the Author insisted that they, who were already anointed and empowered by Jesus' Spirit, must consider how to rouse one another to love and good works. Their gathering as church community should become a fireplace of rousing the participants in the religious community rituals to encourage one another to live a life of faith, hope and charity.

Jesus in his life asserted himself as the Light of the world; he also indicated his disciples too can be empowered to be a shining lamp on the housetop. Ascertaining such unbelievable ability for all his disciples, as we see him in today's Gospel, he demanded from them not to escape or flee from such splendid chance bestowed to them. He argued: *Is a lamp brought in to be placed under a bushel basket or under a bed, and not to be placed on a lampstand?* Plus, he cautioned them: *The measure with which you measure will be measured out to you, and still more will be given to you. To the one who has, more will be given; from the one who has not, even what he has will be taken away.*

The Spirit of Jesus today encourages us first to be the light like himself with shining faith-filled life of justice and love and truth. Then he urges us to let it grow with glow.

As today's Responsorial Psalm indicates, only those of us whose hands are sinless, whose heart is clean, and who desires not what is vain, can ascend the mountain of the Lord or who may stand in his holy place as his lamp. By the Baptismal Grace of God our personal access to Jesus, the holy Priest, was made possible through the Holy Spirit and all we have to do is to call on the Spirit in prayer to help us to assemble fearlessly but gracefully with our fellowhumans and encourage one another to be the same shining lamps in the world.

Prayer: *Almighty God! Our discipleship with Christ continuously calls us to strive for greater things, giving one's best, and doing the utmost as a process of growing your kingdom on earth. We too are looking forward to the time when we see your face in eternity. Grant us Lord, the inner strength to experience continuously your Son's peace, calm and assurance even our efforts of being your lamp may be infrequent and not fully shining. Amen.*

Friday

Remembrance of our past with God brings better life
(Scriptural Passages: Heb. 10: 32-39; Ps. 37; Mk. 4: 26-34)

It is said that 'remembering the past brings healing in us.' It is absolutely true in our relationship with God. In OT we often hear God pointing out this truth through his Prophets and Sages. For example, we read this factual norm of human life as the wisest lifestyle even in the Book of Wisdom, where almost all its 19 chapters talk about how to live wisely and fruitfully our earthly life, astonishingly concludes in its last chapter with the amazing sentence of remembering God and his marvelous deeds: *Lord, in every way you have made your people great and glorious. You have never disdained, (despised, held in contempt, and looked down on them), but stood by them always and everywhere.*

While we should always remember the past deeds of God in and around our life, today's first reading reminds to us the first century Christians who remembered their own personal acquaintance with God in the past: *Remember those earlier days when, after you had been enlightened, you endured a hard struggle with sufferings, knowing that you yourselves possessed something better and more lasting.* The Reading also includes an instruction that spontaneously follows after those green memories: *Do not, therefore, abandon that confidence of yours; it brings a great reward. For you need endurance, so that when you have done the will of God, you may receive what was promised.*

The Psalmist testifies today that it is only by such firm trust in the Lord and endure our hectic lifesituations with good heart and mind, that we will be blessed with salvation of spiritual security and prosperity. As Jesus too expounds today in his parables, this is how God's Kingdom sprouts secretly and grows mysteriously both in and around each one of us and produces abundant fruits. As I titled one of my books of daily meditations: *'Daily Dose for Christian Survival,'* Christian life in this modern world cannot survive, more than any centuries, without the two virtues of Faith and Hope. Jesus knew this in his life and therefore he included in the beginning of his remarkable Prayer he taught us, *Our Father, who art in heaven,* as a creed of faith and *hallowed be thy name, thy kingdom come, thy will be done on earth as it is in heaven,* as an assurance of hope.

We certainly need faith and hope in this world, which is so full of natural disasters, social evils and so many other misfortunes. As our forebears, we have to endure a great contest of suffering and we need endurance to do the will of God and receive what he has promised. We must sing the Psalm of our faith that salvation comes from the Lord, who is our refuge in times of distress. And as Jesus' parables indicate, we need to firmly believe and hope that all the promises and dreams Jesus shared with us and the multiple efforts we do together with the church, may seem to be small seeds of God's Kingdom at present but surely growing into a fine harvest one day and that too in God's time.

Prayer: *Lord of Goodness and Graciousness! Remembering all that you had done for us through your Son and all the good and bad we did in the past, we entreat you to help us in allowing your Spirit to work in our lives, so that whatever good we do will bring glory to God, and not to ourselves; let our Church be a community which, growing like the mustard tree, may offer a safe shelter for all who are damaged by this wordly life. Amen.*

Saturday

*By true faith we are able to see the Lord
who has come to us as Dawn*
(Scriptural Passages: Heb. 11: 1-2, 8-19;
Lk. 1: 67-79; Mk. 4: 35-41)

In our daily crossing from one lifesituation to another, we feel frightened or frustrated, like Jesus' disciples, who, as today's Gospel narrates, were terrified in rowing their boat when they were crossing from one shore to the other, not only because they were facing violent squall, that came up and waves were breaking over their boat, so that it was already filling up; but also, because during such critical times, they noticed their Master, a powerful Prophet, was insensitively in deep sleep on a cushion. Hence, they cried out to him: *Teacher, do you not care that we are perishing?*

Certainly, the good Lord's mindset was not at all as frustrated disciples complained. He intended to teach them the reality of their faith through this natural event. After calming down the fury of the wind, he put before them two simple questions: *Why are you terrified? Do you not yet have faith?* He underscored that his disciples' faith must be built on the awesome greatness and goodness of the Lord who is the One who is the Sovereign Lord of the nature.

As an extension of Jesus' teaching about our faith, God's Spirit instructs us today through Letter to the Hebrews about the real definition of faith as demonstrated by our forebears: *Faith is the realization of what is hoped for and evidence of things not seen. Because of it the ancients were well attested.* And through the Canticle of Zachariah, which we recite today as Responsorial Psalm, we are told that our faith must be founded on the realization that Jesus is the God's New Covenant promised in the past with an *oath to our father Abraham: to set us free from the bonds of our enemies, free to worship him without fear, holy and righteous in his sight all the days of our life.*

Moreover, our faith should be focused on our eternal life as the fruit of Jesus' coming. This is what John writes in his Gospel: 'God so loved the world that he gave his only-begotten Son, so that everyone who believes in him might have eternal life'. Amazing faith of our forefathers nurtured them at times when they did not receive what had been promised, the Redeemer. They relentlessly believed they would one day indeed see the promise fulfilled. They were willing to sacrifice anything as God demanded, even be it the beloved son like Isaac.

The same kind of uncompromised faith Jesus expected from his disciples in their turbulent times. This is why he sadly rebuked them: Why are you terrified? Do you not yet have faith? As he demanded the nature to be quiet and be still, he too expected from his disciples upholding their faith in his powerful Presence, to be quiet and still liberated from fear and anxiety. To signify such faith-filled spiritual and psychological stillness, God made the High Priest Zachariah be dumb until his faith in God's promises blossomed out.

Prayer: *Father and King, we place into your care all of us who are vulnerable and fragile in living our faith as expected of us. Kindly enlighten and strengthen our inner spirit so that we may row our lifeboat with faith in your Son, who possesses the power to calm all the storms disturbing the unity and dignity of our human life; and growing in respect and understanding of one another, we may work together for the peace of this world.*

WEEK - 4

Monday

Jesus is the only refuge for all who are tormented by evil spirits
(Scriptural Passages: Heb. 11: 32-40; Ps. 31; Mk. 5: 1-20)

We hear from the first reading about the glorious victory of all OT patriarchs, judges, kings and prophets over the evil invaders of their personal and social life by their faith and righteousness. The Letter also verifies even ordinary men and women prevailed against their evildoers, by enduring in faith and patience, all the tortures, mockeries, and atrocious bleeding sufferings of scourging, chains, and imprisonment.

Nonetheless, we who battle today against such evils are better off than those forebears due to our privilege of being redeemed by the bloodshed and brokenbody of Jesus, who in his life, as we read in today's Gospel, demonstrated such invaluable victory over the legions of unclean spirits, tormenting our personal and social life. We may give them so many names such as lies, disinformation and immoral attractions which we hear and see in all kinds of sources and by which sometimes we are being tempted to succumb to their evils.

Indeed, so many of us, who have been filled with the graces we receive from the Eucharistic Lord, either escape from or fight victoriously those unclean spirits and try to lead a life of spiritual peace and joy. As the Psalmist today underlines, the great goodness of the Lord is hiding us in the shelter of his presence and continues to preserve our inner spirit comfortable and restful. The one and only thing Jesus demands from those of us who are healed by the Eucharistic Lord, is, as he expected from the one whom he cured, to *go home to your family and announce to them all that the Lord in his pity has done for you.*

Prayer: *Gracious Lord, you have shown us the wonders of your love through your Son, Jesus Christ who, by his power over the forces of evil, brought calm to a tormented human. Today through him we confidently entrust all our relatives and friends who are tormented by mental illness. Help them with your medical and emotional support which will alleviate their distress. Fill all those who work with severely mentally ill people with courage and compassion, and always show respect for those in their care. Amen.*

Tuesday

*The cry of the brokenhearted touches the
compassionate heart of Jesus*
(Scriptural Passages: Heb. 12: 1-4; Ps. 22; Mk. 5: 21-43)

As the Writer in today's first reading reminds, we are privileged *to be surrounded by such so great a cloud of witnesses, who have liberated themselves from every burden and sin that clings to humanity and persevered in running the race that had been designed for them by the Creator.* The only secret of their relentless perseverance in their journey of sufferings was, again as the First Reading points out, *while keeping their eyes fixed on Jesus, who has been their sole Leader who won unimaginable victory by carrying his cross of death patiently.*

Our leader is not a bogus figure or any fairytale hero; rather he was a suffering Messiah and bore all our diseases which are the post-effects of sin. Above all, through his healing miracles, such as those which are narrated in today's Gospel, he demonstrated his power to take away all our infirmities and diseases which we all suffer spiritually, emotionally and physically.

For such holistic healing from him, he places before us only one requisite: A strong faith and hope in his enormous power to heal and in his immense compassion toward us. He loves to hear from us with that Faith as the Official was pleading: *Please, come lay your hands on her that she may get well and live."* And as the lady suffering from hopeless infirmity: *If I but touch his clothes, I shall be cured."*

Shockingly, the same divine Healer, who liberated countless afflicted people from their pains and sufferings, earnestly cried out to his Father at the peak of his ignominious passion with the words, which we recited in Responsorial Psalm, *My God, my God, why have you abandoned me? Why so far from my call for help, from my cries of anguish?* We also find in him during those moments of crises strong trust and hope in his Father affirming: *God has not spurned or disdained the misery of this poor wretch; did not turn away from me, but heard me when I cried out.* It is how all Jesus' followers prevailed against the atrocities shoved by the evil forces.

Prayer: *Lord, kindly increase our faith in your compassion and power to heal, so that we may first be healed from our personal maladies and become worthy vessel in which you would fill all your graces and consequently we earnestly look for more* occasions to bring the healing to our own relatives and friends, including our enemies. Amen.

Wednesday

In our Gospel Life with Jesus there is no gain without pain
(Scriptural Passages: Heb. 12: 4-7, 11-
15; Ps. 103; Mk. 6: 1-6)

In our human birth we are surrounded by so many mysteries; one of the most disturbing mysteries is the human sufferings. The surprising matter is, in portraying the life of Jesus, the Son of God, all Gospel writers have been keen on sharing with us large portion of his life's sufferings more than his glorious deeds. His sufferings were caused not only by his social, religious opponents, but also by his relatives and friends. In today's Gospel we hear, while Jesus' kith and kin were astonished at his teachings, and praised him for his mindblowing wisdom and power, they took offense at him.

But Jesus only pitied them for their lack of faith. With his wisdom, he knew all the answers to the mystery of sufferings. However, he was keen on teaching us, his disciples, who are limited in our understanding that mystery fully. He, as his Father, was kind and compassionate on his fellowhumans; for, as the Psalmist underlines today, *he knows how they are formed; he remembers that they are dust.* That is why, John's Gospel would state about Jesus: *No one needed to tell him about human nature, for he knew what was in each human's heart.*

There is one more main remarkable lesson Jesus taught us in handling our sufferings as his disciples. At every horrible suffering incident, he smiled at them because he was so happy to suffer them because it was God's will for his Mission-fulfillment; he was not only sympathetic and forgiving, but also, he used every such suffering-time as an occasion either to reveal his Gospel values or to bring peace and conversion to those who hurt him. It is this Good News all NT Writers testify, as we read in the Hebrews.

While we encounter our regular, chronic or terminal diseases, or face rejection, hatred, slander and violent treatment from our own neighbors and friends, we should perceive in all those events the loving hands of the just God being there. Those loving hands of God are the disciplinary hands of our loving Father. He disciplines only those whom he immensely loves; and he scourges only those whom he acknowledges as his beloved sons and daughters. Hence in no way we should lose heart when reproved by him.

Prayer: *Heavenly Father! From the beginning of your Son's ministry, he suffered with opposition and rejection; yet he continued in a spirit of trust and joy. Help us in our sufferings to be always filled with the strength of Jesus, so that we may carry our daily crosses with dignity since suffering is part of our learning and maturing in Christian discipleship that produces the fruits of peace and goodness in and around our life. Amen.*

Thursday

God of fear, seen in man-made temples,
exists in Jesus as a God of Love
(Scriptural Passages: Heb. 12: 18-
19, 21-24; Ps. 48; Mk. 6: 7-13)

Today's first reading clearly explains to us how our New Way of life with Jesus is broadly different from the OT religion. As the Author points out, the OT Israelites were following a religion of fear: They experienced God in a blazing fire and gloomy darkness and storm; they heard his voice speaking words such that those who heard begged that no message be further addressed to them; they were stunned to hear from God as a command: *'If even an animal touches the mountain, it shall be stoned.' Indeed so fearful was the spectacle that Moses said, 'I am terrified and trembling'.*

However, we, the new Israelites, Jesus' followers, as the same Author underlines, inherited a new and splendid kind of religious environment, which is like that of Mount Zion and the city of the living God, the heavenly Jerusalem and countless angels in festal gathering. And boldly we can get closer to and even enter into that classy environment of love and friendship. It is, as the Psalmist prophesied, an *amazing temple or city of mercy and justice.*

Our religious circle is mystically the assembly of the firstborn enrolled in heaven and God the judge of all; where the spirits of the just made perfect through Jesus, the mediator of a new covenant. It is with Jesus, who is powerful and merciful Founder of our religion, as Mark emphasizes, in our church, starting from the Apostles' time upto this day, all his disciples hold *a power to preach the genuine repentance; to drove out demons from humans; to anoint with oil those who are sick and to cure them.*

Thanks to Jesus' sharing of his healing power, all his disciples as well as those who see and hear their Gospel words and deeds are free from harmful dreams, from fears and terrors of the night; and being withheld from their dark desires and thus feel enabled to prevent themselves from eternal fire.

Prayer: *Lord, let the knowledge of salvation enlighten our hearts; so that, freed from fear and from the power of our* enemies, we may serve you faithfully and better the lives of our fellowhumans by our compassion and justice, all the days of our life. Amen.

Friday

Not defiling our human relationships is the Highway to heaven
(Scriptural Passages: Heb. 13: 1-8; Ps. 27; Mk. 6: 14-29)

When the Lord God gave humanity his Ten Commandments, he made sure the neighborly love to be continued, being undefiled and unstained. In a special way he was concerned about the purity of human sex and marriage-relationship and therefore he included two exclusive commandments. This is also what Jesus persistently preached as one of his Gospel values; and as we read in the First Reading, the Church has been teaching the same truth but with emphasis on God's judgement: *Let marriage be honored among all and the marriage bed be kept undefiled, for God will judge the immoral and adulterers.*

In fact, sex is very personal to humans; therefore, when somebody criticizes us about its use, we are boiled with anger. One among these historical upheavals of human beings is what we hear in today's Gospel. King Herod, violating God's Commands defiled his marriage bed by marrying Herodias, the wife of his brother Philip. Knowing such defilement John the Baptist, condemned Herod's sin saying to his face: *"It is not lawful for you to have your brother's wife."* It was for such prophetic deed, John had to be imprisoned, tortured and cruelly beheaded.

The Biblical heroes, like John the Baptizer, were strong in this risky path of truth upto bleeding and dying because, they were filled with the spirit of the Psalmist, who utters in today's Psalm: *The LORD is my light and my salvation; whom should I fear? Though an army encamp against me, my heart will not fear. For he will hide me in his abode in the day of trouble.* The Letter to the Hebrews also exhorts us to remember the words those saintly sages spoke and to try to imitate their faith.

Today the Lord calls us for living such heroic life of truth and for the truth and with the truth. It is indeed harder to be faithful to the Truth and live by it, especially in these modern days, where so many liars and deceivers are around us and sadly, related to us. But still our Master expects us to witness to the Truth, nothing but his Truth.

Prayer: *God the Holy One! You have shown the pure way of living our Christian life through the exemplary life of St. John the Baptizer, who showed his courage in stark contrast to the evil desires of Herod and Herodias. We pray that all those who manipulate other people for their own ambition, may come to respect the dignity of others without fear or favor. Keep us faithful to Jesus your Son so that by leading a chaste and just life, we may be blessed with your abundant salvation. Amen.*

Saturday

God's goodness and kindness follow us all the days of our life
(Scriptural Passages: Heb. 13: 15-
17, 20-21; Ps. 23; Mk. 6: 30-34)

In today's Gospel event we notice Jesus very much pleased with his disciples who had returned from their missionary trip and admired at their good deeds as he intended. At the same time, as a compassionate Master, he realized his disciples were so much wearied and tired after their long trip and as being humble and meek of heart, he too thought his disciples might be tempted to glory in their new-found power and the resultant fame and popularity. Hence, he decided to withdraw with them for a while to a solitary place where they would be left to themselves for reflection and rest.

Surprisingly, while Jesus and his disciples crossed the lake in a boat, and as they stepped out of the boat, they were faced by a huge crowd. Though Jesus knew why most of the crowd were after him for mere material and earthly needs to be fulfilled, he was still deeply moved by the people's need. He found out: *They were like lost sheep in need of a shepherd's guidance.* As the Psalmist sings, Jesus proved his inheritance of the Shepherdship of the Father who is *our shepherd; we shall not want. In verdant pastures he gives us repose. Beside restful waters he leads us; he refreshes our soul.*

That is how Jesus wants us, his disciples, to live through our life. First, focusing fully on God, the One who gave birth and redemption and still provides all that we need, we should spend sufficient time to renew contact with the Heavenly Father, to recharge our batteries. Otherwise, we may become active for activity's sake or performing things for less worthy motives. At the same time, if we clearly discern a situation, as Jesus and disciples were called for accomplishing some neighborly and community actions for uplifting our fellowhumans, we should as Jesus, abandon our restful solitude of prayer and rush to assist the needy people as best as we can.

True it is with the life of every Christian, about which the First Reading teaches us: It is primarily to offer God as prayer, an unending sacrifice of praise by acknowledging His name, and to keep doing good works and sharing our resources, with other Christian communities in need of assistance and support. Both of these are "sacrifices that please God".

Prayer: *God, Shepherd and King, the compassion of Jesus for the crowds continues to inspire all of us to have a love and concern for all peoples. Guide us along the right path of Jesus, not only in finding that quiet place where we can be personally commune with you in prayer but also in doing good works and sharing our blessings with those who are struggling, so that by your goodness and kindness we may be brought to our eternal home. Amen.*

WEEK - 5

---•◆•---

Monday

God through his Word makes creations good, better and best
(Scriptural Passages: Gen. 1: 1-19; Ps. 104; Mk. 6: 53-56)

In the Book of Genesis, we hear Moses narrating that God is the One who by his word created the entire universe and all creatures in it; namely by the touch of his words all creations came forth out of the emptiness and nothingness. Marveling at the mindboggling creational works of God, King David sings: *Bless the Lord, my soul. Lord God, how great you are, clothed in majesty and glory, wrapped in light as in a robe.* However, referring to this revealed fact, we hear David's son King Solomon attesting prayerfully in the Book of Wisdom: *God of my ancestors, Lord of mercy, you who have made all things by your word.*

In extension of such prophetic revelation, John in his Gospel, introducing Jesus of Nazareth as the God's Word became flesh and made his dwelling among us, states that is the same word through which God created the world: *In the beginning was the Word, and the Word was with God, and the Word was God. He was in the beginning with God. All*

things came to be through him, and without him nothing came
to be.

More than other NT Writers, Mark, in today's Gospel,
takes special interest in proving how Jesus of Nazareth
identified himself as God begotten Son and Word who
came to us to recreate, to refresh and to restore the fallen
state of all his creations to its original greatness about
which he was pleased much as Moses writes: *God saw how
good it was.* At every step of his public life not only through
his words of the Gospel Jesus touched the inner spirit of
his listeners but also whoever touched him with belief and
hope were cured of their illnesses.

Prayer: *God our Father, through your powerful Word you
created us and through the same Word-in-flesh Jesus you are
ready to recreate and heal us according to your Dream. Besides
helping us to be renewed by your Word, make us follow your
Son Jesus in accepting our sufferings with patience. May all of
us, who suffer pain, illness, or disease realize that we have been
chosen to be saints and know that we are joined to Christ in his
suffering for the salvation of the world! Amen.*

Tuesday

*Let us serve God by our discipled hearts
rather than by mere lipservice*
(Scriptural Passages: Gen. 1: 20–2: 4; Ps. 8; Mk 7:1-13)

After creating everything in the universe, as a climax,
God brought the humanity out of clay. And as he found
everything, he created, was good; he was overwhelmed
with joyful nostalgia about all that he had accomplished.
The wonder of wonder is his creation of humanity.
Reading such marvelous creative deeds of God and see

them also in our day today life, we wonder at God's love and greatness in going out of his heavenly way, our hearts begin to sing today with the Psalmist: *What is man that you should be mindful of him...You have made him little less than the angels, and crowned him with glory and honor.*

Yes, we are right to say, God went out of his mind and his holiness; only his mercy and compassion prevailed. We were created with the same nobility, greatness, glory and plenitude as he breathed into us his own Spirit and made us in his image and likeness. Together with interior beauty and greatness, we would be hearing in OT Books and from God's Son, our Creator bestowed us some instructions for how to maintain outwardly our nobility and greatness. Bible calls those instructions as 'God's Words, God commandments and so on.

But, forgetting all of God's instructions, how silly we have been behaving in our day today dealings with God and our neighbors! Most of us act like the Pharisees we hear about in today's Gospel. They behaved as silly as possible and nullified God's Commands all for the sake of their fake supremacy, fake prestige and wounded pride. While God was speaking about the necessity and importance of spiritual efforts and practices, people like Pharisees have been declaring many trivial external practices of purifying themselves as carefully washing their hands and feet, the purification of cups and jugs and kettles and beds and so on.

That is why, our Lord rebuked them, pointing out that they disregarded God's commandments but hung on to mere human traditions; they honored God with their lips, but their hearts were far from him. Moreover, it is a historical fact that by such insistence of silly, exterior traditional practices, humans have lost their true original

45

nobility, greatness and glory and ended up in hatred, violence, infights, and wars.

Prayer: *God the Creator, we are grateful to you that you created us in your image and likeness; but we have been failing you and out of your immense love you sent your Son to redeem us from our messing-up of our nobility and greatness and through him you lifted us up. Grant us your Spirit, Gracious Lord, so that being conscious of your dwelling in our breath, we may purify our silliness by your Fire. Amen.*

Wednesday

In Jesus restoration of our dusty and
perishing status is guaranteed
(Scriptural Passages: Gen. 2: 4-17; Ps. 104; Mk. 7: 14-23)

By nature, every creature, and in particular every human, is connected intrinsically and ontologically with our Creator God. That is what the Psalmist sings today: *All creatures look to you to give them food in due time. When you give it to them, they gather it. If you take away their breath, they perish. When you send forth your spirit, they are created.*

In the Book of Genesis we hear how in the benevolence of God, bestowing his breath of life, humans become living beings. His original dream was, we would be intimately related to him and he could enjoy our reciprocal love; keeping that in mind, he planted an amazing Garden of Eden, evergreen, ever beautiful, and ever fruitful and made it a unique settlement for his human friends. He gave them one and only suggestion that they should obey to his order of 'stay back from a tree', which would cause them a horrible result in their life to be doomed.

Jesus' words and actions, we read in today's Gospel, were simply to realize such divine Dream of humanity. Pointing out the silliness of his opponents who were adamantly crazy about only the external practices but never bothered about the beauty and nobility of their interiority, he reminded them to see the marvel of God's existence within them; he exhorted them to freely make the best use of that power to manage all their earthly and bodily engagements outside. His only concern was about their honest and sincere reciprocal love to God and their voluntary reverence and respect to his Greatness, his wisdom and above all being obedient to his directions in dealing with their rare gifts of freedom and knowledge.

But as Jesus foretold, almost all of us fail God by abusing our inner Godly power; the endresult is everything within us and outside of us become topsy-turvey, uncontrollable, messy, twisted, unholy, and permit thirteen and more evils, as Jesus enlisted, coming out of our filthy interiority. We know it is not at all a fairytale. Everyone's life story will testify to the reality of how we have become Pandora boxes in our lifetime.

Prayer: *Benevolent God, by our disobedience and carelessness, we become victims of evils; but through your Son's gift of amazing grace we are trying our best to rise up and return to our original settlement. Please Father, purify us, shape us, mold us, fill us and use us as long as you let us to be settled in your Kingdom forever. Amen.*

Thursday

*Maintaining equality between male and
female uplifts human dignity*
(Scriptural Passages: Gen. 2: 18-25; Ps. 128; Mk. 7: 24-30)

Women are center-stage in today's Scriptural readings. We read in the Book of Genesis, the first woman, Eve, heals the loneliness of the first man, Adam, corresponding to him in a way that no other creature could, and the two are united as equals, in one flesh. Genesis suggests that either the woman or the man in isolation would be deficient and incomplete. The union, by which they complement one another, enables the image of God in both of them to flourish. In this way marriage sets the pattern for all human friendship and community.

Though the Jews in Jesus' time knew how women bring joy and fulfilment, and stability into the life of men, they regarded women in low-esteem; out of their patriarchic and male-controlled tradition, they kept their women, as homemakers or only as their cooks and servants; in addition, they cursed pagan women as responsible for apostasy in Israel. But in today's Gospel we find a pagan woman surprising Jesus with her faith and humble perseverance and got from Jesus praises as well as her healing-request being granted.

Many of the women in the Scriptures can be models for men as well as for women, just as men provide examples for both women and men. This is what we celebrate Mary the Second Eve but always Number One Woman in history. Because of her feminine humility, womanly tenderness and motherly perseverance and love for her children, she has become part and parcel of life of all disciples of Jesus; not only she intercedes for us in heaven, but also appeared many times and in many places and proclaimed her Son's way of life and inspired us by instructing 'do as Jesus tells you.'

As today's Psalm indicates, since those, who always fear the Lord and who walk in his ways, are blessed, and humble women, like Mary, are prosperous in their handiwork; and they have been blessed and favored.

Prayer: *Lord God! In your creation of man and woman you stated your eternal romantic manifesto to be held in our relationships. So many times we drifted away from the fidelity and truthfulness in our human relationship. Grant us the grace to welcome humbly your Loving Word that has been planted in us so that our souls will be wholistically healed and saved. Amen.*

Friday

In Jesus we can reclaim our 'Innocent Paradise-Lost'
(Scriptural Passages: Gen. 3: 1-8; Ps. 32; Mk. 7: 31-39)

Today's first reading brings home to us about the sin of our First Parents. According to our Church doctrine, their sin became a sort of original source of all our sins and the evils we face in daily life. And it is our strong belief also that by baptism we are cleansed from that Original Sin. However, if we go deeper into the message of the Genesis story of the First Sin, we simply discover a pictorial explanation of what every human being experiences in this world.

Every baby born in this world is as innocent as an angel, even little than God. What attracts us to newborn babies? Besides all their physical beauty, their openness, their playfulness and their innate humor, they are attractive because they possess the quality of innocence, containing guileless ignorance; unthinkable imagination; and most of all, simplicity and purity not yet spoiled by mundane affairs. It is this innocence that was exactly bestowed by the Creator to the First Parents as his First Love-Gift.

Unfortunately, as they lost that splendid innocence by the subtle and smarty plus cunning Satan, you and I too have lost that innocence of babyhood by listening and following the words of certain persons in the family, in the community, in the peergroup, in the media, and especially in the circle of religion. Almost all of us can testify to this tragedy.

Fortunately, God's Spirit didn't leave us only with the story about the loss of the paradise of innocence. Through Master Jesus we received another joyful story of regaining the same Paradise of innocence. Through the miraculous healing of a speech-impaired man, as we hear in today's Gospel, Jesus paved the way for reclaiming our innocence with his consistent authoritative but compassionate power-sharing with us to reclaim our Innocent Paradise-lost. He too opened our mouths to cry out, like the Psalmist, our confession of our acknowledgement about his capacity to grant a renewed innocence to us; also acknowledging our foolish sins and guilts; and resolutely promising him our faithfulness in maintaining the renewed innocence up to the finale of our life.

Prayer: *Father God, as our First Parents, we are ashamed of our past when we lost your Gift of innocence. Thanks to the redemptive healing of your Son Jesus, we are now able to reclaim our innocence. Kindly refresh us with your Spirit's counseling and light, so that we may try our best to maintain and enhance our reclaimed-innocence during our pilgrimage to eternity. Amen.*

Saturday

We may fall repeatedly inside the mud
of sin; Jesus is still our refuge
(Scriptural Passages: Gen. 3: 9-24; Ps. 90; Mk. 8: 1-11)

During my time of meditation, as I recited today's Psalm, I was struck by the verse: *"In every age, O Lord, you have been our refuge."* When I lisped the phrase, 'in every age', which is interpreted as 'in every generation' or 'in every century' or 'in every stage of human and social development', I was convinced that the personal life every one of us live with God in this world can be divided into different phases or 'ages' in personal and social human dimensions:

Like that of Adam and Eve, at the beginning of my Age, I listened to cunning people like the serpent, disobeyed God and disfigured and defiled my own original status of angelic innocence; and above all, I offended my Creator by pooh-poohing and dismissing God's Masterplan for my life and destiny. Then came the second age when, as my First Mom and First Dad, I felt ashamed, felt guilty, and tried to hide myself behind or under certain of my sinful undertakings. Within me I did visualize my conscience raising hell over me, throwing at me so many cruel arrows that pricked and hurt.

In the third stage of my life, as my First Parents had encountered, I had to eat my food only by my labor of sweat and blood; I have to climb up the life's ladder to be promoted or to be qualified for my social role, I have to gamble my life in this competitive lottery-fied world. In between I get sick, I get all kinds of maladies, as my First Parents got. And life goes on that way. Despite all that are occurring in different ages of my life, surprisingly

God's Spirit instigates me from within to say aloud to God in full confidence: *In every age, O Lord, you have been our refuge.*

The only reason for such relentless behavior toward God is that the God who was mad at me and my First Parents because of our sins, has sent to us his Word, his Son Jesus, as we are informed in today's Gospel, who possesses a heart that is moved with pity for the hungering and crying crowd of sinners who are on the verge of collapsing. Plus, he is so powerful to make miracles, like multiplication of loaves and fish, to stoop down on me a sinner and to uplift me from the miry muds of sinfulness.

Prayer: *Almighty father, we clearly see your Son Jesus' humble but powerful behavior in performing miracles not out of ambition, but only of compassion. His only concern and happiness has been to restore us to life of joy and fullness. Grant we pray the grace of living firmly attached to this faith in Jesus so that at our times of temptations and evils we boldly say: "In every age, O Lord, you have been our refuge." Amen.*

WEEK - 6

Monday

Our dignity is preserved only by controlling our natural feelings
(Scriptural Passages: Gen. 4: 1-15, 25; Ps. 50; Mk. 8: 11-13)

From the beginning of human history upto our own present Age, besides the sin of pride that brought unsurmountable sufferings in human life, the wickedness of violence and murdering stays with us as a reality of life. According to our Scriptures, the real reason for such atrocious human behavior is that our human indepth-self has been twisted and defiled by disproportionate hunger for being satiated in our basic needs.

This uncontrollable desire made the Pharisees, who, as we find in today's Gospel, argued with Jesus, for getting more signs from him. In fact we know Jesus was performing so many miraculous deeds, like multiplication loaves and so on and had proven his origin from the heavenly Father; yet, these Pharisees belittling all his miraculous performances, came back again and again to test him. We can understand why Jesus sighed from the depth of his spirit, and why he denied their request.

Also, today we are reminded by the Spirit, through the first reading, that our uncontrollable craving for worldly things can make us feel of jealousy, which then becomes the cause of evil deeds, as it happened in the life of Cain, who, out of sheer envy, performed terrible and horrible action against his own brother.

In the long run, if those natural cravings are not controlled, most of us consider our self-image is wounded by God's cold response; worst still, when we notice the abundant blessings, our neighbors enjoying, more than us, we become slaves to harmful feelings of resentment, inferiority, and envy; and we begin to use all kinds of violent reactions against our neighbors. Thus, we may move on living low-spirited and make a world of our own full of violence and killing.

It is about such pathetic human personalities God regrettably speaks in today's Psalm: 'Why do you recite my statutes, and profess my covenant with your mouth, though you hate discipline and cast my words behind you? You sit speaking against your brother; against your mother's son you spread rumors. When you do these things, shall I be deaf to it?'

Prayer: *God of goodness! You have blessed us abundantly, yet often forgetting your love, we are ungrateful to you and out of our wounded pride, we even don't pay heed to your Spirit's summon to offer you proper sacrifice of praise in truth and obedience. Please Lord, open our eyes to see all the wonderful signs, which your Son did, to prove himself as our Redeemer and open our ears to hear and follow his life-giving words, so that getting stronger in our faith in him, we may control all our evil-feelings. Amen.*

Tuesday

Going beyond the externals takes us to our highest birthright
(Scriptural Passages: Gen. 6: 5-8, 7:
1-8; Ps. 29; Mk. 8: 14-21)

The first reading narrates the story of deluge. When the Lord saw the man's horrible wickedness on earth, he regretted that he had made man on the earth. With this regret, he planned to wipe out all his humans along with other creatures from this world. At the same time, being compassionate enough, he decided to save the family of Noah, who alone in that period he found to be truly just. He asked Noah to prepare a huge Ark in which Noah's family will survive safely from deluge along with other chosen creatures. As God intended, an unprecedented deluge destroyed all creatures, except Noah's family and his chosen creatures.

When God seems to be such kind of destroyer of his own creatures, why in the world there are people, like the Psalmist, continuing to advise us loudly: *Give to the Lord, you sons of God, give to the Lord glory and praise?* This prevalent question is answered by the same Psalmist who tells us: It is because the same God who is the Sovereign Lord bless his people with peace. And in today's Gospel Jesus shares the shame thoughts to his disciples, who were fretting over that they had forgotten to bring enough bread for their survival in their voyage across the Sea of Galilee.

Jesus regretted about their faithlessness and reminded them about his powerful ability to feed thousands of hungry people by multiplying seven loaves. Yet, they saw only the external happenings and satisfied with surfaced level of their life. God in Jesus expected them to dig into what was visible and tangible and to see the internal workings of God who deals with them always in justice, love and peace. However, they did not really understand who he was or what he was about. Sadly, many of them misunderstood him and eventually abandoned him.

Thus, today's Scriptural passages attest that God through his Son is eternally faithful to us, even when we are less faithful or even unfaithful to him. Once we begin to get into his internal deeds, we find him going ahead of us into all the places we find ourselves in. Then with Paul we can dare say: 'We know that all things work for good for those who love God, who are called according to his purpose'.

Prayer: *God our Creator! Please cleanse us from our evil attitudes and deeds, with which we make your heart grieve and regret. As we plan to survive daily successfully and peacefully and safely, and desire to join your Son's salvific works, grant us strength to follow the footsteps of Noah in obeying and trusting your directions and shelter your Ark of love in the midst of our modern age challenges. Amen.*

Wednesday

If our inner eye is enlightened, we will always walk in light
(Scriptural Passages: Gen. 8: 6-22; Ps. 116; Mk. 8: 22-26)

As the Spirit of God never fails to offer us a deep symbolic meaning through the miracles of Jesus, in today's Gospel he shares with us some factual truth about our Christian life through a simple healing story. This story is undoubtedly linked with come events we know when Jesus was regretting about the arrogant blindness of the Pharisees to recognize the power of God found in his words and actions and scolding his disciples about their indifferent blindness to his caution against corrupted interiority of the Pharisees and the Herod.

In connection to this story, we should be aware of the rare gift, God has endowed humans at our creation. It is an inner ability to see through the reality, the depth and height of God the Supreme Spiritual Being's interactions with fragile humans. By healing the physical blindness of a resident at Bethsaida, Jesus emphasized that every one of his followers needed healing of their inner blindness and he claimed that it was possible if they reached out to him. By curing the blind man gradually he also taught them, due to their human inability and corrupted freedom, it would take a slow and gradual process.

Our understanding of Jesus is also a gradual process and it never ends. We prefer God's intervention in our spiritual growth should be like the instant coffeemaker or one-minute cooking of microwave. In God's parental love and wisdom, he has been dealing with his human children enduringly, patiently, slowly but steadily. We hear about Noah and his children in today's first reading that they found out the immense and enduring love and wisdom of God, when they were checking the natural disaster-situation of the flood. They glorified God for his faithfulness and his love-based repenting about the evil he had permitted. They were so happy to hear him saying to himself: *Never again will I curse the ground because of human beings, since the desires of the human heart are evil from youth; nor will I ever again strike down every living being, as I have done.*

Many of us seem to settle into a complacent level of understanding beyond which we never go. Because of our quick-fixing tendency, we forget very easily the eternal truth that even though we are unfaithful, he is faithful to us and will never fail us. More regrettably, we fail to offer, as the Psalm directs, the sacrifice of praise and thanksgiving for all the good God has done in our life. Nor do we pay our vows to the Lord publicly to demonstrate the immense goodness and greatness of our Master who saved us. As a result, our spiritual growth is blocked and also our ability to have a growing faith declines.

Prayer: *Our Sovereign Creator God! In our blindness filled with pride, we want to be like you God by creating our own gods. But our faith assures us that you will keep providing us some means of healing our miserable blindness. With filial hope we entreat you to bless us with the repeated healing action of Christ, so that finally we would clearly see everything that is truthful and heavenly. Amen.*

Thursday

*Living in God's covenantal love we will
never fear of life's challenges*
(Scriptural Passages: Gen. 9: 1-13; Ps. 102; Mk. 8: 27-33)

In the middle of his Gospel, after narrating many miraculous events in the life of Jesus, Mark makes the disciples respond to the question, who is Jesus?: While the public described the identity of Jesus in various ways, the Lord asked his disciples, 'who do you say that I am?' And Peter, on their behalf, responded: *"You are the Christ."* As Jewish Galilean, Peter surely knew what he was stating. He professed that Jesus was the Messiah, the Christ, and the Anointed One.

In that single word 'Christ', so many of Jesus' Characteristics are included. In the eyes of Jesus Peter's reply didn't come from his full understanding of the whole truth contained in that term 'Christ'; rather, he was only referring to one side of Jesus' identity of his glory, divinity, prophetic role, and his powerful mission and action. Hence in order to make Peter and other disciples understand his true and whole identity, Jesus responded: *The Son of Man must suffer greatly and be rejected by the elders, the chief priests, and the scribes, and be killed, and rise after three days.*

Peter showed he did not still understand what the Lord meant. As an impetuous person, he took seriously the first part of the Master's response about his future sufferings and death, and he never bothered about the most amazing second part of the answer: *The Son of Man will rise from death after three days.* Again, Jesus rebuked Peter not with anger but with lots of love and surely a bit of frustration, and said: *"You are thinking not as God does, but as human beings do."*

When sufferings affect us, when we are diagnosed with chronic and even terminal diseases and so on, almost all of us do the same as Peter rebuking Jesus; out of insecure feelings about our future life we resent against God and religion. But the Good God ceaselessly reminds us about his eternal covenantal promises he has made to humanity from the day of Noah. We hear him in today's first reading saying to Noah: *See, I am now establishing my covenant with you and your descendants after you.*

Our Master Jesus too does not want us, his disciples, to sit in fear as if in our dark days. Through the Psalmist he tells us we should never miss to declare that our God will never leave us in our lifesituations of sufferings; rather he continues to stoop down from his holy height, and hears all our groanings and liberates us from death.

Prayer: *Sovereign God, you have established your loving covenant with us and continuously confirming it faithfully. But often we are thinking not as you; yes Lord, we are fully convinced that your thoughts and ways are not ours. Hence we pray longingly that you liberate us from evils and rebuild our life with your Spirit so that following your Son Jesus in the times of our trials, our yoke become easy and burden light. Amen.*

Friday

God's Eternal Plan can never be foiled by our perverted behavior
(Scriptural Passages: Gen. 11: 1-9; Ps. 33; Mk. 8: 34-9: 1)

We all have challenges as our crosses to bear in daily life. Commonly, we, humans, tend to get upset about anything and everything, particularly if it happens by nature, by neighbors and surely if some such things come under the permission of the Almighty. Unfortunately we forget, most of the times all kinds of those crosses are generated by our own personal wounded pride, unduly-puffedup fake self-image. As an example of it, in today's first reading we read a world-classic event, occurring in the beginning life of human race.

Bible underlines, the whole world of humans once had the same language and the same words. But due to the human perverted use of their freedom and deviant view of human sovereignty among all creations, they started building the city and the tower with its top in the sky, and so make a name for themselves, became a cause of alienation among the people, violence, corruption, and all of the sins and crimes of overcrowding. Therefore, God intervened and prevented the so-called powerful people from achieving long term success in their fake self-glorification.

In Jesus' time, the people, as the Psalmist proudly sings about, whom God has chosen to be his own, took the same sort of abominable detour against God's sovereignty. Hence, we find Jesus challenging them and insisting that those who want to participate in the peace and joy of God's reign must deny their ambition, take up their cross, and let God be in charge. In other words, he advises us through his Gospel to get over ourselves. *"Whoever wishes to come after me must deny himself, take up his cross, and follow me."*

In his counseling on our bearing of life's crosses, first he fondly suggests: 'Take it easy; don't let these little things get to you. You are my close friends'. Secondly, he directs us: 'Look at me and how I bore my own crosses from the day I came down from heaven. Also look at your other fellowhumans who truly more than you are burdened with heavier burdens and hardships. You are not alone.' Plus, he too reminds us about a valuable benefit we would be drawing from all the crosses we bear. He invites us to follow him in his redemptive bleeding mission, carrying our crosses willingly and consequently we become sources of salvation of others as he won by his bloodshed and broken body.

Prayer: *Benevolent and truthful God! Rather than trying to accomplish something to make a name for ourselves, we are invited by your Son to let our name disappear and let the name of Christ be glorified by our work. Since such anextraordinary attitude has been difficult for most of us, we pray that we be granted by your Spirit his gifts of wisdom, humility and truth. Amen.*

Fr. Benjamin A Vima

Saturday

We pledge till our death we will be true
to our forbearers' faith in God
(Scriptural Passages: Heb. 11: 1-7; Ps. 145; Mk. 9: 2-13)

By expounding about the exemplary faith of Abel, Enoch and Noah in this short passage and continuing in the next chapter sharing a lengthy list of the examples of faith found in Abraham, Sarah, Isaac, Jacob, Joseph, Moses, the kings and prophets after the exile, the Letter to the Hebrews defines today our faith correctly: *"Faith is the realization of what is hoped for. But without faith it is impossible to please him, for anyone who approaches God must believe that he exists and that he rewards those who seek him."*

The Psalmist, sharing his spirit of such glorious faith, consisting in recognizing and proclaiming the invisible God's greatness and goodness, sings: *"God's grandeur is beyond understanding." "One generation praises your deeds to the next and proclaims your mighty works." They speak of the splendor of your majestic glory, tell of your wonderful deeds."*

Today's Gospel also takes us to hilltop with Jesus and his beloved Apostles to feel rightly what is all about faith we profess and what it demands: It tells us, first and foremost the unique identity of the Leader whom we follow and how to relate ourselves to him, as we hear from the Heavenly Father: *"'This is my beloved Son, listen to him.'*

Our faith includes to hope confidently our fragile and vulnerable life also would be transformed by the help of our Master. This is what the disciples encountered in that 'split-second' moment of seeing the Transformation of Jesus. Through Peter's babbling words, we understand well how the human hearts are craving for such moments permanently. *"Rabbi, it is good that we are here! Let us make three tents: one for you, one for Moses, and one for Elijah."*

Very importantly the fact of faith demands that we have to live our earthly life contently and joyfully in the midst of its dungeon and fire. It would be sad, as soon as we finish our religious rituals and devotions, we would be heading to the downhill with the same weakness, limitation, with the same diagnosed illness, riding in the same wheelchair. This is what Apostles went through. They found Jesus, walking with them as weak as a lamb; as innocent as a baby; as fragile friend as they were.

Prayer: *Lord, Our Father! We love to walk not by sight but always by the amazing and incredible faith, as the one and only way to be 'great'. May we stand and walk in daily life like a mighty ram in the midst of burning fire, chosen out for sacrifice from a great flock, a worthy victim made ready to be offered to God. And this is how we want to please you in proclaiming our faith in you and your Son Jesus. Amen.*

WEEK - 7

Monday

Godly wisdom offers us unique power blended with humility
(Scriptural Passages: Sir. 1: 1-10; Ps. 93; Mk. 9: 14-29)

We read today in the Book of Sirach that wisdom is the rare gift bestowed to us by the Creator: *There is but one, wise and truly awesome, seated upon his throne–the Lord. All wisdom is from the Lord and remains with him forever. And the fear of the Lord is glory and exultation, gladness and a festive crown.* In reaffirmation of this truth, today's Psalm underlines: *'The Lord is king; he is robed in majesty'*. The psalmist reminds us of the theme of God's power and wisdom and leadership in our lives.

In continuation of this teaching about the excellence of wisdom, God cautions us about the post-effects of knowledge and wisdom, when it is not properly handled. God reminds us also that the wrong way of storing of knowledge in our brain backlashes at us bringing psychological, emotional upheavals and horrible deviation and perversion of our attitudes, behaviors and deeds as we are reaping in this modern society.

Hence, God in Jesus offers us in his Gospel today a wonderful solution for proper managing of our wisdom and knowledge and making it a source of blossoming of human life with dignity and glory. We notice Jesus' disciples, though they were slowly filled with the knowledge about Jesus and his unique power and authority, being blamed in front of Jesus by a person whose son was possessed by evil spirit: *I brought my son and asked your disciples to drive that evil spirit out, but they were unable to do so."*

Immediately our Master expressed his frustration over his disciples' incapacity, saying to them: *O faithless generation, how long will I be with you? How long will I endure you?* He indeed cured the sick man only after he was sure the father of that sick man demonstrated his faith in Jesus' power. Then in private he gave the reason why his disciples could not drive the evil spirit out: He said to them, "*This kind can only come out through prayer."*

When we pull together Jesus' behavior and his words, we find, Jesus exposed to his disciples their lack of trust in God, their little faith and scored their lack of prayer, i.e., of conscious reliance on God's power when acting in Jesus' name.

Prayer: *Father of immense wisdom! Jesus exhorts us, not to be satisfied merely with our knowledge, acquired by our education and experiences, and by storing in our memory large amount of Scriptural and religious data information about you and Jesus; rather, he wants us to blend it with our strong faith and trust in you; and with intimate connections with you through prayer. We sincerely entreat you to share with us more of your wisdom that can keep us level-headed and grace-filled. Amen.*

Tuesday

If you want to be first, then be last
(Scriptural Passages: Sir. 2: 1-11; Ps. 37; Mk. 9: 30-37)

We come across so many references in Scriptures about human childhood, and childlike behavior. Through today's readings the Spirit of God clearly offers us what and why of such stunning advice to us. He underlines in the Book of Sirach that such advice of behaving like child is given only to those sons and daughters who in their matured life, start serving the Lord in justice and fear, never be distracted or disturbed even in the time of adversity and always patiently waiting for the glorious coming of the Lord God. It is to them the Spirit proposes the childlike attitude: *Trust God and God will help you; trust in him, and he will direct your way.*

The Psalmist too explains to us how and for what we, as adults, should be like little children. He exhorts us: *Commit your life wholeheartedly to the Lord; the salvation of the just is from the LORD; he is their refuge in time of distress; he helps them and delivers them from evil time.*

Above all, Jesus has clarified to us, in today's Gospel, the importance of this incredible advice of behaving like little children in an appropriate occasion where he saw all of his followers like you and me, standing there with an impending problem of life, in the midst of his disciples. Jesus noticed his Apostles, who were recruited by him to be matured enough to serve God through him by living his life and witnessing to it and his Kingdom, arguing among themselves: *Which of them was the greatest?*

To them he articulated very candidly that this sort of powermongering attitude is not going to help them in any way in the matters of God's Kingdom. Therefore, he asked them: Do you want to easily bear the yoke of challenges of life? Do you want to feel lightly the burdens of darkened future light? Do you wish to gain the genuine fruits of joy, peace and contentment in this world and the world to come? Then he proposed to them: *"If anyone wishes to be first, he shall be the last of all and the servant of all."*

Prayer: *Gentle and Gracious Father! According to the splendid advice of Jesus to us to be last, to lose, to serve, and to be little like children, we decide to travel light in our life-journey. Offer us your Son's Power to be powerless and his Brave heart to be little. Also, Lord, bestow us a tiny portion of your compassion so that we can plunge into sponsoring, feeding, supporting and performing charitable deeds to uplift the fallible, vulnerable, needy, sick, dying, and inflicted people by many evils. Because we believe by being like child and helping the needy as their sponsors, is the only way to alleviate our own pains in facing our life's challenges. Amen.*

Wednesday

Jesus, the New Law of Wisdom brings true peace and joy in human deals
(Scriptural Passages: Sir. 4: 11-19; Ps. 119; Mk. 9: 38-40)

All the words of God we hear today from the passages of Sirach and the Psalm, include not only the praises toward the greatness of the Word coming out from God as Wisdom and Law, but also some valuable instruction for us on how to lead our earthly life in true peace, joy, and contentment with this magnificent gift of God. Psalmist sings: *Those who love your law have great peace, and for them there is no stumbling block.* Sirach augments such eternal truth, writing: *Wisdom, namely God's Word, breathes life into her children and admonishes those who seek her. Though she tries us with her discipline she comes back to bring us happiness and reveal her secrets to us.*

In the Gospel today Jesus, emphasizing all that has been said in OT, demonstrates to us about how to apply such revealed truth in practical life. We find Apostles James and John, demonstrating their zealous attitude toward their Master and his values. When they had found out that someone, outside of Jesus' Primary Team, was casting out demons in his Name, they complained to him. Unfortunately, their Master was not happy about their kind of zealous move.

Jesus, the Wisdom, perceiving the evil spirit possessing his disciples, offered an incredible advice: *Do not prevent him. There is no one who performs a mighty deed in my name who can at the same time speak ill of me.* He reprimanded them for their envy and fear. His reply was decisive, based on his unique wisdom. It reflects a person at peace, and therefore strong and secure.

Affiliated to Christianity, so many of us feel good whenever we join with people of one mind and one heart in worship and more in performing good deeds. Unfortunately, some among us, like the sons of thunder, may even possess an evil-attitude; while defending the worth of our racial, denominational or national culture of religion, we may refute and disregard the growth of some other religions and their works, and foolishly, we may even demand Jesus even to destroy those 'others'. And Jesus warns us today that attitude is not at all his 'kingdom-Policy'.

Prayer: *Lord of Wisdom and Love! We confess sincerely our human hearts are being thwarted by silly attitude we have developed even in our religious adherence to you and your Son and consequently we encounter our values or practices are in* *conflict with those outside our 'holy' campus. Father, Send your Spirit of Wisdom into our minds and hearts so that rereading our own sinful background and insincere, unjust and arrogant abuses we indulge in; and we may follow your Son as our Life, Way and Truth in every neighborly deal that can please you. Amen.*

Thursday

A lie has no leg, but a scandal has wings
(Scriptural Passages: Sir. 5: 1-8; Ps. 1; Mk. 9: 41-50)

Absolutely it is true, all humans are good; this is because it is the way the God designed and created the entire universe and its creatures; and at the completion of his job, he was totally satisfied about his creation work, shouting loud: *It is good.* However, Biblically it is true, soon after the days of creation, humans behaved so wicked that the same God was found regretting for creating such evil-producing humans. The main reason for such wickedness pervading the human race is either they temporarily or permanently become victimized by their perverted intellect and will.

By Teacher Sirach, we are told today that human intellect and will are enslaved first by human perverted lust and trust on the power of wealth; by finding strength in following the earthly desires of the heart and foolishly thinking no one, including God, would prevail against them. Plus, the worst mistake they do is they can go on committing evils because there is a compassionate God who offers forgiveness ceaselessly. Today's Psalm echoes the same truth, that the eternal blessings are bestowed only to those who hope in the Lord and act accordingly. When we live the way God shows to us, all sorts of positive outcomes can be expected both on this earth and beyond. Conversely, the Psalm also confirms the bad and unpleasant outcomes of human wickedness.

In keeping with the thoughts of Sirach and the Psalmist, we hear Jesus, in today's Gospel, sternly condemning those of us, who take such perverted stand in our human deals. He was terribly angry and very critical of those who were a stumbling block to the faith of others: *Whoever causes one of these little ones, who believe in me, to sin, it would be better for him if a great millstone were put around his neck and he were thrown into the sea.*

Moreover, Jesus pointed out to us, that every evil action originates from our evil inclination, and therefore, he exhorted us to take care of our inner spirit, as Sirach advised: *Don't walk "according to the desires of your heart".* He demanded us forthrightly to control our physical lust, emotional outburst, and fake freedom of licentiousness. Being so serious on this matter, he even prescribed for us some inhuman and undignified actions of self-mutilation.

Prayer: *Father of unimaginable compassion and uncompromising Justice! As your Son demands, we are ready to 'circumcise' our heart of its evil inclinations before they are resulted in scandalous and abusive deeds. We are really sorry that forgetting your immense power, we are prone to rely on only our fragile and sinful inclinations. Kindly salt us with your amazing fire of love, so that we love you wholeheartedly and love and respect our neighbors, especially little children who are certainly your special favorites. Amen.*

Friday

Human friendship gets its fullness when
it is bonded in fidelity to God
(Scriptural Passages: Sir. 6: 5-17; Ps. 119; Mk. 10: 1-12)

If we are asked "What will make you happy?" some of us might acknowledge that, to be happy, 'we want enough to eat'. Many others may answer, 'we want to have a goal in life. But almost all of us would say that we want a friend to love and to be loved. The Grand Teacher Sirach, reading our minds, offers his valuable and realistic thoughts on friendship. First, he appreciates the greatness and nobility of the faithful friendship: *Faithful friends are sturdy shelter to us; they are precious treasure to us; they are life-saving remedies.* Then, listing out the countless human beings who come into our life charming us with friendliness, he advises us: *When you gain a friend, first test him/her, and be not too ready to trust him/her.*

In other words, we are told that if we expect to reap best fruits from our friendships, we first need to test and choose a right person. As we ourselves have no proper ability to do it, the Teacher concludes, *such admirable and noble friendship is possible only when we include God in our friendship.* To include God in this process, the Psalmist, joining with the Teacher, urges us today to pray to the Almighty to become more open to the Spirit in order to be able to discern God's Will in this process of courting friendship.

Jesus the heavenly Teacher, as usual applying the same principles and ideologies of Sirach regarding genuine friendship, teaches how all men and women, who are bonded as lifelong friends by human laws and regulations, should treat this friendship. He offers this magnificent

71

instruction of friendship to be followed in a weird but real 'two-in-one' married life. In his reply, to a question of his inimical critics about 'divorce in marriages', he expounds it well.

It is natural for a boy to be attracted sexually to a girl and both may start developing their friendship; but it is immature. It is social for them to make their friendship legitimate by lawful rituals and by signing an incredible contract of their friendship. But still their friendship is immature. As Sirach had stated, without God's active presence the friendship would be jeopardized. Hence, Jesus reminds us: *what God has joined together, no human being must separate."*

Prayer: *Lord God! We are truly blessed in Christianity, finding thousands and thousands of your Son's disciples continue lifelong as faithful and joyful friends. At the same time, we know how those marriage-friendships are being damaged; even one party misses you, everything is collapsed in their friendship. Kindly bless all those still struggling in their married life to be faithful and friendly to you and your values. May they be freed of encountering so many evils prowling around them and inside the families they buildup. Amen.*

Saturday

*Be childlike to live a fruitful, peaceful
and joyful life in this world*
(Scriptural Passages: Sir. 17: 1-15; Ps. 103 Mk. 10: 13-16)

Through the Teacher Sirach, today God speaks again to us: *Keep on living a well-balanced, and level-headed life in between two extremes.* Namely, on one side, we share God's power, knowledge, and his authority over all creatures;

and on the other, we are limited with our weaknesses, and our short term of earthly life. In this precarious situation, God expects us to avoid all evil and be controlled not going too far extremes of the two sides.

As a support system, God has set before us knowledge, a law of life as our inheritance; an everlasting covenant he has made with us, and he has revealed to us his justice and his judgments. He has also put the fear of himself upon our hearts, and showed us his mighty works in our day today life.

In addition to the exhortation of Sirach, Jesus instructs us to be childlike, if we desire to lead our life in balance and levelheaded way: *"Let the children come to me; do not prevent them, for the Kingdom of God belongs to such as these; and whoever does not accept the Kingdom of God like a child will not enter it."* By this he means: That only those humans who possess a transformed heart of complete openness and unprejudiced mind. From his own life pattern we also know that God's kingdom can hold seats and mansions only for those who embrace willingly and voluntarily poverty in spirit, full dependence on God, and live a simple and humble life until their last breath.

I underline the adverbs: "Willingly and voluntarily", because of our human physical and emotional limitation by nature every dimension of our greatness, strength, and all the supreme gifts God has bestowed us in our birth will be shrunk automatically and turn out to be nothing but dust. However, one thing would be staying stable and powerful, and that is the inner innocent spirit the Creator has endowed us with. Through the Psalmist we are also encouraged on this day by God with an eternal truthful fact: Even if we forget all that God has done for us, and even if we are unfaithful to God by ignoring all his precepts and performing all kinds of evils, he is always faithful to us as a kind, compassionate Father. He is waiting eagerly to embrace us if we go to him as his beloved children.

Prayer: *Lord our Savior, you want us to be pure of heart like little children so that we get a place in your Kingdom; you too expect all our human affections are purified so that you would shine through. Fill us with your divine grace so that being liberated from the selfish temptations of today's fake culture we may attain our glorious ultimate destiny. Amen.*

WEEK - 8

Monday

Bettering life of the needy with our riches
our joy becomes complete
(Scriptural Passages: Sir. 17: 24-29; Ps. 31; Mk. 10: 17-27)

In Psalm we hear today the Spirit announcing that our true happiness in this world can be attained, if we are consciously aware of all our sins forgiven by God. *Happy the person whose offence is forgiven, whose sin is remitted. O happy the one to whom the Lord imputes no guilt, in whose spirit is no guile.*

Echoing the same Spirit's words, and holding the OT understanding that humans after their death would be dumped in Sheol, a darkened gloomy state of living, where no trace of happiness would be found, Teacher Sirach urges us today to do all that we can before we die, in order to enjoy God's happiness by a non-stop praising of his divine glory. He also instructs us: *While we are alive, we should repent from sin while we still can; we must turn to the Lord, plead before his face and lessen your offence. Return to the Lord and leave sin behind, plead before his face and lessen our offence.*

Jesus foretold and promised us that human life after death would be a blissful state of living where we would be praising God in joyful singing and dancing together with hosts of angels and saints. However, such promise is guaranteed only to those of his disciples who accept and live his evangelical counsels.

As he points out in today's Gospel, while we still live alive in this world, besides praising and thanking the Lord, we should continuously observe the Commandments of the Lord faithfully as the good-willed young man whom he meets in his public ministry.

Also, Jesus warns us not to be too much excited with our moral goodness. He indicates this to us, in warning the same young man: *"You lack one thing; go, sell what you own, and give the money to the poor, and you will have treasure in heaven; then come, follow me."* Jesus was asking him to do something very positive, namely, to share his prosperity with his brothers and sisters in need. Unfortunately, the young man didn't relish the Master's advice, and went away from Jesus.

Prayer: *All Benevolent God! We confess honestly, that as the young man hurt Jesus by his preference of hoarding his riches, we too stupidly misbehave by not caring our Master, who is standing at our door and knocking and begging us to feed, to shelter, to clothe and to educate the needy people around us. Graciously grant us the enlightenment and sufficient strength to listen and obey to Jesus' counsel, so that joining Jesus' plan of bettering the world, we may dispose all the worldly goods we have gathered to help the needy neighbors and consequently we may be filled with heavenly joy in praising you and your glory. Amen.*

Tuesday

Whatever connection we think we have with God, is His 'dole'
(Scriptural Passages: Sir. 35: 1-12; Ps. 50; Mk. 10: 28-31)

Among many profound promises God has made in his covenantal deals with his upright and faithful humans, the most enlivening and encouraging one is to "give back" in abundance. In the Book of Sirach we are told: *The Lord is one who always repays, and he will give back to you sevenfold.* And more surprisingly in today's Gospel, replying to Peter's valid question, what reward he, his comrades, who have given up everything and followed him, would be offered as rewards, Jesus said categorically that *those disciples, who have given up every earthly possession and relation, will receive a hundred times more now in this present age.* Additionally, in today's Psalm we are astounded to know the reciprocal gesture that God will show us even in his unbelievable saving power.

Such beautiful promise of the Lord surely excites us and strengthens us to go forward to attain that incredible abundance. But what the Scriptures give us, as conditions to be fulfilled to possess such gorgeous future, is bit hard to digest and that is the 'narrow Highway' of God in Jesus.

Through Sirach God demands us to keep his laws as great oblation; to observe the commandments as sacrifices of peace offering; to please the Lord by refraining from evil and to avoid injustice as an atonement; to give to the Most High, as he has given to us, generously, according to our means. And above all, while doing such almsgivings and charitable deeds, we must never think we are doing them in order to, as if, bribing the Lord; rather we should esteem them as our sacrifices of praise to the Almighty;

plus, we should do all love-performances in the generous spirit of joy.

According to the Psalmist, the prerequisites of receiving God's gifts abundantly are: That we should be upright; must have made a true covenant with God by sacrifice; must fulfill our vows to the Most High; and we must lead a life in God's right way.

Breathtakingly, Jesus, in his heavenly wisdom, places before us one single condition to be fulfilled for attaining his manifold gifts. He proposes that only when we give up all our earthly possessions and relations for his sake and for the sake of the Gospel, we would be offered all his promised eternal and fuller life.

Prayer: *Lord, Jesus, open our eyes. Help us hear your call and believe your comforting promise. Don't let us be blind to the attraction and addiction to a way of life that ultimately excludes you. Let us live more freely. Let us know the joy of being with you, loving as you love us, sharing your mission of compassion for others as you do, and of doing what we can to make a difference in this world for those who are most in need. Amen.*

Wednesday

Let us never prefer human praise to the glory of God
(Scriptural Passages: Sir. 36: 1-17; Ps. 79; Mk. 10: 32-45)

Today Sirach, the wise sage, spells out loudly that our hearts, by nature, intensely demand for the restoration of our self-glory with which or for which we were created by God. Sirach prays to God the Creator this way: *O Lord! Give new signs and work new wonders. Give evidence of your deeds of old; fulfill the prophecies spoken in your name, Reward* those who have hoped in you, and let your prophets be proved true.

The Psalmist echoes the same demand to the Creator: *Help us, O God our savior, because of the glory of your name; with your great power free those doomed to death. Then we, your people and the sheep of your pasture, will give thanks to you forever.*

Jesus too never hesitated to long for being glorified by God; but he always wished, it should be done according to his Father's Will. We hear in the Gospels that, while Jesus declared that his purpose of coming into this world is nothing but to be glorified by his Father, he was troubled knowing how such glorification is going to be fulfilled through his Bloodshed and Brokenbody. Hence, he humbly and obediently said, 'Father, glorify your name'. And God the Father, being well-pleased by Jesus' resignation, declared in loud voice from heaven: *"I have glorified it and will glorify it again."*

Like Sirach, like the Psalmist and surely, like Lord Jesus, the disciples too were longing for the restoration of their original glory. That is what we hear in today's Gospel event. Almost all his disciples, like James and John, were aching for the glory; but they didn't grasp what and how their Master perceived of that glory. He repeatedly explained to them how to covet the true glory. According to him, they have to drink the bitter chalice of human life's events and to be baptized in ignominious death.

This means, the only way for all of us, Jesus' disciples, to restore our original and real glory of divinity is to empty ourselves as he did; to serve all our fellow humans, and to go deeply into the depth of this earthly life as he immersed even to the extent of encountering its hellish quality.

Prayer: *Father God! We, the feeble and weak creatures, with the right of being your Son's disciples, long for vain earthly power, glory, high position, and good name as well as fighting tooth and nail becoming indignant as the Apostles, to be in the first place in the team of Jesus. While we truly feel sorry for such perverted behavior, we beg you to send out your Spirit on all of us to listen and follow your Son's footsteps not only to possess the genuine glory from you but also attain it through drinking the bitter chalice and being baptized in bloodshed and broken body. Amen.*

Thursday

Blessed are we who are enlightened to see God's glory in nature
(Scriptural Passages:(Sir. 42: 18-25; Ps. 33; Mk. 10: 46-52)

Most of us feel frustrated at God because of his continued hiddenness in our physical and earthly life. However, there lived many good people, who have been overwhelmed with the vivid portrayal of the same hidden God's actions for eternity.

Sirach, for instance, recalling God's marvelous works, says in today's first reading: *At God's word were his works brought into being; they do his will as he has ordained for them.* The Psalmist too does the same and teaches us to be grateful for such magnificent deeds of God. It is sad to know that human creatures, being enslaved by sin, become blind to see the marvels of God.

It is for liberating us from that blindness, Jesus came to this world. He said: *I am the light of the world; whoever follows me will have the light of life.* To demonstrate this hysterical phenomenon, we find him in today's Gospel, performing the miracle of curing a blind man Bartimaeus.

In this event, the Spirit offers us some means to be enlightened by Jesus.

On hearing that Jesus of Nazareth was coming by, the blind man cried out: *"Jesus, son of David, have pity on me."* Despite the bystanders telling him to be silent, he kept calling out all the more, "Son of David, have pity on me." As the people encouraged him saying that Jesus was calling him, he threw aside his cloak, sprang up, and came to Jesus and earnestly told him, 'Master, I want to see'. From those movements and words of the blind man, we are offered two means to be cured by Jesus.

First, we must have firm faith in the powerful identity of Jesus of Nazareth. Second, those of us who want to get cured by Jesus, must be very honest and humble in recognizing our own blindness. Very fittingly, Jesus emphasizes that those two requisites are expected of us when we reach out to him for his miraculous help. This is why, he appreciates the blind man saying: *'Go your way; your faith has saved you."* Also Jesus, respecting the freedom of the needy person, gets his authorization to be touched and healed. Thus, we are told by the Spirit that without our personal concern and decisive move, made of faith and hope, even the Light, shining like the sun, cannot cure our spiritual blindness.

Prayer: *Creator God! We are truly blindfolded not to see all the natural splendor that came and still coming out your Hands. Worst of all, we are blinded only to see our creaturely strengths and puny intellectual abilities and seem to be content in vain human glory. Jesus, whom you sent to us as our Light, calls us every moment to come within his Lightline. Father, energize us to go to our Master to get cured; so that we may be freed of being entangled in our own life, our space, and our ideas; and to see the amazing universe and to appreciate all that life has to offer us; and we want to see you in every person we meet. Amen.*

Friday

We are to immensely rejoice to know that God is delighted in us
(Scriptural Passages: Sir. 44: 1, 9-13;
Ps. 149; Mk. 11: 11-26)

In today's Psalm, King David galvanizes all God's people, singing: *Let Israel be glad in their maker, let the children of Zion rejoice in their king.* David adds to his advice: *It is because the Lord takes delight in his people.* Sirach gives today another reason for such rejoicing and praising the Lord. *God will never forget all the virtues of God's people; and their glory will never be blotted out.*

Now a legitimate question arises from our hearts: In what way we can make our God be delighted so that we become eligible for receiving abundant gifts? The solid answer is offered by Sirach that those unending blessings are available only to those people who, not nominally identifying themselves as 'God's people', but live a godly life and that too, being led with covenantal fidelity.

In the Gospel of Mark we hear today the core teaching of Jesus on how to delight God so much that God's benevolent eternal graces would be showered upon us. First, using a metaphor-in-action of cursing a fig tree, which didn't offer fruits for his hunger, even it was not the time for figs, Jesus emphasized that for any God's blessing to be offered to us we must be delighting the Lord in season and out of season.

Secondly, by a wild action of driving out those selling and buying in the Temple area, Jesus wanted to offer us another way of delighting our God. Quoting a Scriptural saying, 'My *house shall be called a house of prayer for all peoples*', and uttering with zealous feeling: '*But you have made it a den of thieves,*' Jesus taught us such zeal for

God and his Holiness is another way of delighting God in order to possess abundant gifts.

In addition, Jesus suggests two more practical and brisk actions we should do in all our prayer-efforts. He instructs us to make sure our prayer to God should be qualified, first with genuine faith in God. We should esteem the magnificent efficiency of faith, with which, as Jesus points out, even if we say to the mountain to be lifted up and thrown into the sea, but always holding very strong, obstinate, and with no doubt whatsoever, it will be done for us. Besides, Jesus recommends that when we submit our prayer to God we should possess a forgiving heart, as our Father God forgives, erasing all our inner grievances against our neighbors.

Prayer: *Lord God of power and might! Your Son chose us from this world to share your heavenly gifts with us and to bear solid and lasting fruits in this world and the world to come. Grant us, we pray, the grace to believe relentlessly you and your Son and enable to encounter you both with your Spirit in nature, and in every moment of our social and religious life so that you may be delighted. Amen.*

Saturday

Let the wisdom of Christ dwell in us richly
(Scriptural Passages: (Sir. 51: 12-20; Ps. 19; Mk. 11: 27-33)

In the beginning of the Book of Sirach, we were reminded the vast gap existing between the power of knowledge and the authority of Wisdom. And as today we read the final passage from the same Book, the Teacher instructs us about the lifelong struggle it takes to attain the wisdom and its authority.

Feminizing of wisdom and its elusiveness, the Teacher expresses his continuous striving for possessing her in season and out of season from the day of his youth. *When I was young and innocent, I sought wisdom openly in my prayer.* Indeed, he was tormented within his soul in pursuing such wisdom-searching; nonetheless, he gladly accepts: *In the short time I paid heed, I met with great instruction. Since in this way I have profited, I will give my teacher grateful praise. I became resolutely devoted to her.* The words of Sirach flow so beautifully articulating an enticing search with great rewards for those who are willing to take this journey and open the gate.

The Psalmist indeed shares with us today a manual of the directions, which God has bestowed to us as his precepts, rules, and commands, similar to those of Sirach, to guide our lives toward wisdom. He sings: *The command of the LORD is clear, enlightening the eye. The precepts of the Lord give joy to the heart. The decree of the LORD is trustworthy, giving wisdom to the simple.*

When God's Son came from heaven, he made that divine counsel clearer and more vivid to us. In today's Gospel we come to know how Jesus with his wisdom approached each challenging lifesituation with a calm, simplistic way. While his opponents tried to trap him by demanding the source of his authority, he turned the table with his question requiring them to address the ultimate authority. Due to their twisted attitude, they were struggling to connect both the political and divine paradigms. On the contrary Jesus used it very deliberately in order to silence and rebuke the half-baked elders' attitudes.

The powerful message of this story is that when we react, like Jesus' adversaries, we too may be unable to answer the questions, which the Gospel proposes to us; if we are stuck to our cobble-headedness, not being illuminated by Jesus' light, we may cut ourselves off from the font of wisdom.

Prayer: *God of Wisdom and Power! We entreat you that, considering Jesus as your Word and Law of Wisdom, we may appreciate him as more precious than any earthly possessions and that, becoming more simple and humble to search for achieving him in whom the divine wisdom is immensely present, we may experience true joy in our hearts that lasts forever. Amen.*

WEEK - 9

Monday

Jesus is the faithful witness to God's mercy and justice
(Scriptural Passages: Tobi. 1: 1-2, 2:
1-9; Ps. 112; Mk. 12: 1-12)

The story about Tobit, narrated in the book of Tobit, portrays how faithful followers of God should show their devotion through the corporal works of mercy, such as sharing one's meals with those who are unable to fill their stomach with sufficient food; and burying the dead, especially when they are strangers and abandoned and neglected by the society. It proves that humans are born charitable by nature, even without the benefit of Jesus' teachings.

In fact, as Tobit, most of us are stymied from doing good works by the coldness, indifference and sometimes hatefulness of some among us. Our neighbors apparently may think we are foolish for taking such risks. If we persistently devoted like Tobit in performing acts of charity in the midst of undesirable situations, such good habits of the heart are formed in this manner, a powerful force for good is at work, which also witnesses to the truth of God's mercy in our midst.

This is simply a vivid testimony to the fact that the God whom we worship is good and merciful. As we sing today with the Psalmist, we will be blessed when we lead an upright and generous life and heavenly light would shine in us through the darkness; and we would be gracious and merciful and just, as God our Creator.

Jesus, God's Son, when he came down to be one like us, noticed so many of his chosen people had a sort of commitment to God different from that of his forebears like Tobit and from his own teachings. He therefore in today's Gospel is seen pricking their perverted conscience through the Parable of the Vineyard and driving into them how wrong they were by being disobedient and unrighteous before God. They would not respect any limits on their desires for autonomy; and they neither feared nor respected the owner and proprietor of their life. Jesus made it clear the terrible judgement from their Owner would soon come.

The Spirit invites us to recall that sometimes we resemble these folks when we decide to follow our own autonomous paths that lead to sin and alienation. We, too, need mercy and reconciliation from our Creator, as we sometimes simply respect the wrong things.

Prayer: *Merciful Lord, teach us to guard our hearts against the hardness that comes from pursuing our sinful inclinations that alienate us from you. Help us build habits of loving and serving you in all things. Infuse us honor you by passing along toward others the same charity and mercy, which we have received from you. Amen.*

Tuesday

Virtuously-leading a just life lies in the middle
(Scriptural Passages: (Tobit 2: 9-14; Ps. 112; Mk. 12: 13-17)

The Psalmist today describes the benefits of blessings that will be given to any just human being. We hear from him a list of virtues which characterizes the nature of that blessed person: *A just person is one who fears the Lord; greatly delights in His commands; firm and trusting in Him; steadfast in fearing Him; and lavishly gives to the poor.* What embarrasses us is the perennial fact that even such just people face in their day today life many conflicts in their human relationships in the family and social and religious situations.

In the first reading we find a conflict occurring between Tobit, who was a just man, and his wife Anna, who was faithful to her husband and even went to work in order to earn her livelihood and for her family's sustenance while her husband lost his eyesight. But, as we hear in the reading, due to some misunderstanding Tobit raised a conflict against his wife and the family lost its peace. It is because of Tobit's failing to manage the dual dimension of human life where both the divine and the human blend together. He seemed to be very good in dealings with God but miserably weak in handling issues regarding human interpersonal relationship.

We meet, in today's Gospel, the same conflicting issue, presented to Jesus but in politico-religious situation. Jesus, handling his 'duality of divine and human' in a proper way, brought to himself glory and victory of resurrection even after his death; plus he too brought salvation to the entire human race. We know how he lived and said that testified his true 'just personality'. As we hear in the Gospel incident, Jesus prudently answered to the mischievous question of his enemies. Though his answer may seem like very diplomatic and cunning and put their mouths shut, it was the perfect declaration of his genuine dual-personality. *"Repay to Caesar what belongs to Caesar and to God what belongs to God."* Here we discover his personality was built on two main attitudes blended correctly.

He was both God-oriented as well as earthly life-loving person. He has never been too extreme in applying and activating these two original dimensions of human life: spiritual and physical; heavenly and earthly; summing up all Scriptural Commandments into two he was obedient to both commandments: loving God and loving his neighbors as well. He never sacrificed one for the sake of the other. Anything he did for the sake of his God never subdue or throw over board his love for his humans and their lives.

Among the characteristics of a genuine 'just person', listed by the Psalmist, the most significant one is *'The heart of the just one is firm, trusting in the Lord'*. This is what the Lord Jesus demonstrated in today's Gospel event. Being a just one, Jesus was observing all that his Father ordered him to do; and simultaneously he never neglected or avoided any human enterprises of justice, love and peace. This is the genuine personality of any human being who wants to be fruitful and successful.

Regrettably, almost all of us, including those who are trying to be just persons before God, have been failing to manage our beautiful duality of physical and spiritual and we always go either extreme and thus hurt ourselves and others.

Prayer: *All-Virtuous God! You have declared through your Son that if we want to enjoy all the blessings and abundant fruits* *in our lives the only thing we have to do is, following your Son Jesus, we should manage the duality of our personhood, always standing, walking, and running in the middle of Your High Road. Kindly fill us with your Spirit of Wisdom and steadfastness in keeping our uprightness. Amen.*

Wednesday

Our God is the Lord of Life and Resurrection
(Scriptural Passages: Tobi. 3: 1-17; Ps. 25; Mk. 12: 18-27)

God's words in our Scriptures consistently portray the importance and efficacy of our human prayer. Amazingly in the Scriptural passages we take today for our prayerful meditation we hear the exemplary prayers of three God's people: Tobit, Sarah, and King David. Tobit accidentally lost his eyesight and he tried all that he could do for healing but in vain. Therefore, the entire community, including his wife Anna, hurt him with insulting calumnies. He expressed in prayer his overwhelming grief and pain.

In the same sort of lifesituation we see Sarah, Raguel's daughter, crying out her prayer. She had been married to seven husbands, but the wicked demon killed them off before the marriages were consummated. Her life-crisis took her to the limit of even suicide herself. And we hear too the same mournful prayer from David in his Psalm as he was being strangled in the midst of horrible trials. He was pushed to the life's edge that was shameful and all his enemies were waging wars against him.

Those prayers were amazingly knocking at the Pearls Gate and the Supreme Being stooped over those prayerful persons and granted all their life's needs. One thing we should remember. Those holy men and women got all rewards from God, not just because their prayers were mournful and pitiable; rather, those prayers consisted of some ingredients of any qualityprayer our Lord Jesus recommends.

In the Gospel we hear from Jesus the core of those ingredients. He firmly confirms the main source of the efficacy of any deed, we do for God and to God, is to hold a clear understanding of God's true identity, nature and quality. He says: *The God to whom we pray is not God of the dead but of the living.* This saying of Jesus was a reply, literally targeted to the resurrected life after death as the question, proposed to him, called for. But in the light of the writings of Church Fathers, it can be said that he used that occasion for referring to the earthly life we are living before we die. During this time of earthly life God interacts only with those who breathe alive or atleast try to be struggling for surviving in their voluntary and close connections with God.

Prayer: *Living God! Very sadly most of our prayers are not qualityprayers that bring miracles in our lives from your hands. Anything we chose, planned or implemented was all gone in the past, namely dead. You, being a God of Life, abhor us like dead-humans walking. Kindly send your Spirit of fervor and trust so that in all our needs, especially when we are sorrow-stricken, we may get up from our deathtrap or from the self-made grave and start walking alive, breathing alive and acting it out for bearing wonderful fruits of love, support and consolation among us. Amen.*

Thursday

True lovers are not far from the Kingdom of God
(Scriptural Passages: Tobit 6: 10-11, 7:
1-17, 8: 4-9; Ps. 128 Mk. 12: 28-34)

Human life is simply a bundle of relationships between God and humans and between human to human. Bible instructs that the norms, codes and disciplines, used for the sake of creating and maintaining well those relationships, must be based on the justice and love-based will of God. In today's Psalm we hear David singing a sort of plain statement that the ever-reliable God would bless abundantly all his devotees, especially the couples, who live their life and conduct their spousal and family relationships according to his commands.

We read in today's Gospel, Jesus was asked by a Scribe *'which is the first of all the commandments?'* The answer Jesus gave consisted of the command of twofold love. 'Love God wholeheartedly and love your neighbor wholeheartedly'. We cannot truly love God if we do not love our neighbor and we cannot truly love our neighbor if we do not love God. These inseparable commandments also mean that we love our neighbor through God and God through our neighbor.

In the Scriptures, a neighbor is anyone in need, and who can be supported by us. Also, the Word of God has instructed us that any relationship among humans, for its successful ending, must be accomplished as tripod action connecting us, God, and neighbors. From olden days, many God's sons and daughters have applied such Godly norm in all their undertakings, especially in their marriages.

The Book of Tobit presents to us the ideal marriage of Tobiah as a model for such God-blessed married life. It started with God, whose help and blessing were invoked by Tobit, the father of Tobiah, before the traveling of Tobiah in search of his God-blessed lifepartner. In its process God-sent angel joined with Tobiah as his travel-companion and counselor. By the guidance of God's Angel, Tobiah found the right and God-blessed woman for his life. As the climax of his wedding story, God again worked marvelous miracle in the lives of the couple. Tobiah recognized Sarah as his neighbor and showed her the appropriate support and love. His action was embedded in his love of God. It is indeed a story teaching us how to win the victory over hardship and deliverance from suffering through loving God and loving our neighbor.

Prayer: *Compassionate and loving God! Your Scripture portrays some of those God-fearing people, who involved in the marriage union help each other with love, but always under their faith, hope and love in you. We beg you to grant us your enlightening grace to seek and obey your clear and straightforward guidelines for our fruitful human relationships, so that being liberated from all clutches of evil spirit, we may be not far from the kingdom of God. Amen.*

Friday

*Total commitment to Love Command is
the key to open God's Treasures*
(Scriptural Passages: Tobi. 11: 5-17; Ps. 146; Mk. 12: 35-37;

There may be many ways to enter into the heavenly and blissful mansion of our God; and there may be multiple different keys to open the amazing treasure-hall where countless divine secrets and mysteries are securely stockpiled; though humans are eligible to enter into the mansion as well as to possess such treasures, they are shut up from us because, while there is an appropriate master-key to open the doors of that mansion and treasure hall, regrettably we try to open those doors with improper keys.

As Gospel acclamation we recited: *Whoever loves me will keep my word, and my Father will love him and we will come to him.* These Jesus' words declare that our firm faith in his divine Sonship and in his redeeming role, is the master-key to possess God's treasures. In Mark's Gospel we see Jesus, claiming such position and role. He says, *"How do the scribes claim that the Christ is the son of David? David himself, inspired by the Holy Spirit, said: The Lord said to my lord, 'Sit at my right hand until I place your enemies under your feet.' And he too added: David himself calls him 'Lord'; so how is he his son?"*

Undoubtedly our faith in Jesus takes us to believe also in the salvific deeds of God the Father. we read in OT about many God's people, full of such faith, enjoying the heavenly treasures in earthly life. In the Book of Tobit we find this truth in the consistent prayers of Tobit and his wife Anna, who were enlightened in latter years, his son Tobiah, and his wife Sarah, who even in their your years were committed to the Lord. In all their life's experiences-both good and bad as well, we find these family members constantly held love, trust, faith, and mercy not only among themselves but also toward their God who was their Creator and Redeemer.

They expressed this both in their behaviors and prayers. It is noteworthy we discover in them on one side, a total devotion to one's family; and on another side, their strong commitment to belief that God would be able to make anything happen. With the Psalmist their hearts lisped daily that *I will praise the LORD all my life. Because it was you who scourged me, and it is you who has had mercy on me.* It is this dual commitment all of us are in most need today.

Prayer: *Almighty and merciful God! What you have done through your Son becoming flesh as Jesus is always more than we can fully grasp. The only right response to that revelation of your amazing love is our love for you and every other creature that we meet in the family and the society. As we promise to love you and your human children wholeheartedly, we beg you to grant us the grace to continue walking in your presence and possess your treasures in your wonderland. Amen.*

Saturday

Our tiny gift with big heart pleases the Lord most
(Scriptural Passages: Tobi. 12: 1-20; Tobit
Canticle 13: 2-8; (Mk. 12: 38-44)

In Gospel acclamation we recited the words of Jesus: *Blessed are the poor in spirit; for theirs is the Kingdom of heaven.* He was fully correct in underlining that all God's miraculous happenings in this earthly life are seen clearly only by those who are poor in spirit. Besides, they are the ones who possess the guts to sing joyfully, as we recited in Responsorial Psalm: *Blessed be God, who lives forever. He scourges and then has mercy; he casts down to the depths of the nether world, and he brings up from the great abyss. No one can escape his hand.*

In addition, they are the ones who can see their God in the needy, the weak and the downtrodden. We hear in OT that it is this kind of heavenly-connected life, about which the Angel Raphael exhorted both Tobit and Tobiah: *"Thank God! Give him the praise and the glory. Before all the living, acknowledge the many good things he has done for you. Do good, and evil will not find its way to you. Prayer and fasting are good, but better than either is almsgiving accompanied by righteousness.* Besides, the Angel also revealed to them that in all their good and pious undertakings and in their hope-filled prayers of sufferings, their God had been glorified and he granted them all his blessings.

Jesus repeatedly proclaimed his Good News of being poor in spirit and promised us that God our Father would bend to assist only such humble and simple people and not the arrogant people like some of the religious leaders of his time as well as of our time. Especially in today's Gospel he compares and contrasts the gift of widow's mite with the richest contribution of wealthy people in the temple. He cautions us about the deceptive and fake personalities around us, and presenting to us a simple widow as our rolemodel in our dealings with God and our religious practices, he says: *This poor widow put in more than all the other contributors to the treasury. For they have all contributed from their surplus wealth, but she, from her poverty, has contributed all she had, her whole livelihood.*

The Spirit of the risen Lord is ever reminding us about the right way to be blessed by God; and that way is to be merciful as our heavenly Father is merciful. Though he scourges us with his justice but then has mercy. His only aim is that we must be holy and perfect as he who is the Lord of righteousness.

Prayer: *Generous and holy God! We are truly happy to know from your Son Jesus that you are pleased very much with our heart-felt and sincere offerings. Such thought makes us to* *offer more generously even our very life as total sacrifice of praise and thanksgiving. Kindly make us, persevere in that mindset and lead our life with humility and honesty as our Master Jesus Christ. Amen.*

WEEK - 10

Monday

God-blessed people are true blessings to others
(Scriptural Passages: 2 Cor. 1: 1-7; Ps. 34; Matt. 5: 1-12)

The content of today's Psalm has been a common prayer of good-willed people, like Mother Mary, who inwardly understood well the greatness of the Lord as he was filling them with happy and positive messages constantly. Jesus, God's Son also continued to fill the same inspiring messages as we hear him pronouncing in his beatitudes.

This list is simply another highly-enlightening version of the Ten Commandments, which OT had listed out. While the first four beatitudes deal with our relationship with God, the last four deal with our relationships with others. Jesus declares the right and truthful ways of maintaining our relations with God are: One, by totally depending on God; two, by mourning to God when we fall short of God's holiness; three, by submitting ourselves to God with a passion-filled meekness and compassion in our dealings with the sinners; and four, by desiring to live morally and putting an end to injustices that we witness.

And the other four of the Beatitudes is a list of fruits that are produced by the spiritual growth that we gain in the first half. One, when we are poor in spirit and place our trust in God's mercy, we gain the spiritual maturity to be merciful to others; two, due to our sincere regretting of our sins, we are led to greater holiness, and then we see God working through us; three, we become peacemakers, because we submit ourselves to God's will and we handle conflicts the way Jesus does; and four, when we are suffering and being persecuted because of our trying to live like Christ, we are fully filled with tremendous blessings, because of our patient sufferings we feel that we are indeed living the Beatitudes.

Though the entire Paul's Letter to Corinthian deals with serious problems he was having with the Corinthian community, Paul starts his Letter with beautiful doxological greetings; and he includes his prayerful meditation on the experience of both suffering and comfort, he and Corinthians, faced for the sake of Jesus. As an echo of Jesus' beatitudes of consoling the weak and the afflicted, Paul too professes the ageold Christian faith that God, through Jesus, is the source of all comfort and consolation in every affliction we can experience.

Prayer: *All consoling God! You are the eternal Source of consolation and encouragement for all those downtrodden, afflicted in earthly life. As we meditate on your Scriptural words, we pray first for ourselves to be strengthened by your never-ending consolation; also after we are strengthened, help us to become comforters and consolers of others in their difficulties and sorrows. Amen.*

Tuesday

With the salt of 'yes'- spirit to God, we can do marvels
(Scriptural Passages: 2 Cor. 1: 18-
22; Ps. 119; Matt. 5:13-16)

The Psalm and the Gospel today repeat the most conspicuous greatness of light. We often use the words "seeing the light" when we understand something or when someone comes to share our perspective on something. Whenever we clarify meaning in our lives, we speak of coming out of the darkness and into the light. Thus, the metaphor of light is associated with good, purity, warmth, and comfort.

Knowing well our inner darkness of ignorance, arrogance and weakness, we recognize that it is only through the divine enlightenment that we can be brought out of that darkness. Hence, as the revelation of God, through his words and statutes, sheds light and gives understanding to the simple, we repeatedly request God as the Psalmist: *Let your countenance shine upon your servant.*

Correspondingly, in today's Gospel we hear from Jesus an encouraging message for us who are yearning for the splendid fortune of being enlightened by God. Being God's Son and, as he credited himself, being the Light of the world, Jesus assures his followers, especially who are voluntarily discipled by his Gospel, are also the light of the world, as his proxy. He compels us to *be like the lamp;and having been set by him on a lampstand, we should shine before others, that they may see our good deeds and glorify our heavenly Father.*

And if we deeply pay attention to his breathtaking message, we can be easily shocked because, as a requisite for managing such brilliant role of being the light to others, he included another identity of his disciples as the salt of the earth. As light, Jesus uses the salt also as a metaphor to instil in us that without inner spiritual fervour and flavour, we can never be the proper and effective light to others.

In this connection, God's words from Paul explicate the essence of that salt. Paul writes to Corinthians about how his good work of preaching got authentic and valid. He says: *As God is faithful, our word to you is "yes" has been in Jesus, who anointed us is God. The Amen from us also goes through him to God for glory.* In addition, he writes: 'God has also put his seal upon us and given the Spirit in our hearts as a first instalment'.

Prayer: *God, the Source of Light! Though we know the wonder and greatness of your commands for us to walk in right path; but we are sidetracked often and fall into dark pits. Kindly turn to us in pity as you turn to those who love your name. Pour out your Light of the saving grace, so that, being filled internally with the faith-filled yes to you and Jesus, we may become shining lamps to our fellowhumans who can be able to encounter your glory. Amen.*

Wednesday

*Love is the only Rocket to take us speedily
to prime seats in heaven*
(Scriptural Passages: 2 Cor. 3: 4-11; Ps. 99; Matt. 5: 17-19)

Jesus in today's Gospel passage indicates that he came to this world, *not to abolish the Law but to fulfill it.* Explaining this statement, Jesus lists out the Commandments of God deliberated in OT. He too exhorts us that if we break any one of them we will be called least in the Kingdom of heaven; if we obey and teach them, we will be esteemed as greatest ones.

Jesus showed in his life that he himself was the embodiment of that amazing fulfillment of God's Law and secondly for our easy understanding and fulfilling them, he put them all in one package of double but total love. *Love the Lord God as well as your neighbor with your whole heart, mind, body, and soul.*

It is this love-based spirit of the law that makes the law life-giving. The law that we have now should point to the Divine lawgiver who dispenses justice tempered by love, understanding and mercy. Paul, in today's first reading, talking proudly about his apostolic qualification, says: *Our qualification comes from God, who has indeed qualified us as ministers of a new covenant, not of letter but of spirit; for the letter brings death, but the Spirit gives life.*

The Psalmist too emphasizes the perennial fact of God and humans relationship as two persons though different from each other: God is Holy residing in holy abode but humans are sinners who are worthy only to stand at his footstool. At the same time, he has been a forgiving God to them; though requiting their misdeeds, he permitted them to worship him in holy places.

The Spirit urges us today to continue obeying faithfully any kind of laws or regulations or rubrics, presented to us by the Church, in the name and spirit of Jesus; not as mere obligations under penalty, but because we want to fulfil the intentions of the law or the spirit of the law, which is not only to love the Emmanuel, God with us, who is present in the Church, but also to love every neighbor journeying with us on the Highway to our destiny.

Prayer: *God of all-surpassing Love! Reminding us through your Son that love is the only right and valid path to be esteemed* as the greatest ones in the Kingdom of heaven, you make us understand that true love is in the details and the details magnify the glorious fulfillment of your law of love. Help us Lord, to look for the smallest of opportunities in daily life and to be attentive to all the big and many small ways we are called to love you and others. Amen.

Thursday

To encounter God in truningpoints
requires forgiving others as Jesus
(Scriptural Passages: 2 Cor. 3: 15-
4: 1, 3-6; Ps. 85; Matt. 5: 20-26)

Human life is filled with so many turningpoints-may be as accidents, may be as extraordinary events, or may be as some sort of regular uphill and downhill happenings. Whatever the kind, all those turningpoints have been truly the sources and occasions for our individual growth and development. We are today reminded by Paul in his Letter about one such turningpoint, occurring in every Christian's life. Comparing the veil-experience of us, the new Israelites, with that of old Israelites, Paul says: *Whenever the Scriptures were read, a veil was covering the hearts of the children of Israel, but whenever a person turned to the Lord the veil was removed. But today whenever we hear Jesus' Gospel, all of us, gazing with unveiled face on the glory of the Lord, are being transformed into the same image from glory to glory, as from the Lord who is the Spirit.*

In other words, whenever we privately or in group willingly listening to the proclamation and explanation of the Gospel of Jesus, a tremendous turningpoint occurs that can be on regular basis or occasionally but always according to the Spirit's freedom. However, while so many human beings in all the religious circles, claim such experiences of God, being unveiled to them, we know not all are genuinely spiritual but only a sort of emotional, psychological or even intellectual presumptions. Hence, the most important matter in our Christian spiritual turningpoints is, to be proven as valid and legitimate of the work of the Holy Spirit.

Any such turningpoint must be followed by our external performances in our daily life. Jesus instructed us on this point, as we hear in today's Gospel. He says: *Unless your righteousness surpasses that of the scribes and Pharisees, you will not enter into the Kingdom of heaven.* Jesus means, any external action we perform should not be worldly and fleshly as many of the OT Israelites and their leaders led a life that came out of their veiled hearts.

Rather, our every external action should be measured in accordance with his command of loving our neighbors totally and wholeheartedly. If we claim we have been gazing at the face of God with no covering when we listened to his Gospel, then, instead of feeling complacent with only avoiding the sin of killing those who disrupt our peace and joy, we must not even get angry with them; and much more, in all our religious practices, if we recall that our brother or sister has anything against us, we should make sure we forgive and reconcile with them. This is how God's Masterplan of salvation would work. And therefore we can profess with the Psalmist today: 'Kindness and truth shall meet; justice and peace shall kiss. Truth shall spring out of the earth, and justice shall look down from heaven'.

Prayer: *God of Righteousness! From your words today we see you long for our right-tracked way of living your righteous life. Kindly assist us in making the best use of the admirable*

Christian spiritual turningpoints your Son shares with us and thus we may support one another with the amazing wholehearted love as Jesus demands. Amen.

Friday

For Jesus' friends, human body is a treasure-trove
(Scriptural Passages: 2 Cor. 4: 7-15; Ps. 116; Matt. 5: 27-32)

All genuine religious persons esteem their earthly life as a favorable opportunity to offer sacrifice of praise and thanksgiving to their Creator God. They long to sing uninterruptedly with pure and contrite heart with the Psalmist: *Lord God! I am greatly afflicted; no man is dependable. To you will I offer sacrifice of thanksgiving, and I will call upon the name of the Lord. My vows to the Lord I will pay in the presence of all his people.* But we read in human history countless men and women, being unable to fulfill such a heavenly wish due to their physical and sexual concupiscence, left from this worldly life to the deserts and forests.

But today we hear from Paul a beautiful and amazing positive thought about the same human physical life. He says that we hold a remarkable treasure in our body, which is a breakable and vulnerable earthen vessel. According to him, that incredible triple treasure is: the treasure of faith that we are *always carrying about in our body the dying of Jesus, so that the life of Jesus may also be manifested in our body;* the treasure of relentless hope that *the Father who raised the Lord Jesus will raise us also with Jesus;* and the treasure of love for God and other humans: *Everything indeed is for you, so that the grace, bestowed in abundance on more and* more people, may cause the thanksgiving to overflow for the glory of God.

When we hold such positive and realistic view about our body and the earthly life, we are not satisfied only by fulfilling what our body demands. Basing an argument on the eternal truth that we are greater than what we feel we are, Jesus proclaims in today's Gospel, changing and enhancing the old Commandment: *"You have heard that it was said, 'You shall not commit adultery.' But I say to you, everyone who looks at a woman with lust has already committed adultery with her in his heart.* Then he sounds scary and ruthless about maintaining such renewed Law under the penalty of even amputating our external bodily organs.

Prayer: *God the Source of Life and Love! You know how difficult it is for us to observe Jesus' new way of esteeming and exercising our sexual desires and accomplishments in our personal, family and community life. We hear you exhorting us that if we give a willful commitment to Jesus' advice and Paul's recommendation of upholding the treasure of faith, hope and love within us, such yoke would be easy and such burden would be light. Grant we pray your enlivening Spirit within us to be committed to your directions so that we can possess all heavenly treasures. Amen.*

Saturday

Truth should be the second name of every Christian
(Scriptural Passages: 2 Cor. 5: 14-
21; Ps. 103; Matt. 5: 33-37)

Our Christian belief is that the sacrament of Baptism washes away all our sins and reconciles us with God. Since at baptism we are baptised into the death and the resurrection of the Lord Jesus, we are born anew. About this glorious status of every baptized Christian, Paul proclaims: *God has reconciled us to himself through Christ and given the Church and her ministers as the ambassadors of Christ the ministry of reconciliation, namely, to reconcile the world to himself in Christ. So, whoever is in Christ is a new creation: the old things have passed away; behold, new things have come.*

The Scriptures and our Christian Tradition, remind us that those gorgeous results of Baptism are only initial step with abounding potentials from which we are supposed to climb up the Mountain or House of the Lord in order to reach the Gospel idealism of *being holy as God is holy; being merciful as the Father is merciful; and being perfect as our Father is perfect.* Our ideal Father, as we hear from the Psalmist, *is kind and merciful. He will not always chide, nor does he keep his wrath forever. Not according to our sins does he deal with us, nor does he requite us according to our crimes.*

And for attaining such peak of divine life, we, the sinful children, are advised by the Lord that we should first be reconciled with our God the Father. One area that may need reconciliation, as we hear from Jesus in today's Gospel, is the sadness or loss we may have caused to others by our false promises. *"You shall not swear falsely, but perform what you have sworn"*, is a law, set down by the Creator himself. Jesus therefore exhorts us that we should be totally trustworthy and completely honest, when we make our vocational vows, such the marital vows, the religious and evangelical vows and so on. Jesus underscores this important factor by his concise and precise statement: *Let your 'Yes' mean 'Yes,' and your 'No' mean 'No'; Anything more is from the Evil One."*

Prayer: *God of merciful and selfless love! We, the baptized Christians, who start our new life in Jesus through Baptism, are instructed by your Son to be persons of known integrity and honesty. Not even a single word coming out of our mouth should* carry any lie. Forgiving our sins of infidelity to your Truth, kindly grant us your merciful power to be true in words and deeds until we attain our blissful life. Amen.

WEEK - 11

Monday

To return evil for good is devilish but to
return good for evil is godlike.
(Scriptural Passages: 2 Cor. 6:1-10; Ps. 98; Matt. 5:38-42)

In our daily walk of life, more often we are hurt by the wrongdoings of others against us; and we strongly feel the need to personally either see to it that someone pays for the hurt they have caused or jump into the arena of boxing to exchange blows to them in the cruel spirit of retaliating with vengeance. We take such reactions for granted as the outcome of our basic instincts for our life's survival, safety and security. But today our Master Jesus exhorts us, in the Gospel, not to hold such nonsensical attitude of *'an eye for an eye and a tooth for a tooth'.* Instead, he commands us to *'offer no resistance to one who is evil.'*

Asking us not to take this saying of Jesus literally, our Church Fathers and Biblical Scholars tell us that what Jesus is asking us to do is not to harbor a spirit of resentment and not return violence with violence. Instead, according to Jesus' heartbeat: *If someone injures us, we must show ourselves the masters of the situation, by doing something*

*to the adversary's advantage. Despite one gets some pleasure out
of hitting us, if we let that person hit again, we are performing
an act of grace!*

This may sound folly and weird. But this is the way, all
our saints and faith-filled men and women, for centuries,
who were faithful in following Jesus' way of non-violence
and forgiveness as he himself verified it in his life. This
is because of the conviction that through Jesus they
have been made 'new creation'. David prophetically asks
us in his Psalm to *sing joyfully to the Lord, all you, lands,
and to sing to the Lord a new song.* God's Spirit urges us
to sing acknowledging joyfully and gratefully, the fact
that we have been made by Jesus' redemptive deeds as
'new creation'. And in the Gospel he points out one main
dimension of such new life, namely the way of living in
non-violent love.

Accepting the Master's call of non-violence, Paul, an
ultimate Disciple of Jesus, in his Letter today, testifies to
this marvelous Christian saintly attitude, by mentioning
how he handled all his hurting lifesituations patiently
and with grace and magnanimity, and underlines also the
wonderful results of such non-violent endurance of evils
done against him. He too advises us, to follow our Master
as he did, and thus not to receive the grace of God in
vain. In other words, once we are fervently committed to
follow our Master, we are granted with abundant graces
and heavenly benefits from God, to walk the non-violent
walk of Christ.

Prayer: *Good and gracious God! Our human sense
of justice naturally prompts retaliation to unprovoked and
malicious assault. But as servants of God, we are advised by
your Son to leave justice to God and to resist evil with goodness.
As we find difficult to follow Jesus' way of non-violence,
graciously help us with your Spirit so that we may make the*

best use of all your graces to witness Jesus and his Gospel in our earthly life. Amen.

Tuesday

Come what may! Let us follow Jesus' Highway of Love
(Scriptural Passages: 2 Cor. 8: 1-9; Ps. 146; Matt. 5: 43-48)

Our Christian life's unique greatness consists in the proclamation of a 'single way', in order to attain and maintain the fullness of the divine and human connection even in this world. It is nothing but the Gospel Way of love. Today we hear from Jesus and his Apostle Paul two of the dimensions of that Gospel Way of love.

In the Gospel, Jesus commands us, illustrating how to bring the teaching of the Old Law to a higher and more perfect plane, *Love your enemies and pray for those who persecute you.* And Paul, in his Letter, begs us to share our love-gifts with the needy and the strangers as he writes: *I say this not by way of command, but to test the genuineness of your love by your concern for others.*

While Jesus uses the Greek term *'agape'* to explain about love to be used in loving our enemies, Paul, to explain the love to be shown in our helping the needy, uses the Greek word *'charis'.* Agape-love is nothing but God's unconditional love, a unilateral way of loving others, not minding about the attitudes, actions, reactions on whom we love. It is simply a one-way flow of love generated by the longing of the other person's well-being.

As for Paul, he uses the term *'Charis',* which means 'Grace'. It denotes the experience of being loved by God or God's love tangibly experienced. This sort of gracious favor from God may come as a direct gift from God or through another person or through some blessing which comes into our life. In other words, Paul tells us, anything we do to help the needy people out of love by the sharing of our available and possible possessions, even our very self, is simply as an outcome of our thanksgiving to God's immense helps and supports to us and also as an occasion for the beneficiaries to witness the same merciful, compassionate *Charis* of God through our charities.

The Psalmist declares today that *he will praise the Lord, that his hope is in God.* Why? Because the Lord made everything, keeps faith, secures justice for the oppressed, gives food to the hungry, sets captives free, gives sight to the blind, raises up those who are bowed down, loves the just, and protects strangers. It is for such unrivaled relationship between God and ourselves, we are today called for doing the maximum possible in reciprocating to our God's love.

Prayer: *Benevolent God! Though all that the Spirit of Jesus teaches about love may seem and sound very hard and unrealistic, it's worth to be swallowed by us as bittersweet capsule. We are indeed very eager to abide all his love-demands. Grant us, your weak children, the fire of your love so that, we may attain our Christian peace and joy, not only in this world, but mainly at the end of the day, we may win our ultimate victory of heaven. Amen.*

Wednesday

Let our superfluities give way to our neighbors' conveniences
(Scriptural Passages: 2 Cor. 9: 6-11;
Ps. 112; Matt. 6: 1-6, 16-18)

In every religion there is a tradition of appeasing and pleasing God with different rituals and performances.

Our religion too, in close connection to Judeo culture, demands from us such religious practices and rituals. They can be categorized as: 1. Almsgiving; 2. Prayer; 3. Fasting. In today's Scriptural passages God teaches us about how properly we should perform those practices for reaping heavenly harvest in life.

Jesus in today's Gospel exhorts us whenever we perform any religious or spiritual practices to please our God we should possess a purity of intention, focusing our attention only to our God and not contaminating ourselves and our religious performances and make them all in vain, as most of us are capable of doing them with a showoff-mindset to procure human temporary praises and rewards.

Paul in his Letter today affirms on the same teaching of Jesus to perform all religious deeds with heavenly intention, especially in our sharing of our money, talents, time or any material possessions toward the welfare of needy people. He stresses we should keep in mind always a few truthful and practical factors which God's Spirit proclaims elaborately in the Bible: When we give out our possessions to the poor, going beyond our personal gratification and beyond the people who are related to us by blood or by any other artificial networks, such as caste and race and so on, our righteousness would endure forever. Also, we should make sure to perform all our good deeds without sadness or compulsion, because our God always loves a cheerful giver.

On this matter, God offers one more advice through today's Psalm. First he underlines that people faithful to him will have their riches, but also be lavish in their generosity, which will endure forever. In addition he cautions us also telling us: There is an ideal connectedness that is not born out in this world, where sometimes the just suffer and the unjust seem to prosper. In this precarious situation, we need faith to see that all that glitters is not gold; we also need faith to see the hollowness of the fickle praise of others and walk matured enough not to be bent down to any worldly fulfillment.

Prayer: *God of abundance and generosity! Through your sages you had taught us that whoever sows sparingly will also reap sparingly, and whoever sows bountifully will also reap bountifully. Especially through your Son you instructed us to give and gifts will be given to us; a good measure, packed together, shaken down, and overflowing, will be poured into our lap. While we are becoming more and more aware of the needs of people around us, help us to see ourselves not only as part of all poverty-stricken humanity, but also as part of your own squad of agents in sharing with your needy children the abundance you have entrusted to us. Amen.*

Thursday

*Be faithful to Gospel as God's adopted
children and betrothed lovers*
(Scriptural Passages: 2 Cor. 11: 1-11; Ps. 111; Matt. 6: 7-15)

Whether we like it or not, we are a sinful people, easily duped by the enemy, and distracted by the false lights that move our lesser selves. This is why, Church constantly makes us think of the greatness of our holy God and his marvelous deeds as the Psalmist sings repeatedly today: *I will give thanks to the Lord with all my heart. Great are the works of the Lord, exquisite in all their delights. Gracious and merciful is the Lord.*

But unfortunately, most of the secular philosophers and teachers deceive humanity by offering untrue and shallow guidelines for our hazardous lifesituation. This damaging obsession for novelty seems to have been crept even into early Christianity. In today's first reading, Paul straightforwardly warns his Christians against accepting such new gospel which is different from the one they had accepted from him.

Paul seems to be so fervent and obsessed by his call to proclaim Jesus' Gospel that he declares any message he preached as the Gospel of Jesus is nothing but the intimate words of love being exchanged between God the Bridegroom and us his brides. So, he writes *I am jealous of you with the jealousy of God, since I betrothed you to one husband to present you as a chaste virgin to Christ. But I am afraid that, as the serpent deceived Eve by his cunning, your thoughts may be corrupted from a sincere and pure commitment to Christ.*

Our Lord Jesus in his divine style, in order to augment the validity and magnanimity of his Gospel teachings, has been deliberately expressed the only source of his Gospel is from God and he defined his intimate relationship with God, by many metaphors. One of the most striking one is spelt out in today's Gospel passage. It is the famous prayer he taught to his disciples. He wants us to relate ourselves intimately to God, as he does, and address God as Abba, Father. "Abba" is a term of endearment for the Father.

This shows that God is not just the Almighty or the All-Powerful. God is so much more. God is our loving Father and we are the Father's beloved sons or daughters. Jesus and his disciples are closely connected to God only by the covenant of love and fidelity, which has been established starting from the compassionate and condescending Father God, through his faithful Son Jesus and ending with his disciples.

While the Bible uses those two metaphors of spousal and parental relationship existing God and us, it is God's earnest will that we all should accept willingly and wholeheartedly the Gospel he conveys through his Son Jesus. As the scriptural passages suggest, we need to surrender ourselves to whatever God may want to do with us and with our world and be ready to do the best we can in cooperating with him according to the Gospel, that his Son has proclaimed.

Prayer: *Heavenly Father! As our Master reminds us, we do believe that you know us and all we need better than we do. Graciously grant us your Spirit of the spousal and parental fervor and fidelity that abides in you so that we may trust and surrender ourselves to you and your Son's Gospel throughout our earthly life. Amen.*

Friday

Freedom from earthly riches is the first step to gain heavenly assets
(Scriptural Passages: 2 Cor. 11: 18, 21-30; Ps. 34; Matt. 6: 19-23)

Human experience teaches that almost all our dealings with earthly riches make us victims of fear, distress, anxiety and loss of peace. As the Psalmist cries out today, we are exhorted by our Creator that in all those high-risky dealings with worldly goods, we should never lose heart but preserve it humble and honest through glorifying and praising the Creator and his love affairs with us. Besides, God also through today's scriptural passages offer us some wonderful guidelines to focus our attention on enjoying his ever-content heavenly life.

116

In today's Gospel passage, we hear Jesus one more of his Gospel teachings: *Do not store up for yourselves treasures on earth, but store up treasures in heaven.* Saying this, he never retracted or belittled his first order that his disciples should perform good deeds as the Light shining brightly; but his main thrust has been while the good deeds are performed externally, the disciples' inner spirit must be attuned to God and heavenly rewards. Because Jesus knew well how the humanness works. He accentuates: *Where your treasure is, there also will be your heart.*

In order to accumulate the heavenly treasures by using earthly good, Jesus provides for us one practical advice. Using the 'inner eye' as a metaphor to describe the human inner spirit of heart and mind, he advises that our inner eye should be good, filled with the necessary light to see the good results coming out of our external actions and in particular, from our reactions toward others' faults and idiosyncrasies. With the help of "good inner eye" we should always recognize their good side. We should commend them for their virtues, not condemn them for their vices.

Saint Paul frequently repeats in his Letters about his ardent ambition to covet the heavenly treasures, which Jesus has indicated, through the accomplishment of his good works. To our surprise, we hear him today emphasizing that his success in the pursuit of possessing Jesus' promised-treasures consists mostly in his weaknesses and sufferings. He offers a long list of the trials and hardships he has been enduring in the missionary endeavors. For the sake of Christ and for the preaching of the Gospel he has been through far more than any of his contemporaries. All those unstinting efforts were aimed to offer the message of Christ to as many people as possible.

Prayer: *Almighty Father! We truly long to covet abundant heavenly treasures as well as to occasion the overflow of your grace in us and in the entire world. Today you advise us through your Scriptural words that we can possess those heavenly treasures both by our unrelented good works and enduring sufferings and hardships we may meet in this august pursuit. Kindly pour out your Spirit in us to tread in the amazing path Jesus and Paul walked and finally attain the heavenly treasures. Amen.*

Saturday

Whenever we feel weak, then by God's grace we are strong
(Scriptural Passages: 2 Cor. 12: 1-10;
Ps. 34; Matt. 6: 24-34)

Worrying is part of the human condition. It is a God-given tool, included in our life's First Aid-Kit for our survival, safety and security. Therefore, when we hear Jesus' words in today's Gospel, *Do not worry about tomorrow; tomorrow will take care of itself. Sufficient for a day is its own evil,* we should know clearly that he doesn't necessarily mean advising us never to worry about anything. Many preachers and church teachers hold that Jesus means by his words that we should not be worrying about the worrying.

In other words, we should not be worrying overanxiously or unduly about the negative things happening in our earthly life. Through the saying of Jesus about our anxieties and worries regarding earthly happenings and needs, we are told by the Spirit that we should work singleheartedly with sincerity and justice; if we fail in our effort, we must redo it as many times as it takes but hopefully and double-forcefully; we need to allow others as much as possible in our undertakings but wholeheartedly; we must make sure we see God's hands in our and other people's actions; moreover, we must never lose our focus on pursuing our ultimate goal in life.

Apostle Paul writes in his Letter today about the most superbly enlightening point for how to take both good and bad happenings in life, worse and better situations we meet in daily chores, together with both our weaknesses and strengths. He was fully aware of the amazing hands of God intervening in his life by sharing with him personally many supernatural revelations which made him fully convinced of his dignity and loving acceptance from God that he has been a favorite disciple of Jesus.

In addition, Paul clearly realized that not only God acknowledged the severity of his feelings of pain from a thorn in his flesh as a messenger of Satan tormenting him; but also God energized him to bear such natural human frailties and sufferings by his exquisite but most stunning divine words: *My grace is sufficient for you, for power is made perfect in weakness.* These words of the Lord to Paul "My grace is sufficient. Trust me," indeed has already been proclaimed in the message of today's entire Psalm. The Psalmist makes us convinced of the eternal fact that the angel of the Lord encamps around those who fear God. Those who seek the Lord want for no good thing.

Prayer: *All-powerful and Compassionate God! Your Spirit today reminds us that our weakness must lead us deeper into prayer and dependence on you. Nonetheless we fret over about many earthly needs and the risks we face daily. Inebriate our life, Lord, with your power by your encouraging grace-filled touching so that we may lead a life fully relaxed and relied on your loving hands as Jesus' words ringing in our mind: 'Don't worry about tomorrow. Your heavenly Father knows all that you need'. Amen.*

119

WEEK - 12

Monday

Go beyond; judge, and treat everybody
and everything with eyes of God
(Scriptural Passages: Gen. 12: 1-9; Ps. 33; Matt. 7: 1-5)

In Scriptures we read God often making unthinkable but very relevant and necessary promises to his people through his faith-agents like Abram, Moses, and above all through Jesus. One of such Godly promising moments we hear in the first reading when God promised Abram. *Your relatives, and from your father's house to a land that I will show you. I will make of you a great nation, and I will bless you; I will make your name great, so that you will be a blessing.*

Since those promises are Godly, they are also very costly. In every one of such occasions the Lord hooks his human children to his singular salvific plan. In this event God before listing out his breathtaking promises orders Abram: *Go forth from your land.* In other words, God wanted Abram to leave from his tradition, culture, and even his beloved birthplace, and thankfully taking with him all his family members, family possessions. One more striking dimension in God's order is that Abram was asked to leave his own, well-known place called Ur, to an unknown land of strangers.

The valid reason for such inconceivable divine order is revealed and augmented both in today's Psalm and mostly in the Gospel. The Psalmist says that *when the Lord looks down from heaven, he sees all mankind as the people he has chosen for his own inheritance.* The only way to get all his promises fulfilled for us and for the whole humanity is that we warmly welcome and accept his decision of a lot of different kinds of faith and culture gather together.

Converting everyone to Christianity won't guarantee that we all think alike or live out our faith alike. This is exactly what our Lord tells all his disciples in the Sermon on the Mount. We know he asked us to make our prayer as a universal cry of human beings as God's children, calling Him 'Abba Father'; plus, he expected all his disciples' religious and social deeds must be not merely personalized nor individualized but more importantly to be universalized. In continuation such universalism of his Gospel teachings, he underlines in today's Gospel passage that we can't be the ones to decide which measure we can use to judge others. Every human person should be respected and esteemed as God's beloved child.

Prayer: *Lord, God of eternal wisdom and justice! As Jesus has affirmed, you are the only judge, not any human beings, even himself. We pray that, going beyond our human strength and weakness, we may be concerned about our spiritual connection with you and by walking in the footsteps of Jesus we may discontinue our habit of wrongly judging our neighbors but relate to them with the measure you measure us personally. Amen.*

Tuesday

A good neighbour is better than a bag of money
(Scriptural Passages: Gen. 13:2, 5-18;
Ps. 15; Matt. 7:6, 12-14)

World history narrates that our forebears, who lived mainly in small towns and villages, were closer to their neighbours. They never felt the burden of hunger, thirst, and the lack of life's conveniences, because they were more dependent on each other. But today, in the fragmentation of contemporary sophisticated life, most of the people live in great isolation and distance from each other; plus, their daily life has turned out to be darkened by fear, hatred, and indifference to each other.

Today in Jesus' Sermon, we hear him offering us two of the most basic recommendations for our peaceful, just and fulfilling community life: The first one is an ageold advice, found in almost all the cultures around the globe, which is proudly labelled as a Golden Rule for every human's social life: *Do to others whatever you would have them do to you.* Again, quoting a general suggestion prevalent among the so-called righteous Jewish people, Jesus offers us a second counsel that emerges from his positive attitude, which was demonstrated in his grand Commission of evangelization, *Go and make disciples of all nations.* We can take his second counsel as applying to our dealing with our neighbors who are hard-headedly stubborn in their evil ways and very hardheartedly obstinately unrepentant.

To follow these two basic counsels of Jesus are indeed very difficult as he himself states as if walking through the narrow gate. In practical life we experience when we seriously practice those admonitions our individual life is being squeezed, infringed, and sometimes debilitated. But the story of Abraham illustrates in today's first reading, that the God of love who is the source of all blessings takes care of those who are generous and unselfish with others. Abraham, following the Godly counsel, allowed his cousin brother Lot to take the better portion of his land. And as today's Psalm underlines, that Abraham walked blamelessly, and always thinking the truth in his heart and did justice as best as he could. This is why, he was blessed to be very rich in livestock, silver, and gold. And he became the Father of all believers.

Prayer: *All-wise God! Thanks for sharing and confirming through Jesus the golden rule of thumb by which we should live. We want to be respected, to be treated with dignity, and to be treated fairly. But on an even deeper level, we want to be loved, understood, known, and cared for. Our selfish tendency is to demand and expect love and mercy from others while at the same time we hold ourselves to a much lower standard regarding how much we offer. Grant we pray to empower us with the attitude of Jesus to put into practice his counsels in our dealings with neighbors. Amen.*

Wednesday

*Christian life is an admirable blend of
godly and earthly connections
(Scriptural Passages: Gen. 15: 1-12, 17-
18; Psalm 105; Matt. 7: 15-20)*

In today's Gospel passage, Jesus talks about the prophets who boast themselves as God-sent prophets. He exhorts us to discern who among those prophets are the true ones or false ones. For such wise discerning, he offers a tip with a metaphor of the intrinsic connection existing between trees or plants and their fruits: *Do people pick grapes from thornbushes, or figs from thistles? Every good tree bears good fruit, and a rotten tree bears bad fruit.* The same way we can find out the goodness and falsehood of a prophet by his/her fruits.

In this regard, let us remember Jesus' today's advice is for all of us who are baptized and anointed to be prophets. There are two most important scales of question and answer, closely connected to our judgement whether we are true or false prophets: First, an answer to a question: To what is the intrinsic connection that should exist between our interior so-called Godly connections and our exterior behavior? Second, an answer to the question: what the fruits Jesus pointing out are as the endresults of our prophetic words and deeds?

Such admonition leads us to understand the core message of Jesus. He expects us to uphold a twofold awareness or consciousness in our daily living in this world: Personal awareness about who we are in reality; and social awareness about our place, role, and relationship in a social environment we move and have our living while we are in the world.

In this duplex process of consciousness, from the day of human creation, God entered into our life to assist us in realizing the most results out of our interior conscious efforts. Those deeds of God with humanity are called 'making mutual covenants'. One of those covenants, we hear in today's first reading, as the first one of the formal covenants, made between God and Abraham and later between God and the Israelites. It begins with a general promise from God in a vision to Abraham: *"To your descendants I give this land, from the Wadi of Egypt to the Great River the Euphrates."*

As the Psalmist sings repeatedly, Abraham kept in his heart firmly that *The Lord remembers his covenant forever.* With this relentless faith, hope, and devotion, he obeyed God's directions in every moment of his critical situations. This is why Bible underlines in beautiful words: *"Abraham put his faith in the LORD, who credited it to him as an act of righteousness"*

Prayer: *Almighty God! While so many among us are prone to behave like sweet- talkers who say and promise in order to get them to do what they want, help us not to be deceptive and misleading and degrade our prophetic integrity. Also enliven us to try our best to stop either doing the right thing in the wrong way or doing the wrong thing in the right way; instead, as our Master advises us, let us always do the right thing in the right way. Amen.*

Thursday

We are handworks of God as well as His handymen
(Scriptural Passages: Gen. 16: 1-12, 15-16; Ps. 106; Matt. 7: 21-29)

There are some popular but very truthful sayings we hear often from our preachers about the supreme power of our God over us, such as: *When humans write lines crooked, God will straighten them out.* Also, *human proposes God disposes.* Surprisingly, the reverse is also true. *When humans write straight lines God can make them crooked.* And when God proposes, humans can also dispose. All these sayings take their roots in all Scriptures, especially our Bible.

In the story we heard today from the first reading, we notice the three characters Abraham, Sarah and Hagar who held within them a certain plan for their comfortable and painless family life. When they encountered some weighty problems and consequently, hitches between each other, they acted too hastily, without regard for the feelings of others. Abraham tried to opt out of a difficult situation and disown his responsibility; Sarah was driven by envy and spite; and Hagar, being abused by Sarah, was running away from her mistress to the wilderness.

Yet, the Sovereign God intervened in the grim lifesituations of his specially chosen children. God used Hagar, an underprivileged handmaid, who was filled with fear and trembling in front her employers but very much obedient to God's words, to set right the critical situation occurring in Abraham's family and prestige.

Such kind of stories are numerous in God's Kingdom. In today's Gospel, Jesus reminds us many critical situations may come in our personal and family life. We may be victimized by the problems and dangerous disasters, like the torrent of rain falling, the tsunami-like floods spiraling, and the stormy winds and Tornadoes blowing and buffeting our family, and anything we buildup for our personal and social life. But according to Jesus nothing will affect our undertakings if we listen to God's words and act on them. He says: *Everyone who listens to these words of mine and acts on them will be like a wise man who built his house on rock.*

This is because, as Jesus himself states, we are not alone in those crises. Heavenly Father and His Son would be inside the house or family we build as a loving and caring support. Let us continuously link on to Jesus' encouraging words and be prepared for facing any eventualities in daily life. Today's Psalm too invites us to praise the Lord continuously in those dark situations, and not behaving like the Old Israelites, who believed God's words and sang his praises at one time, but then they soon forgot all he had done because they had no patience for his plan to be fulfilled.

Prayer: *Lord God! We are not only your handmade creatures, but also your handymen to continue your work of building your Kingdom until it is established fully. Today Jesus makes it clear to us that anything we build here on earth will have a solid foundation only when we listen to your words and act on them. Help us to patiently keep our focus upon you through all of life's challenges and to trust in the reality of your unfailing presence and your amazing love for us. Amen.*

Friday

Christ's kingdom is in this world but not of it
(Scriptural Passages: Gen. 17: 1, 9-10,
15-22 Ps. 127; Matt. 8: 1-4)

Jesus began his public ministry stating that the kingdom of God is at hand; it is among us; and it is within us. However, at the end of his earthly life he told Pilate very strongly that the same kingdom of God is not of this world. In other words, as Vat. II would assert, *though anything that pertains to the earthly life and its progress is to be carefully distinguished from the growth of Christ's kingdom.* Undoubtedly Jesus taught us to hold deep awareness about the intrinsic and close connection between our earthly, physical realm and God's heavenly, spiritual realm, since he is the entire creation's source, process, and end.

Jesus underscored repeatedly this crucial fact through his miraculous deeds. One among them is narrated in today's Gospel passage. We notice Jesus relating his miracle to two elements expected in God's Kingdom in this world. One, the beneficiary's faith in the Sovereignty and power of Jesus, the Son of God. That is what we hear in this miraculous event. The leper approaches Jesus; does him homage; and tells him: *"Lord, if you wish, you can make me clean."* Two, the beneficiary's religious duty in his earthly life. After curing the leper, that is what Jesus asked from his beneficiary: *"See that you tell no one, but go show yourself to the priest, and offer the gift that Moses prescribed; that will be proof for them."*

Jesus plainly followed the way of his Father, when he made his covenantal dealings with our Patriarch Abraham. In the first reading we hear, before promising some unthinkable earthly benefits of inheritance and prosperity in the life of Abraham, God asserts that he is God the Almighty; he also advises Abraham: *'Walk in my presence and be blameless'.* Plus, God spells out very clearly the religious duty of Abraham as requirement for all the good he would be enjoying in this world. He says: *On your part, you and your descendants after you must keep my covenant throughout the ages.* In today's Psalm, we are also reminded that the Lord blesses in this world those humans who fear him. For that admiration and respect, he gives us all that we need, fruitfulness in all we do, and prosperity.

Prayer: *Sovereign Lord God! Despite seeing the healing and prosperous Christ, your Son, so close to us, our head, heart and hands so far away from his project of connecting both his Kingdom and our own petty earthly kingdoms we build and manage. In spite of his almighty and compassionate presence in our midst, he expects from us our voluntary and firm collaboration. Only thing we request from you, Lord, that we may all learn to see our many blessed occasions nearer to Jesus as the means by which God works in and through us. Amen.*

Saturday

Faith and Humility go hand in hand
(Scriptural Passages: Gen. 18: 1-15;
Canticle Lk. 1: 46-55; Matt. 8: 5-17)

We hear in today's Gospel Jesus praising the centurion, though he was a pagan soldier, for his unprecedented virtue of faith. In his amazement Jesus loudly said to his followers: *"Amen, I say to you, in no one in Israel have I found such faith.* He added another exceptional future benefit of the centurion's faith. Comparing and contrasting him with the chosen children of God's Kingdom, he said that the centurion would be one of those who would come from the east and the west and would recline with all Patriarchs at the banquet celebrated in the Kingdom of heaven. Moreover, he granted the centurion an immediate miraculous help of healing for the sick servant, uttering: *"You may go; as you have believed, let it be done for you."*

What sort of amazing element Jesus found in the centurion's faith? As the centurion approached the Lord and appealed to him, and stated about the sickly condition of his servant who was lying at home paralyzed, suffering dreadfully, the Lord immediately expressed his willingness to go and cure the servant. But the centurion held stronger faith in the healing power of Jesus, whose *word alone would be sufficient; his servant would be healed however far away.*

In addition to his robust faith in Jesus, the centurion did not let his hierarchical ego get the best of him and therefore did not act as if he was deserving of Jesus' coming to his home and do the healing to be seen by his fleet. He shunned his pride and glory and humbled himself saying to Jesus: *"Lord, I am not worthy to have you enter under my roof; only say the word and my servant will be healed."* The centurion allowed his castle wall to be broken open by showing his vulnerability. This allowed him to receive and to be "healed".

To highlight the greatness of such 'quality-faith' that can do marvelous deeds in our midst, today's first reading narrates a beautiful story of how Abraham also demonstrated this same faith with simplicity and humility in God's power to do what seems impossible. He conveys his strong, complete, and unquestioning faith in his God's relentless benevolence and mightiest power by putting himself at the service of humans who were strangers and travelers, offering them hospitality and rest. His spirit of humility urged him to serve others, to welcome them and show them hospitality, and keeping his ego under control.

Consequently, we see him enjoying grace-filled moments of receiving breathtaking promises from the Almighty to become the father of the nations. Even in today's meditative canticle Mary gloriously sings her ardent faith and sincere acceptance of her mindblowing role with humility and with trust she possessed in the words of the angel Gaberiel: *'Nothing is impossible for God'.*

Prayer: *Powerful and Compassionate God! While so many around us, like Sarah, belittle your eternal plan of salvation for humanity and scorn us as foolish when we convincingly declare your almighty power and your miraculous interventions in our lives as Mary, Abraham, and centurion believed in all humility. Grant us the Spirit's wisdom, faith, humility, and love so that we may gratefully experience every miraculous interaction and intervention you bring about in our daily life. Amen.*

WEEK - 13

Monday

Let us not put off until tomorrow what we can do today
(Scriptural Passages: Gen. 18: 18-
33; Ps. 103; Matt. 8: 18-22)

We hear God, in today's first reading, expressing to Abraham his anger and grief regarding the wickedness pervading in the cities of *Sodom and Gomorrah*. We know, this is not the first time the Creator was regretting about the perverted and twisted and malicious attitudes and actions of humans against his dream about the goodness and greatness of his human creatures. Moses already in his Book of Genesis writes about another incident of the same kind but against the entire humanity in Genesis chapter 6. *When the Lord saw how great the wickedness of human beings was on earth, and how every desire that their heart conceived was always nothing but evil and full of lawlessness. Therefore, the Lord regretted making human beings on the earth, and his heart was grieved...*

But Bible also verifies the fact that whenever those sinful humans came back to him with humble and contrite of heart, he forgave them, as we recited today in today's Psalm: *The Lord is kind and merciful. He pardons all your iniquities; he heals all your ills. He redeems your life from destruction, he crowns you with kindness and compassion.* This message of justice, blended with forgiveness, was the core of Jesus' preaching; he also placed a stern plan of action for those who are forgiven by God so that they may not incur any punishment under the wrathful justice of God.

We hear his amazing actionplan in today's Gospel. He tells us to persist in focusing to God and his Kingdom with no desire of returning back: *"Follow me, and let the dead bury their dead."* Plus, he too demanded us to uphold his spirit of poverty as the bulwark of protection for our spiritual safety, purity, and security. *"Foxes have dens and birds of the sky have nests, but the Son of Man has nowhere to rest his head."*

Today God's Spirit confirms the fact of closeness between the compassionately-just God and his sinful-but-contrite people. He, by all means, expects his human children to yield to his wisdom and sovereignty. When today we hear Jesus' harsh sayings, we would be, like Abraham, annoyed and even begin to argue against them. Like him, we may feel that justice and decency are on our side. But we should understand those shocking words of Jesus deeply possess some heavenly exhortations and truths. For example, the phrase, *Let the dead bury their dead* is a figure of speech to emphasize the urgency of following God's call when it comes. Even if we still want to argue, we should trust that God, who is the Source of life and not death, always wants to give healing and life to us.

Prayer: *Amazingly gracious God! We are truly ignorant and weak to understand all that you share with us especially through your Son Jesus. Today we humbly stand before you to acknowledge that following Jesus' actionplan, we have been pardoned many times; and we pledge to commit ourselves to* *following your Son wherever he goes. We choose your most holy will above all things. Kindly help us to live faithfully in accord with your divine will and to say "Yes" to you every day. Amen.*

Tuesday

Superb faith never ceases to tell Jesus: 'My life is in your hands.'
(Scriptural Passages: Gen. 19: 15-
29; Psalm 26; Matt. 8: 23-27)

The two stories we hear in today's Liturgy of the Word enforce us to believe the merciful and powerful greatness of God and teach us how to draw out that power through brave faith.

In the Book of Genesis, we hear the high-stakes experience of Lot and his wife just before the unimaginable destruction of Sodom and Gomorrah, performed by violent and wrathful God, as the deplorable punishment for the vile sins of the citizens. At that moment of perils, merciful God came to rescue only the families of both Abraham and Lot his brother. God, in consultation with Abraham, advised Lot and his wife to head for the hills. But with the bold faith in God's merciful nature, Lot asked God to allow him to escape to a tiny town Zoar. God in his mercy granted his request. The town of Zoar is spared, only because of the power of the faith dwelling in Lot. Unfortunately, his wife, careless in her obedience to God's admonition, was punished to become a pillar of salt.

The second story, narrated in today's Gospel, depicts the disciples, being overwhelmed by the turbulence of nature-winds and the sea, as they were rowing the boat. They, of course, were scared to death; the worse issue was, they saw their Master being *in deep sleep while they faced a violent storm coming up on the sea, so that the boat was being swamped by waves.* However, due to some faith and hope they had in the Messianic power of their Master, they wake him and shouted: *"Lord, save us. We are perishing."* Once Jesus was alert, he not only rebukes the wind and the seas, but he also rebukes the disciples addressing them as "Why are you terrified, *you of little faith."*

Like Lot and his wife, we find, the disciples too were tossed around by the earthly perils. At those moments they were conscious of the loving presence of God and his Son. But unfortunately, either they forgot the justice and compassion of the Divine or they were more conscious about their own safety and security. Fortunately, in both events the Divine seemed to be considerate and merciful to the humans. Only Jesus revealed the underlying truthful fact that, while God's greatness deals always with fragile humans in justice-filled compassion, humans' weakness fails to consider about such goodness of God.

Almost all of us, like Lot's family and the disciples continuously, especially when we experience the tilting and shocking and painful natural disasters, may raise in our hearts as our routine creed in awe: *What sort of man is this Jesus of Nazareth?* In that usual confession we always forget to include the unending compassion of God in Jesus. If we see such amazing compassion to the divine justice in everything, happening in and around us-be it good or bad, as totally either performance of or with the permission of God but ultimately everything will help us to enjoy the betterment of our life.

And like the disciples we may cry out: *Lord, save us! We are perishing!* But Jesus' cool words with amazing actions he would say: *Don't be afraid. I am always with you and in your midst with full divine power, divine love, and divine* concern. As we sing with the Psalmist today, keeping God's mercy before our eyes, let us try to walk in his truth and integrity; and make sure our foot stands always on level ground. In other words, to lead a life in a levelheaded way.

Prayer: *Almighty and all-compassionate God! Kindly help us to spend time close to you. Kindly awaken our sensibilities, which may be dulled by sinful dimensions of our environment that keep us from seeing our need for mercy. Help us to be fully aware of your infinite goodness, blended with justice, found in all your initiatives to care for us. Grand us superb faith as your Son demands from us. Amen.*

Wednesday

By persistently trusting the Lord we are strengthened and filled
(Scriptural Passages: Gen. 21:5, 8-20;
Ps. 34; Matt. 8: 28-34)

Today the Psalmist echoes loudly the virtue of trust in God and his Son, which is an apt theme of this day readings. We recited: *My soul will glory in the LORD; let the poor hear and be glad. Magnify the LORD with me; and let us exalt his name together...Fear the LORD, you his holy ones; nothing is lacking to those who fear him. The rich grow poor and go hungry, but those who seek the LORD lack no good thing.*

While today's Psalm is, like most of King David's Psalms, knitted on this theme of trust in the Lord, it also can be taken as the main backdrop against the other readings because it has been the resource for so many canticles we read in the Bible like 'Magnificat' of our blessed Mother Mary and the Spirit-filled prayer of Hannah, the mother of Samuel.

In today's first reading we notice that Abraham was excited and thrilled, and overwhelmed at the same time. God surprisingly accepted Abraham marrying a second wife, plus he grants a beautiful son through her. Being overwhelmed with a newborn, Abraham faced quarreling wives delivering demands. In such critical situation God promised Abraham that he would take care of Ishmael, born of a slave. Abraham, being a faith-filled person, trusted God and God did fulfill those promises.

Coming to the Gospel passage of today, Matthew repeatedly augments the strong faith of the Apostles who were stunned what they experienced in their boating in the midst of storm and exclaimed: *"What kind of a man is this? Even the winds and the sea obey Him."* The Evangelist today, narrating about Jesus' miracle of casting out demons, underlines Jesus as powerful healer, deliverer from demons, and forgiver of human sins. Hence we, the followers of Jesus must continue to put relentlessly our whole trust in Jesus and get all his gifts for attaining eternally blessed life.

Prayer: *Generous and Wise God, you allow in our daily life so many occasions that will drain us emotionally, physically, and financially as you did in the lives of your friends like Abraham and the Disciples. As the townsfolks who came out to meet your Son, and begged him to leave their district, we, out of our narrowness and stinginess, are prone to refuse and discard manytimes Jesus the Emmanuel, the Bearer of healing and saving, the true Light which enlightens everyone. Grant we pray to esteem all overwhelming lifesituations, as watershed moments granted by you to cling to Jesus tightly, and esteem them all for our own transformation, and for the fulfillment of your masterplan of salvation. Amen.*

Thursday

God cannot bear any misguided-orthodoxical faith and practice
(Scriptural Passages: Gen. 22:1-19; Ps. 115; Matt. 9: 1-8)

Commonly, good-willed people are thwarted by two critical questions regarding their religious faith and practice. One, as the Psalmist points out to God in his frustration, is the question proposed to them by pagans: 'Where is your God?' And the other, as we hear in the first reading Isaac asking his father Abraham, 'Where is the sheep for the burnt offering?' The first one, about one's faith and the second, about his/her religious practices. The Spirit of God today enlightens us how to deal with those questions.

First and foremost, we should never harbor within us blasphemous thoughts and questions as the Pharisees were filled with as we hear in today's Gospel. Most of us are paralyzed and bedridden to rise up and walk in just ways. Many a time our sins dump us into such deplorable condition. During those occasions, in order to get up and walk we need Divine Being like Jesus who, with his authority would perform marvelous deeds of both forgiving our sins within our spirit and curing our illness outside our body.

This is exactly Abraham did in his interactions with God the Almighty. Since he had already put forth many questions to the Lord and received from him well-enlightening directions, when the Lord ordered him to sacrifice his only son Isaac, he didn't repeat any question but he trusted God wholeheartedly and conducted himself serene, faithful, and obedient. Isaac also did the same. However, he asked the question and accepting his father's answer to it, he obediently behaved as directed by his father who was truly directed by God himself.

The endresult of all such sincere religious faith-filled practices was that God was well-pleased by Abraham's trust and fidelity and he admired at his religious disposition and said: '*I know now how devoted you are to God, since you did not withhold from me your own beloved son.*' Besides, God too blessed him and his posterity with remarkable promises: '*I swear by myself that because you acted as you did in not withholding from me your beloved son, I will bless you abundantly; and in your descendants all the nations of the earth shall find blessing.*'

Prayer: *Loving God, with the Psalmist and with all your saints we profess that you are totally different from all other godfigures; you are in heaven; whatever you will, you do. You are very personal in your interactions with us. And we promise fervently we will always walk in your esteemed presence in the land of the living and never in that of the dead. Amen.*

Friday

We survive only through the merciful interactions of the Lord
(Scriptural Passages: Gen. 23: 1-67; Ps. 106; Matt. 9: 9-13)

Today we repeatedly hear as refrain, in today's meditative Psalm, the gratitude-filled heartbeats of the Psalmist: '*Give thanks to the Lord, for he is good*'. For such amazing heart-filled song, the Psalmist underlines the valid reason for such uplifted prayer is because he was experiencing the Lord's magnificent goodness and providence whenever he was making choices in his life at its every step of growth. He saw that '*The Lord's mercy endured forever which were demonstrated through his mighty deeds'.*

In today's first reading we hear two of such critical choices Abraham had to make. First was about the burial of his beloved wife Sarah, and the other about the marriage of his son Isaac. In both cases he found it hard to make right decision because he was torn between his personal earthly attachment and his God's covenantal mandate. He was not ready to compromise to avoid one for the sake of holding the other. On one side, he was very much concerned with his personal loyalty to his own blood-related people, to the 'purity' of his family line related to his native land of Mesopotamia; and on the other, he longed to comply with God's covenantal mandate to take possession of his adopted home in the foreign land of Canaan.

Such personal and social issues are strangling all of us, especially when we prefer Creator more than the creatures, including ourselves. In this critical human situation, Christ the Lord comes and shocks us by his ways, full of surprises. In today's Gospel we find one such mindblowing unorthodox behavior of Jesus. He calls to become a member in his primary team, a person like Matthew, an unlikely character, a tax collector, a public sinner, to be his friend and goes on to share a meal with such tax collectors and sinners. We see him not following the path of exclusion and avoidance. He was not afraid of being contaminated by others.

On the contrary, he wanted to change others and draw them to a better lifestyle. His Godly and lovely hardheadedness never look for pacifying his own inner urge of natural and artificial network-based relationships, breaking through the man-made ugly divide-lines of culture, caste, and creed, and of fake righteousness.

139

His only mantra was: *'I want mercy, not sacrifice.'* He also expounded it very vividly: *'It is not the healthy who need the doctor, but the sick. Indeed I did not come to call the virtuous but sinners.'* Jesus turned the tables on the Pharisees by looking at the situation from a completely different perspective. He still continues to do the same capsizing of our own twisted and perverted cultural, national, racial, religious, and political views and dealings.

Prayer: *Dear Lord Jesus, you want always your own merciful spirit to find expression in the lives of your followers. You made such spirit as a key principle for Christian morality. You call us to transform others with our openness and compassion. Help us to live as faithful agents of your transforming love and mercy. Thus we may become a gift of mercy and love to any needy neighbor with no expectation whatsoever. Amen.*

Saturday

Divine Diplomacy is intertwined with Truth and Justice
(Scriptural Passages: Gen. 27: 1-5, 15-29; Ps. 135; Matt. 9: 14-17)

Many religious and political leaders may probably interpret the diplomatic action of Rebekah, which we heard in the first reading, as legitimate and according to God's will. God seemed to use Rebekah, Isaac's beautiful wife, in her old age, who instigated her younger son Jacob to deceive his blind father Isaac to obtain his blessings, which were meant for the elder son Esau. It looks like everything our Sovereign God plans and does for his Masterplan of human salvific accomplishment, may seem very diplomatic. But if we, joining in faith, recite with the

Psalmist *'Praise the LORD, for the LORD is good; for I know that the LORD is great; our LORD is greater than all gods'*, and recognize his goodness and greatness, we will find in his action immense justice, truth and love.

In performing a deceptive action, Rebekah probably would have thought that the future of her family would be better served with mild mannered and peace-loving Jacob, than with Esau who was of wild behavior, and carefree, and hence, God would be pleased with her action. But in doing so, she completely forgot that she was making a big mistake in doing a great injustice to Esau. But we should know, in God's Kingdom, there is an eternal fact that good end doesn't justify any bad means.

The entire Bible, especially Jesus, the Word that came from heaven, revealed that what pleases God is above all our truthful and non-deceiving love for our neighbour. More than anything else in our discipled life, pure neighbourly love is the one and only command he wanted us to follow. As he verifies it in today's Gospel, he calls his message of love as *'the new wine and said that neither is the new wine put into old wineskins'*. What he meant was that to safely receive this new wine of love we must first rid ourselves of our thinking that we can please God even though we do harm to our neighbours, by performing either evil for evil or even evil for the sake of attaining or maintaining the good.

In Spirit and in Truth we know our human weakness. In order to survive, compete, and succeed in life at any cost, at times we deploy and utilize some cheating and cunning actions and coolly label them as prudent and diplomatic performances. Thus, as the Lord refers today, we may lose the intimate relationship of our heavenly Bridegroom, the Christ. In those situations, Jesus tells us that act of fasting can help free us from many sinful and twisted untruthful thoughts and behaviors. Fasting has the potential to strengthen our will and purify our desires. Fasting can take on many forms, but, at the heart, it is simply an act of self-denial and self-sacrifice for God. It helps us overcome earthly and fleshly desires so that our spirits can more fully desire Christ and his Truthful Way of Life.

Prayer: *God of the universe, we appreciate and accept anything happening in human history brings home to us the mystery of God's ways in salvation history – his use of weak, sinful people to achieve his own ultimate purpose as we notice in the OT narration. We too agree that the new cloth and the new wine Jesus spoke about are the valid metaphors to denote the spirit of your Kingdom. Those metaphors remind us of a paradigm shift Jesus brought, a radically new understanding of how you are to be loved and served. As Jesus did not measure religion by external actions like fasting or keeping other requirements of the law, help us to consider our religion, as a matter of the inner spirit we possess and renew daily in the light of your Son. Amen.*

WEEK - 14

Monday

The heart that trusts fully in Jesus is the true 'Bethel'
(Scriptural Passages: Gen. 28: 10-
22; Ps. 91; Matt. 9: 18-26)

As many renown writers have said, *'Today's dream, tomorrow's achievement'*, almost all of us develop our life on the basis of the dreams we are frequently dreaming about our future. One among us was Jacob, about whom we read in today's first reading. According to the OT narration, Jacob had a dream: A stairway rested on the ground, with its top reaching to the heavens, and God's messengers were going up and down on it. He too heard the Lord telling him that he would be possessing the land he was lying; he would be blessed with numerous descendants; through them the entire world would be blessed. As the highlight of all, in addition the Lord also promised: *'I will protect you wherever you go; I will never leave you until I have done what I promised you.'*

One more interesting, a little bit embarrassing incident, we read in this OT passage, is: Jacob was the cute and beloved baby of Rebekah and Isaac. He was believing that the true God of his father was the one who appeared and spoke to him in dream. As intelligent and favorite child of God, he even made an unprecedented vow to God but with cautionary profession of his faith in him. He said: *'If God remains with me, to protect me on this journey I am making and to give me enough bread to eat and clothing to wear, and I come back safe to my father's house, the LORD shall be my God.'*

This event depicts vividly how chosen people of goodwill had been dealing with their God in an interpersonal way. This is what we notice in every page of OT Books, especially in the Psalms. While the Psalmist throughout his writings, jubilantly and confidently proclaims, as we hear in today's Psalm that the God, whom he worships, is his refuge, and fortress, in whom he places his trust. Plus, he also advises all his readers and friends to do the same.

When Jesus, God's Son, came to us, he willed the same from his followers that they personally, as little children, must place their trust in him as 'our Savior Jesus Christ has destroyed death and brought life to light through the Gospel'. He demonstrates this factual truth in today's Gospel passage. We find in the Gospel event two needy people approached Jesus for help in this valley of tears. One was a synagogue official who came on behalf of his daughter and the other a woman with a hemorrhage who came on her own behalf. Though their ways of approaching him are quite different, in one point they were together. They wholeheartedly placed their trust in Jesus' mercy and power.

Taking stock of the events, narrated in the Gospel, we learn in the Spirit's wisdom: Our approach to the Lord should always be unique in our way of relating to other people, like that of Jacob of OT, the official, and the bleeding woman in NT; namely, we should be people of faith and trust in Jesus. Jesus will respond tenderly to us as he and his Father had been behaving. The Triune God will be equally responsive to our need and our cry for help.

Prayer: *Lord, you are our refuge and our fortress in whom we trust. We heard from today's first reading how your angels are continuously descending upon us from heaven, as Jacob dreamed, and bringing our prayers back to heaven. And we also are confirmed by today's Gospel events, that our Master Jesus, not minding about our sinful and weak background as unclean or untouchable, is always ready to heal our sickness and wounds and to offer us a renewed and resurrected life either by his touch or by our efforts to touch him. Kindly grant us the grace to approach your Son Jesus with our full faith-filled trust and get his heavenly help every day. In this way may every moment and every place in our life become our Bethel, the House of God! Amen.*

Tuesday

Abundant harvest requires plentiful but worthy Laborers
(Scriptural Passages: Gen. 32: 23-33; Ps. 17; Matt. 9: 32-38)

Matthew brings before us today Jesus, who is lamenting on the shortage of laborers in God's Kingdom, and requesting his followers to implore God, the Master of the Harvest, to send plentiful laborers to do the abounding harvest of saving humans around the globe. He says: *Ask the master of the harvest to send out laborers for his harvest.* Most of us would be wondering at Jesus' ordering us to pray for sufficient laborers for the harvest work, even though he tells us that God is the Eternal Master of the

Harvest, who alone has the ability and right to choose the best and worthiest laborers for his harvesting job. Jesus verified this fact when he strongly pronounced to his Apostles: *It was not you who chose me, but I, the God's Son, who chose you and appointed you to go and bear fruit...* (Jn. 15: 16)

The prayer, that Jesus asks of us, should emerge from the conviction that God is the One who decides who will work, where to put them, and what they'll do. Therefore, we can conclude Jesus's proposal of Harvest-prayer from us is mainly to demonstrate our personal interest and ambition to join the crowd of God's laborers whom he has been after. Through our Harvest-prayer we beg the Lord to make us worthy enough to be placed by him to accomplish the harvest work with the mindset of Christ.

To become such worthy laborers, first we should be compassionate and concerned laborers as Christ has been: *His heart was being moved with pity for the humans because they were troubled and abandoned, like sheep without a shepherd.* Second, not stopping with merely sympathizing over the deplorable conditions of our human brothers and sisters, we should walk the walk of Jesus who demonstrated his compassion in action by curing sick people by casting out demons who prevail over them. Thirdly, we find Jesus not trying to glorify himself, but always giving full glory to the Father in his accomplishments. When the spectators saw his power of healing and amazed saying *"Nothing like this has ever been seen in Israel,"* he never stuck himself to the company of those glorifying him; rather, as the Gospel underlines, he continued his harvesting journey, moving around to all the towns and villages, teaching in their synagogues, proclaiming the Gospel of the Kingdom, and curing every disease and illness.

Prayer: *Almighty Father, through Jacob's story today you make us aware of your readiness to show your mighty and compassionate face to us who are your chosen ones. And through the Psalmist we are taught how to commune with you as trust-filled children to enjoy your justice-based spiritual profits. As Jesus is now planning to reap the harvest of your heavenly fruits together with us, and asking us to express our strong will to accept your invitation, kindly bestow on us your grace to see your brightening and joyful face more so that after being strengthened spiritually, we may go forward to the harvesting job of compassionate and just undertakings to liberate and heal all those who are troubled by evil demons. Amen.*

Wednesday

Trusting in the Lord we can win the win in his Kingdom
(Scriptural Passages: Gen. 41: 55-
42:24; Ps. 33; Matt. 10: 1-7)

We confess relentlessly our trust in the Lord God, as we recite today with the Psalmist: *Lord, let your mercy be on us, as we place our trust in you.* The main reason for such consistent trust in him is, as the Psalmist himself sings, that we are fully aware of the eternal conduct of God, who seems to bring to nought the plans of nations and their leaders; he foils the designs of peoples who manytimes make unfair and malevolent decisions. As the old saying goes: *Man proposes and God disposes.* His grand merciful and just plan stands forever; more importantly, he holds an eternal kindness toward all those who hope and trust in him and he never fails to deliver them from all harms, and perils.

Jesus' Gospel proclamation in Palestine largely included Heavenly Father's merciful and just behavior and he continues it among us today and tomorrow. That was the manifesto of his ministry, which he handed over to his Apostles as he ascended to his Father's Mansion. He called such God's regime of the universe as 'the kingdom of God.' As we hear in today's Gospel, he entrusted to them that duty of proclaiming and enlarging God's Kingdom. He sent his chosen disciples to the world of the poor, the hungry, the thirsty and all those in need of wholistic healing. He shared with them the Bread of his Word to satisfy their deepest hunger privately so that they could go out to the world to share the same Bread of his Word with their neighbors.

Human history testifies, especially through our Bible and Tradition, to the fact of God the invisible, the untouchable, and the incomprehensive, working out his compassionate deeds of mercy and justice through his chosen ones. For instance, we hear in today's OT reading how God chose Joseph; how he saved him from all his earthly miseries and conflicts; how he elevated him to be the dignitary position in a foreign land; and how through Joseph God brought the first Jewish family to Egypt from where he started deliberately his magnificent salvation for the Jews and through them for all other humans with the saving hands of his Son and his Apostolic Agents.

Prayer: *Father in heaven, fully recognizing all your continued salvific works in our midst today, we are grateful for choosing us, as your Son's disciples by our baptism and confirmation, to go and proclaim his good news of your Kingdom's Principle of salvation. In this sacred work, Lord, help us to be energetic like your Apostles and be forgiving like Joseph all the evils we encounter from our fellowhumans. Amen.*

Thursday

Let us take pride in proclaiming the marvels of Jesus' Gospel
(Scriptural Passages: Gen. 44: 18-
45: 5; Ps. 105; Matt. 10: 7-15)

The entire Bible is filled with God's chosen people's untold feelings of awe, admiration, and gratitude towards their God, the Creator and Redeemer. We hear them loudly exclaiming, and prompting their fellowhumans do the same by saying with the Psalmist: *Remember the marvels the Lord has done.* He, in most of his Psalms, never ceases to list out to his readers those marvels of God. They are all the miraculous and merciful unprecedented deeds, done to faith-filled individuals, as well as through them to the community of God's people.

This is what we hear in the story of Joseph, an individual person, exclusively favored by God. Having been tortured, humiliated, and sold out as a slave by his own siblings, fortunately, at his own appropriate time, God moved miraculously the Egyptian king to release Joseph from the bondage of slavery, and to elevate him to highest rank-and-file position as the lord of the palace as well as ruler of all king's possessions.

More surprisingly, we find the same good Lord using Joseph in a breathtaking and very emotional way to satisfy the hunger and thirst of his own family members as how 'the rejected stone becomes a cornerstone' in God's Kingdom. Realizing such marvelous truthful fact of the spectacular deeds of God happening in his life, we hear Joseph telling his siblings in tears: *"I am your brother Joseph, whom you once sold into Egypt. But now do not be distressed, and do not reproach yourselves for having sold me here. It was* really for the sake of saving lives that God sent me here ahead of you."

Today's Gospel passage tells us that those marvelous deeds of God continue till this day but, thanks to our Redeemer Jesus the Lord, more imminently and greater intensively. Sending forth his elected Apostles to the needy and poor people in humanity, he commits them to proclaim his one and only Gospel message 'The Kingdom of God is at hand.' Thus, advising them to take their role of Gospel-proclamation as imminent and urgent, he too exhorted them that their proclamation should not stop with mere words and rituals, but much more it should be blended with action of healing people's illnesses, and especially casting out evil spirits from them.

Most importantly he instilled in their hearts that they should never forget their frailty, neediness, and emptiness in all dimensions of earthly life; and therefore he commanded them to trust totally God and his Providence in every step they take in his Gospel proclamation.

Prayer: *God of love, today we are reminded by your Scriptural passages, about our Christian missionary responsibility to proclaim your Gospel of justice and love in word and action in your Son Jesus' name as well as with his power. Grant us the grace to recognize the greatness of your Son's marvelous deeds of renewing the concept of your Kingdom, which is far surpassed the marvels of the old law. As Jesus continuously tells us that we are now called to go ahead and proclaim your saving works to demonstrate that the Kingdom of Heaven is at hand, help us with your Spirit first to repent ourselves and to believe in his Gospel and then, to perform our missionary works as best as we can. Amen.*

Friday

Salvific Gift is offered unconditionally but reciprocated willfully
(Scriptural Passages: Gen. 46: 1-30; Ps. 37; Matt. 10: 16-23)

From our Scriptures and world history we are fully aware of the fact that there is a perennial war between the Source of Goodness whom we call God and the source of evil, who is Satan, the archenemy of God. In this hectic war, as we read in today's Psalm, God never fails to shower his graces to those who take refuge in him wholeheartedly; they find delight in him; and they turn from evil and do good. To such just humans God promises salvation.

God's salvation-project to humanity contains the objectives of not only helping them and delivering them from evils; but also granting them their heart's requests; offering refuge in the time of their distress; and in days of famine sharing with them plenty of food. It is those kind of discipled persons who gather together as church to worship the true God. They are the ones Jesus chooses as his agents to help him in the implementation of God's salvific project.

As a matter of fact, the Church, made of Jesus' agents, has to deal with a world, which is, being not a neutral reality but a structure isolated from God, obeying the evil-oriented lord of this world. Therefore, we read in today's Gospel, Jesus offered certain forewarnings to his disciples, who were ready to be sent to proclaim the Gospel of Goodness. He confirmed very positively that they were his favorite sheep. He wanted them to be in the know of what kind of environment they would be working in. He ascertained that it would be an inimical milieu where people would behave like wolves to be waiting to devour them by nasty persecution and cruel murder. Surprisingly,

151

these kind of human wolves would exist not only outside but also within their families and kith and kins.

Jesus advised them to be shrewd and simple; he too encouraged them not to be worried about those evilmongering wolves. Jesus reiterated the merciful and encouraging words of his Father to his beloved agents like Jacob, to whom we hear God saying in the First reading: *I am God, the God of your father. Do not be afraid to go down to Egypt, for there I will make you a great nation. Not only will I go down to Egypt with you; I will also bring you back here, after Joseph has closed your eyes.*

He too promised that they would be empowered by his Spirit in the times of such struggles and conflicts. *You will be given at that moment what you are to say. For it will not be you who speak but the Spirit of your Father speaking through you.* He too underlined that if they endure all the persecutions to the end they would be saved. Finally he bid them goodbye saying, *Amen, I say to you, you will not finish the towns of Israel before the Son of Man comes.*

Prayer: *Creator God, as the joyful and hopeful journey of Jacob to Egypt with all his kith and kins, our life-journey too began in this world as Christians with the same Jacob's spirit of faith, hope and charity. We firmly trust in your goodness and fidelity and try our best to be just and do good deeds to others for your sake so that you may dwell in our heart, family, community and in our nation. However, as Jesus foretold, many times we see ourselves moving around like sheep among wolves. Lord, kindly help us with your Holy Spirit to patiently bear our daily life's burdens so that persevering in your love, we may be fully saved. Amen.*

Saturday

We are Christians, the discipled followers of Christ
(Scriptural Passages: Gen. 49: 29-50:
26; Ps. 105; Matt. 10: 24-33)

We feel proud of our religious name 'Christians', that indicates we are the 'discipled followers' of Christ. This is because, as Peter writes in his first letter, which we recited in today's Gospel Acclamation, *anything we do and bear in the name of Christ, we will be blessed because the spirit of God would rest upon us.*

In the Gospel passage we hear today Jesus promising such kind of positive thoughts on being Christians. According to him, if we are truly his discipled followers, at the end of the day he will acknowledge us before his Father and grant all that we need not only in this world but also in the world to come. He would openly own and acknowledge us as his ministers; he would speak in the praise and commendation of our works and labors; and he would introduce us into his Father's presence, and recommend us to him, to be honored, blessed, and glorified.

However, for attaining that sort of testimony from him, Jesus proposes: First and foremost we should fully aware of our worth in the eyes of heavenly Father. *You are worth more than many sparrows.* We are indeed worth more than all birds and animals God takes care of. At the same time Jesus too wants us to be afraid of only one person and that is none other than God himself. Secondly, he exhorts us that it is enough for us to follow him and accepting his Gospel values, we can imitate him, go with him wherever he takes us to go. *It is enough for the disciple*

153

that he become like his teacher, for the slave that he become like his master.

Furthermore, he confirms that if we behave in this humble and obedient way, then we would not be afraid of any life's obstacles, and hurdles. We will never be affected by the rejection, by the hatred and by the evil deeds of our opponents, who are always behaving as agents of Satan and performing all kinds of atrocities against God's favorites.

There is one more benefit that comes from the Lord when we commit ourselves to be his genuine followers. In today's first reading we hear from Joseph in his emotional conversation with his siblings that if they follow God in trust and sincerity, they need not be afraid of anything because God can never deceive us nor will he withdraw himself from the promises he have made to us. Joseph said: *Have no fear. Can I take the place of God? Even though you meant harm to me, God meant it for good, to achieve his present end, the survival of many people.* that would be the endresult in our life too if we uphold Joseph's conviction about the Triune God.

In addition, God's spirit advises us in today's Psalm, that our everyday life's words and actions must be like that of our ancestors forebearers, like Abraham, Jacob, and Joseph, giving thanks to the Lord, invoking his name and making known his deeds among the nations, and singing praises and proclaiming all his wondrous deeds.

Prayer: *Your Son Jesus instructs us today, Lord God, not to be afraid of any evils we face in this earthly life but to commit our lives to your care. He points out to us your powerful presence and loving providence among us as valid reasons for such fear-free feeling. We entreat you, Father, to help us to appreciate and cherish your benevolent caregiving providence. Do not withhold your Spirit from us but help us find a life of peace during the days of trouble. Amen.*

WEEK - 15

Monday

Loss of our transient life gains God's never-ending life
(Scriptural Passages: Ex. 1: 8-14, 22;
Ps. 124; Matt. 10: 34-11: 1)

In many past weekdays, we have been reading passages from the Book of Genesis, where we find God the Creator had been dealing more with his human creatures' individual and family problems. But as we start reading today in the Book of Exodus, we see God, after the death of Patriarch Joseph, facing their social and political problems, as they have been blessed by him as numerous and powerful people, compared to Egyptians. Local leaders and officials were afraid of God's people and started harassing them, even tried in many unjust evil ways to stop their increase. It went on so many decades. But God later rescued them from those social and political atrocities. As we recited with the Psalmist, they recognized his marvelous saving deeds and proclaimed: *Our help is in the name of the Lord. Had not the Lord been with us, when men rose up against us, then would they have swallowed us alive.*

Such cruel political and social situations of persecutions and adversities have been continued for ages for the disciples of Jesus. Our Master confirms the possibility of our facing political and social dangers despite our following him as he forewarns us today in a stunning way: *Do not think that I have come to bring peace upon the earth. I have come to bring not peace but the sword.* However, we know from his other teachings, he has promised us that all the social evils we encounter in day today life are for the better end of possessing God's true peace and complete joy.

But, in order to realize his promising gifts of peace and joy, Jesus advises us to endure our sufferings patiently with two strong convictions: One, let us never forget, no pain no gain: *Whoever finds his life will lose it, and whoever loses his life for my sake will find it.* Two, in our bleeding discipleship-life we are not alone. He and his Father are together with us. *Whoever receives you receives me, and whoever receives me receives the one who sent me.* Plus, *whoever gives only a cup of cold water to one of these little ones to drink because he is a disciple—amen, I say to you, he will surely not lose his reward.*

Prayer: *God, King of glory, Lord of power and might! We are aware of the contradiction we find in Jesus, who is, as Prophet Simeon foretold, is destined to be the downfall and the rise of many in Israel, a sign that will be opposed; concurrently he also would be, as Prophet Isaiah declared, the Prince of Peace. We never forget his eternal promise that he would give us true peace and not as the world gives. What he gives is not peace at any price, but a special kind of peace that comes from staying close to Jesus. Lord, give us the wisdom and courage to accept all you have revealed through your Son. Help us to believe, trust, and love you. Being strengthened by you, we will be true to your Son's admonitions. Amen.*

Tuesday

Returning to God in repentance is the starting of salvific revival
(Scriptural Passages: Ex. 2: 1-15; Ps. 69; Matt. 11: 20-24)

It may surprise many of us, when we see Jesus exhibiting in today's Gospel his emotional outbursts in the form of certain cursing-type of words against the towns, Chorazin, Bethsaida, and Capernaum, which made up what scholars call 'The Evangelical Triangle' in the public ministry of Jesus. Apparently, he would have spent 50-70% of his ministry time around those towns; hence their residents would have repeatedly heard and seen all Jesus did. He preached the Gospel of their salvation, cured their sick, and directed them to a deeper understanding of God's plan and the significance of life. His marvelous deeds were meant to lead humans to conversion, to a change of outlook and of lifestyle, a turning away from selfishness and showing new concern for the poor and the needy.

Regrettably, the people living in those towns were not open to his powerful message of the imminent coming of the Kingdom of God. They missed the opportunity to understand his mission, to change their lives and be part of the evolving Kingdom of God. Hence, with divine anger he reproached their hardness of heart. His harsh words were in no way an outburst of his human unbalanced anger; rather, they were an attempt to alert the rejectors of the importance of recognizing and joining his mission. His miraculous deeds of casting out demons and healing all sicknesses showed his immense love for suffering humanity.

Undeniably, by God's Spirit reverberating within us, if we are closely connected to him, we can perceive

157

in the dense pile of our day-to-day experiences, there are moments when God in Jesus intervenes, offering guidance, deliverance, and miracles to its people. Almost all the time he does it through some of our relatives, friends, enemies, and any creature as he designs. In the Biblical event, that is narrated in today's first reading, we see two ordinary human beings-Moses and one of his Jewish brothers, intersecting each other; while the former was very much concerned about his fellowman in slaying the Egyptian who struck cruelly, the latter didn't show any concern for the former but only rebuked him for his killing the Egyptian.

God in Jesus deals the same way in our life. Though he chastises us for our indifference and carelessness toward his loving deeds in our midst, he still continues to shower his mercy and love to us in every moment of life. This is why, today the Psalmist proclaims that in his critical lifesituation like sinking in the abysmal swamp where there is no foothold, and reaching the overwhelming watery depths, he reaches out to the everloving God. And the Lord heard him, freed him from all bonds, and revived his spirit of joy.

Prayer: *Lord, our Father and God forever, we thankfully acknowledge that we have been blessed by your continuous visitation and your wonderful works as the citizens of Chorazin and Bethsaida. But we know well, hearing today your Son's chastisement against his fellow-citizens, how much you are worried about our sinful stubbornness, and how anxiously you and your Son are waiting for our repenting for our hardheartedness and hardheadedness. Here we come Lord with our open and contrite heart. Kindly forgiving us bless all our heartfelt promises responding to Jesus' Gospel, and returning to lead a truthful and compassionate way of just life. Amen.*

Wednesday

Let puffedup-self become a burning bush
where the Holy can work on
(Scriptural Passages: Ex. 3:1-6,9-
12; Ps. 103; Matt. 11: 25-27)

Throughout the drapery of human history, the Divine has been choosing only simple humans, the meek and humble, not only to share his salvific leadership to lead his human creatures but also to reveal his extraordinary truths and ways of living fuller life. Sacred scriptures are brimming with examples of such God's choices.

For instance, in today's first reading, Holy Spirit takes us to Mount Horeb, where God revealed himself to Moses, who was an ordinary man, unassuming and lacking in eloquence, all for implementing his Divine Plan of liberating God's people out of their bondage. In this historical event of God's encounter with Moses, we are informed that our God, who is always ready to share his revealed truths to humanity, continuously seeks human hearts of the meek and humble; he too expects them to possess certain secured guts to accept their limitations and trust in his all-powerful providence.

It is this eternal truth of divine revelation that Jesus reiterates in today's Gospel. In his public prayer of praise to God the Father, Jesus convincingly attests to an unprecedented deal of the Heavenly Father with his chosen children. Hiding so many of his factual truths from those who unduly esteem themselves as wise and learned, God reveals them to the childlike. They are the meek and humble persons, as Jesus, who, *though he was Divine, not regarding equality with God something to be grasped,*

159

emptied himself and took the form of a slave; all for his Father's Will be done.

The Psalmist also highlights today that our God of justice and kindness shares his ways, his plans, and his benefits to humble and simple people like Moses. We find solace and reassurance that divine revelation extends its tender touch to the broken, the wounded, and the contrite of heart. It is the meek and humble who, in their recognition of their need for divine grace, open themselves to receive the transformative power of God's revelation. The Psalm reminds us that in our vulnerability and humility, we find healing, forgiveness, and restoration.

Prayer: *Heavenly Father, Lord of heaven and earth, with your Son today we give praise and thanks to you for your benevolent gesture of sharing all your hidden mysteries with us, your weak children. It is vividly clear to us that only the simplicity, innocence, and humility of a childlike heart becomes a fertile ground for the seeds of your revelation to take root and flourish. Pour out your wisdom and power, Lord, so that we can create space in our life for your revelation to touch and transform us. In doing so, we position ourselves to be vessels for divine revelation and recipients of the profound truths that guide us on our journey toward spiritual enlightenment. Amen.*

Thursday

*Burdensome earthly life becomes easy
when we handle it with Jesus*
(Scriptural Passages: Ex. 3: 13-20; Ps. 105; Matt. 11: 28-30)

The chronicles of world history have recorded the continuous and universal outcries of the humans, who were burdened with loss of freedom and cruelty of injustice. They too were searching for liberation and yearning for a deliverer who would lead them to a peaceful and prosperous lifesituation. Archetype of such groaning people is well-picturized in OT historical stories. They were Israel, a race of humanity, considering themselves as the people of the God of Abraham, Isaac, and Jacob. We hear in the Book of Exodus today that God was very much concerned with their plight. He revealed to them his melted heartbeat as well as his salvific plan through Moses: *I am concerned about you and about the way you are being treated in Egypt; so I have decided to lead you up out of the misery of Egypt into a land flowing with milk and honey.*

He assured his fidelity to fulfill his promising Plan by revealing his one and only Name 'I am who am' indicating that his Essence is 'the eternal and faithful Person'. Significantly God never failed in his promise and expected his people to reciprocate to his compassionate and truthful fidelity by their genuine sacrifices of praise and thanksgiving. Undoubtedly many, like the Psalmist inspired them, pointing out that *the Lord remembers forever his covenant*, and persuading them *to give thanks to the Lord; to invoke his holy name; to make known among the nations his deeds; and to recall the wondrous deeds that he had wrought, his portents, and the judgments he had uttered.*

Intriguingly, it is our belief, the same Israel's God, whom Jesus introduced to us as our and his Father, continues for centuries performing his eternal, and merciful salvific deeds through his Son Jesus Christ. NT Writers and community of Jesus' followers confirm this eminent truth, by quoting the words of Jesus from the Gospel of Matthew: *Come to me, all you who labor and are burdened, and I will give you rest. Take my yoke upon you and learn from me, for I am meek and humble of heart; and you will find rest for yourselves. For my yoke is easy, and my burden light.*

In those consoling words, Jesus reveals himself as the definitive deliverer who brings deliverance to all of us who are burdened and tormented. Not merely standing there uttering these words of consolation to the sufferers, he takes on to himself their yoke, sharing the burden of our sins on the cross, and victoriously rising from the tomb to hand over to them the promised eternal rest and freedom. It is thus Jesus exemplifies his Father's compassion and protection, plus, he offers the Godly and costly advice of how to gain our ultimate rewards of eternal rest through his way of meekness and humility.

Prayer: *Lord, our God and our Savior, you repeatedly declare that you will always remember your covenant forever in saving us from perils and burdens of evil. By the same token, your Son Jesus preserved your covenantal faithfulness and expressed his concern very compassionately about our burdens and yokes we endure, due to our commitment to his Gospel values and demands of love and justice and truth. Actually he wants to share our life's burdens as his own. Lord, help us to be always a friend of your Son Jesus so that both he and ourselves will pull life together and thus all our yokes would become easy and our burdens light. Amen.*

Friday

Godly Ritual is nothing but to be humanly merciful
(Scriptural Passages: Ex. 11: 10-
12: 14; Ps. 116; Matt. 12: 1-8)

We know, through Judeo-Christian Scriptures, that all laws, regulations, rubrics and external observances, which people have been performing in their religious life, were prescribed by God. And by those observances God seemed to be well-pleased and appeased. Since this pursuit of holiness and righteousness was entangled with rigid observance of religious rituals and laws, God's people took meticulous care on their minute details as we hear today in the Book of Exodus. God seemingly told them that they should eat the Passover ritual meal as if those who are in flight, meaning they would be doing all those rituals only as travelers and as pilgrims passing through the transitory voyage to the Promised Land. Plus, very remarkably the Almighty has stated that they should consider every day's religious observances, as if the memorial festive practices, which are celebrated during the pilgrimage to the Lord, as perpetual institution.

Indeed, over the centuries, many holy people obeyed God's command and celebrated their everyday rituals faithfully as their heartbeats, singing with the Psalmist, *I will take the cup of salvation, and call on the name of the Lord. How shall I make a return to the Lord for all the good he has done for me?* This Psalm includes the details of what and how our ritualistic sacrifices must be performed. When the leader of the congregation took up the cup, filled with wine in Jewish pascal rite, reminding himself of the salvation God has promised and granted, and blessing the Lord, he raised his grateful heart to the Creator; he also, placing in the sacred cup his own accomplishments, his sacrifices, his blunders, his ups and downs, and all his burdens, offered his entire life and his family and friends to the Lord.

When Jesus came to them, he observed that most of God's chosen ones, being so attentive to the external observances, forgot to hold the inner spirit according to God's mind. Reverberating the spirit of the Psalmist, he downrightly rebuked such twisted approach. Acknowledging his authority as the Lord of the Sabbath and its external practices, he reminded them an amazing statement: *I say to you, something greater than the temple is here. If you knew what this meant, I desire mercy, not sacrifice, you would not have condemned these innocent men.*

Jesus still continues calling us to a deeper understanding of true holiness, that reflects God's mercy and compassion towards others, and not just offer sacrifices. Our religious practices should not become empty rituals devoid of love and compassion, but rather, they should flow from a heart deeply rooted in God's mercy and grace.

Prayer: *God of power and mercy, we agree with Jesus that all we do as sacraments, devotions and other practices in your name are valuable because they are considered as the enactment of your mysteries, prescribed by Jesus. Grant us your grace to handle them, as he directs us today, with our heart of mercy and love, justice and truth; so that they may not be empty shells and clanging cymbals; faking and fading colorful fireworks. Help us also, Father, to properly perform all our Catholic rituals, devotions and practices with purity of heart and mind filled with mercy and love, justice and truth. Amen.*

Saturday

Becoming bruised reed to our weaklings
we can win the victory of Christ
(Scriptural Passages: Ex. 12: 37-
42; Ps. 136; Matt. 12: 14-21)

From the beginning of his public ministry, Jesus became a figure of controversy and as Simeon the Prophet prophesied, he has been destined for the fall and rise of many in Israel, and to be a sign that would be contradicted. At the same time, as Matthew in his Gospel today refers to the Prophecy of Isaiah, despite the adversaries were plotting to kill him, instead of doing evil for evil, Jesus went ahead preaching the Gospel of mercy and justice in words and actions. It is breathtaking to see his approach to evildoers as a humble and suffering Messiah, performing his works not through crushing power but through sacrificial service. He moved around quietly and, at the same time, he was tolerant and understanding of the weak.

When Jesus' followers approached him to join in his team of continuing his Gospel mission, he firmly expected from them to get into his shoes of meekness and humility, as his heart was ever beating. Church history testifies how his Gospel team of disciples upto this day, face those kind of adversaries to the Gospel values as in his days, with the same prejudices and arrogance. In this regard, regrettably most of his disciples have been disappointing him, not possessing the heart of meekness and humility as the Suffering Servant of God.

As a matter of fact, with the Psalmist we believe God who is good and love cannot but be merciful and cannot but be good even to those who do evil. His mercy endures forever; he demonstrated his meekness and goodness in remembering us in our miseries, tries to free us from our foes, as he did to the Israelites. Hence, from the beginning of creation, specifically in the time of marvelous divine intervention of liberating his chosen people from their lifelong slavery, God expecting from them the same kind of meek and humble attitude in their walk of life.

To enrich their attitude, from the start of their journey to the Promised Land, we hear in today's first reading, when they were leaving Egypt he designed their community to be a mixed crowd of people of different racial background. He wanted them not to value their racial purity as an absolute. The presence of foreigners among them is a factor shared with other oppressed peoples.

God continues to prove himself as the one and only Father of all humans and he is concerned about, not only the just but also the sinners, not only the obedient but also the disobedient. In order to feel that way, through his Prophets and his own Son Jesus, he invites his chosen ones to respect every human with no discrimination whatsoever; in addition, since all his human children are sinful, and weak, everyone of us should be patiently accepting and forgiving each other, especially those who do harmful things to us and avoid doing evil for evil.

Prayer: *Merciful and gentle Lord, we are esteemed by you as your chosen ones; you have gathered us together as one nation under one God, being bonded by your special grace of unity and justice. Lamentably, these days, being unjust and unforgiving, we are divided and fight and hurt each other. Father, we beg you to offer your help to live and proclaim, as Jesus, the Gospel of truth, mercy and justice, without compromise but to do so without any taint of arrogance or bullying; at the same time, fill us with Jesus' patience, meekness and understanding, so that we may continue to proclaim his Gospel of unity in justice and mercy to those who are not yet ready to listen and answer. Amen.*

WEEK - 16

Monday

Jesus is the only sign of our victory from the jaws of evils
(Scriptural Passages: Ex. 14: 5-18; Canticle:
Ex. 15: 1-6; Matt. 12: 38-42)

In today's Gospel we hear the pharisees demanding a
sign from Jesus. But Jesus retorted them with a strong
rebuke: *An evil and unfaithful generation seeks a sign.* In fact,
by such reaction Jesus did not mean that humans' looking
for signs is anything wrong. It is a common strategical
tendency of all human beings to lookout for signs that
might provide direction when we are faced with an
important decision, or just looking for comfort.

Human creatures, even most of other creatures too,
naturally possess a primal feel of fear while they take a
new step for their surviving life-journey. For instance, we
see in the Book of Exodus how Israel had been terror-
stricken as the Egyptian King's blitz of chariots were
bearing down on them. Standing at the edge of the Red
Sea, those fugitives, who were fleeing from the darkened
life to God-promised brightest future, hearing and
noticing the noisy and ferocious army of Pharaoh, getting

closer to annihilate them, would have screamed for Godly sign of support through Moses.

The same was true also in the case of the Scribes and Pharisees of Jesus' time, who were scared and crushed by fear of their own egoistic religious leadership, being threatened by Jesus' unprecedented, authoritative, and Godly Personage. Out of such horrifying situation, they demanded from him to prove himself through performing some signs, as the God of Exodus did.

In fact, though Jesus was fully aware of the hardheadedness of these demanders for the sign, did offer them a remarkable and marvelous sign. According to him, that sign is none other than himself. He confirmed that all the marvelous deeds God had done in the past life of the Israel, such as the fall and rise of Prophet Jonah and universally acclaimed wisdom found in the Kingship of Solomon, were prefiguratively, but most uniquely, symbolizing him as the One and Only Sign of God's Salvation to the entire universe.

God's good news from Exodus to Calvary is nothing but the fact that only through Jesus, who is God's Word, made Flesh, the entire humanity can be liberated from the fears that threaten to paralyze our minds, hearts and bodies. In a world, plagued by fears and phobias of the unknown 'other', we are called by the Redeeming God to stand strong, singing the praises of God, as Moses sings in today's Canticle with Israelites at their encounter of God's marvelous deeds of liberation: "I will sing to the Lord, for he is gloriously triumphant. My strength and my refuge is the Lord, and he has become my savior. This is my God, I praise him; the God of my father, I extol him..."

Prayer: *By reading about your powerful compassion of liberating the panic-stricken Israel at their harm's way to lifesituation by the miraculous sign at the Red Sea, we* *are encouraged to develop a resilient faith and trust in your marvelous deed of salvation for us through your Son, the Word made Flesh. Grant us, Lord, the grace to see Jesus' presence and hear his words around us, constantly guiding us through the dark valley filled with fears and terrors. Amen.*

Tuesday

*Happy are they who do God's will,
seeking him with all their hearts*
(Scriptural Passages: Ex. 14: 21-15: 1;
Res. Ex. 15: 8-17; Matt. 12: 46-50)

Jesus shares with us today one of the best of his Good News: *Whoever does the will of my heavenly Father is my brother and sister and mother.* He uttered this prophetic words when he was informed that his mother and his relatives were waiting for him, standing outside of the crowd of his listeners. He first questioned: *Who is my mother? Who are my brothers?* And pointing out to his disciples, he said: *Here are my mother and my brothers.* He continued to confirm those who do the will of God are his close relatives.

The will of God is nothing but God's Masterplan of humans' salvation and its implementation, which he enacted through his marvelous and powerful deeds, as we read in today's first reading. It is simply a unique heavenly package of God's promises and their fulfillment with the trustworthy and faithful cooperation of humans.

Undoubtedly good many of God's people, as well as Jesus' followers have been striving to fulfill God's will was best as they good. Like Moses, whom we hear in today's meditative canticle, praising the Lord, they were continuously singing grateful songs about God's marvelous deeds for their liberation: *Let us sing to the Lord; he has covered himself in glory. He brought us in and planted us on the mountain of his inheritance, the place where he made his seat, the sanctuary, which his hands established.*

Indeed whenever God performed such amazing deeds for his chosen people, in fear they believed him and glorifying him with mere outward songs, praises and offerings. But we know majority of them failed him and opposed him on every occasion he did things that were displeasing to them. They forgot his eternal goodness and greatness. But those who continued faithfully obeying his will, despite whatever evils happened to them, he blessed and inherited them as his favorite sons and daughters.

It is this understanding and attitude toward God and his Will, as Jesus exhorts us today, to hold in our own earthly voyage to eternity. He underlines, if we sincerely hear and do the divine will, we would be considered not only true children of God, but also thereof we would become Jesus' close relatives and kith and kins. To be a true disciple of Jesus means first and foremost to transform the order of our bonding relationships in this world. Bonding with God as our priority, we start considering all other relationships, including the blood-related, as secondary.

Moreover, Jesus proves this unique relationship with him is more than blood-related, when we see him in today's Gospel event, pointing out to his Mother Mary as our rolemodel. In his view, Mary became his Mother, not only physically, but much more spiritually. If there is anyone who did the will of God most perfectly, it was the Blessed Virgin Mary. She became God's favorite daughter, and faithful and beautiful Bride to the Holy Spirit by her humble submission saying the historical words: *I am the* handmaid of the Lord. Be it done to me according to your word! Thus she was qualified as true disciple of God's Son with flying colors.

Prayer: *Lord, God, the mighty conqueror, we are so glad in believing that your Son Jesus was always considering us part of the disciples' group standing in front of him as we hear in the Gospel. We do desire to be obedient to you and your will in all things. We love to embrace your perfect plan for our salvation. We entreat you, Lord, in that same will, help us to share in your divine life and become a full member of your Son's family forever. Amen.*

Wednesday

Haughty and earthy human spirit is
unfertile to fructify any Godly
(Scriptural Passages: Ex. 16: 1-5, 9-15; Ps. 78; Matt. 13: 1-9)

In today's Gospel we find Jesus introducing us into the mysteries of God's Kingdom. In our day today life, we observe God's one of the most mindblowing mysteries, namely his enduring compassionate dealings with us, despite we behave continuously stubborn, hardheaded and disobedient to him, as his chosen people had done in the desert.

We hear in the Book of Exodus and in today's Psalm that in spite of all that God had done for the Israelites, in liberating them from horrible and gruesome lifesituation in Egypt, they began complaining first about drinking bitter water in the midst of arid desert. And later, as we hear both in the Book of Exodus as well as in the Book of Numbers, they were murmuring bitterly to God through Moses about the scarcity of food.

Clearly we see them preferring a return to slavery in a land where they had plenty to eat, rather than risking the journey to freedom and human dignity through the desert. But as a patient, caring and compassionate Parent, God was tolerating his people's constant complaints because of their short memories of his former help and protection and their weak faith. He immediately listened to their mournful cry for food and rained down bread 'manna' from heaven both day and night; again when they were not satisfied with vegetarian meal, the merciful God had pity on them; he granted both bread and quails falling down day and night for their meals.

God's amazing compassion-filled behavior continues yesterday, today and every day in our midst as a nonstop-providential care for us. In order to uplift us from our sinful and earth-bound nature, he was kind enough to send his Son Jesus in our midst. On his part, Jesus went down to see through the depth of our ignorance and weakness. He explained to us in parables about the expectation of God the Father from our life in this world. In today's Gospel passage he tells us that God, as a powerful and hope-filled Gardener, sows his eternal-life-giving words and deeds, as seeds in every human heart and mind with his immense generosity and magnanimity in many ways with no discrimination whatsoever.

But very sadly, as Jesus reminds us today that we, as puny stubborn creatures, make the worst use of our freedom and independence, and choose God's words and actions according to our whims and fancies; we, as viewers and hearers, react to God's interactions with us-some of us as prejudiced, many of us as shallow, or most of us as busybodies. Only a few among us behave as open minded viewers and hearers, and encounter the expected results of joyful, peaceful and fruitful life.

Prayer: *Loving and compassionate God, help us to become truly fertile soil for your most holy Word. May we receive warmly all that you speak through your Son Jesus! Father, grant us the humility and faith like Peter to tell Jesus: Master, Where shall we go? You have the words of eternal life. We beg you that the seed of faith may be planted deep within us, so that it may grow and flourish and produce abundant blessings to us, and to all our friends and relatives. Amen.*

Thursday

*Only the inner spirit, fixed on Jesus, will
eternally gaze God face to face*
(Scriptural Passages: Ex. 19: 1-20; Dan.
3: 52-56; Matt. 13: 19-27)

From the moment when our first parents committed the sin of disobedience to God's will, the human view of the Presence, Speech, and Behavior of Sovereign God, has been fearful, distancing and trembling. This eternal truth has been well expounded in today's first reading.

At the onset of the encounter of Israelites with God in the vicinity of Mount Sinai, we are told that *there were peals of thunder and lightning, and a heavy cloud over the mountain, and a very loud trumpet blast, so that all the people in the camp trembled.* And at the Lord's coming down, people noticed that *Mount Sinai was all wrapped in smoke, for the Lord came down upon it in fire. The smoke rose from it as though from a furnace, and the whole mountain trembled violently.*

This breathtaking encounter with God has been, through the history of Israel, echoing in the words of the Prophets like Isaiah and Jeremiah and so on. Prophet Daniel, as we recited as today's meditative canticle, repeatedly goes on singing *Glory and praise to the God of our fathers, praiseworthy and exalted above all forever.* Prophet also blesses the holy and glorious Name of the Lord, proclaiming God's blessedness and his holiest glory as found in the temple; he encounters God sitting on the throne of his kingdom and from the firmament of heaven the Lord is looking into the depths.

At the arrival of God's Son Jesus in our midst, as today's Gospel proclaims, he made miraculous change in the old fearful attitude of humans towards God; especially those, who sincerely believed in his testimonies in words and actions, noticed *'God with us', among us, and within us.* Humans, especially the little children of God, began to hear the divine words; and to see the figure of God merciful, lovable, truthful and just.

When the Lord responded to the disciples, who asked him, 'why do you speak to the people in parables?', he implied negatively that he does not talk to his disciples in parables. As many preachers would explain, Jesus was dividing the hearers and followers into two categories: One, the 'insiders', and the other, 'outsiders'. From all his sayings, we can understand the insiders are those hearers and viewers, who more open to listen and observe attentively through their inner spirit about his testimonies of divine kingdom mysteries and assimilate them into their daily life. But in contrast, the outsiders are those viewers and hearers, who shut their inner spirit and fall out into darkened road of Satan.

Very interestingly, Jesus also includes another riddle to his marvelous preaching today. He says: *To the one who has, more will be given until he grows rich; the one who has not, will lose what little he has.* In fact, he has been proclaiming often this positive and glorious result of his 'insiders'. Here he underscores specifically that those insiders in his camp of discipleship, by opening their inner spirit, like a fertile land, will be increasingly enriched in all graces, whereas the 'outsiders' will lose even what they possessed within them and their spiritual situation will be worsened.

Prayer: *Lord God, through your Son we come to know, love, and serve you even with our mortal breakable body and unclean spirit. We thank you and your Son for such lovely gift. Lord, obeying your Son, we promise to be more carefully look at, and more attentively see Jesus so that by learning and practicing in our earthly pilgrimage, we may one day fully gaze at you face to face in heaven. Amen.*

Friday

*More our inner divine intimacy, less we
need outer help for good-living*
(Scriptural Passages: Ex. 20: 1-17; Ps. 19; Matt. 13: 18-23)

Many rationalists and naturalists contend that humans need not have any outside help-religion, scriptures for morality, because it is already embedded in our nature. I agree we are made in the image and likeness of God-in God's goodness, justice, mercy, truth. But our church holds, it is only sowed as a seed initially in our creation. As any other physical and mental needs, we also need help, for our spiritual and moral growth, from outside in the form of parents, elders, religion and scriptures. Let us remember, *it takes a community to build up a child.*

Our Almighty Sovereign God, not only has created humanity as the most dignified creation but also, as we hear in today's first reading, he preserves their dignity and special status of righteousness by offering them his directions, his counsels and admonitions in the form of ten commandments. And as the Psalmist today sings, God's laws, decrees, precepts, and ordinances are refreshing for our souls; and they are trustworthy suggestions and perfect tools for us in leading an everlasting life of joy, peace and holiness even in this world.

Above all, the Lord has sent his Son, as our singular Word that sums up all the directions he had proclaimed to us in the past. In today's Gospel Matthew gives us the explanation of Jesus about his Parable of the Sower. Being an outstanding Gardener, God abundantly sows his words as the life-giving seeds in the inner field of every human person.

So many followers of Christ, like us, started well at the first phase of receiving God's words of eternal life wishfully and happily, but in the second phase of those words' growth within us we fall out, specifically due to the worldly anxieties we are tossed around. In our busy and hectic life our life of grace is choked; our relationship with Christ and the church is being tarnished by our emotional and mental disturbances and thus we make our 'Wordy Field' dry and bushy. This is how so many of us either left the companionship of Christ or play with Christ and ourselves the games, like 'hide and seek' or 'in and out'.

Jesus underlines, if God's words are to be prolifically productive, not only we should hear those awesome words with open heart and mind, filled with joy; not only we must understand them with divine wisdom, so that Satan doesn't steal away what was sown in our hearts; but also we should persevere in obeying God's commanding words faithfully, even in the midst of tribulation or persecution, which come because of abiding by his words, and not permitting any worldly anxiety and the lure of riches choke his words. If we preserve them thus with generous heart, then we will be blessed by him and we will yield abundant fruits.

Prayer: *Lord, God, we truly desire that your words of commands and instructions sink deep into our hearts as we hear them daily. We pledge today to stay strong in our faith and obedience to your Son's New Command of love, no matter the cost. Kindly help us to follow in every moment of our life our Lord Jesus' obedient and humble path that has pleased you very much and yielded plentiful harvest of salvation. Amen.*

Saturday

Having good and evil within, let's not put
others in the box of good or bad
(Scriptural Passages: Ex. 24: 3-8; Ps. 50; Matt. 13: 24-30)

God earnestly seeks our fellowship through the Psalmist today telling: *Gather my faithful ones before me, those who have made a covenant with me by sacrifice.* He too demands from his loved ones to offer to him praise as their sacrifice and fulfill their vows to the Most High. In return of such valid sacrifice, he promises: *Then call upon me in time of distress; I will rescue you, and you shall glorify me.*

On one side, as we read in the Scriptures, God always insists that in our life of warfare against evils, we should abide by the eternal covenant he made with humanity through our leaders like Moses and specifically, through the brokenbody and bloodshed of his beloved Son Jesus. And on the other side, as we hear in today's Gospel, he advises us to be patient and hopeful, especially when we find around us the wrongdoings of our fellowhumans.

177

As a typical resonance of heavenly Father's Voice, through his splendid Parable of the Weeds among the Wheat, Jesus declares that the church will be a mixture of the good and the not-so-good, up until the end of time, when all, that are not of God, will disappear. If evildoers, as weeds, are detected among the wheat-like community of Jesus' disciples, sometimes we do get frustrated and as the servants in the Parable, we beg him permit us to go out and pull them up. Surprisingly we hear God, as a compassionate Farmer, cautioning us, *No! If you pull up the weeds and you might take the wheat along with them.* His words mean that he does not tolerate evil forever, but allow plenty of time for the harvest to be properly brought home.

As individuals, every one of us is a mixture of light and shade, sinful and holy and perfect and imperfect, until we are fully conformed to the image of God's Son in the next life. We are indeed all the time trying to grow more fully like unto Jesus. Yet, we have to accept that sin will always be part of our lives. We are grateful to see that like the farmer in the parable, God is continuously patient with us.

As the Father, so the Son, and in line we, his adopted children also. He expects that we too, as his children, must be patient with ourselves and with each other. We know it is not contentment; it is simply the realistic recognition that we are all a work in progress. You have begun a good work in our lives, and even if it is not perfect in this life, you will bring every work we do into completion in eternity.

Prayer: *Loving God, we entreat you to offer us the grace of patience and tolerance to put up with human faults and failures; though it is hard for us, you demand to offer to you this patient and hopeful attitude as living covenantal sacrifice of praise and* *thanksgiving everyday which you prefer more than ordinary ritual sacrifices. Kindly help us in the midst of evils we encounter in our life, to never fall into their trap or lure. Free us from doubt and despair and give us perfect hope in your promise of justice and mercy. Amen.*

WEEK - 17

Monday

Evangelization means to carry a tiny
piece of heaven wherever we go
(Scriptural Passages: Ex. 32: 15-24, 30-
34; Ps. 106; Matt. 13: 31-35)

As we recited the words of Apostle James in today's Alleluia Acclamation, we, the disciples of Christ, are the "firstfruits" of God's creation; namely, we are identified as the highest creatures of the world above all the rest God has made. It is the will of God that however the dark be our lifesituations, we, his firstfruits, should never forget the enormous good gifts, which God has bestowed to us.

The problem with humans is, we frantically seek, every moment of our life, particularly in the moments of our mishaps and struggles, to see, to hear, and to touch and to feel God as we physically expecting from our fellowhumans. If we don't get what we wish, then we react like the Israelites, as we hear in today's first reading. Aaron reports to God about the people's bad nature and their undertakings against God. According to him, the reason, for people's seeking another kind of god, was that when they were wishing to hear and to get God's help through his leader Moses, they were disappointed by not seeing Moses nor hearing anything from God for some lengthy days.

Therefore they made, by their own hands, a golden calf as worshipped it as their tangible and visible god. As the Psalmist today testifies, the Israelites exchanged their glory for the image of a grass-eating bullock; adorned a molten image; they forgot the God who had saved them who had done wonderous deeds in Egypt in liberating them from their darkened life. Being hurt by the infidelity of his 'firstfruits', despite Moses begging for forgiveness for his people, God proposes punishment to his dissenters.

Many centuries after such horrible event happened in the desert, Jesus noticed among his people the same bitter and sinful behavior was present. In order to inculcate in them an awareness about the hidden and unobtrusive nature but an everloving behavior of God, he explained about it in parables.

Two of those parables are contained in today's Gospel. The metaphor 'muster seed', which Jesus uses in one story, makes us wonder how the Kingdom of God, though seemingly little and inconspicuous, growing awesomely higher, larger and wider to a comprehensive, wide-ranging, and worldwide realm that receives the entire humanity. And by the image 'leaven' used in the second story, Jesus, reemphasizing his first assertion, teaches us that every good work that is done in the name of God's Kingdom, though it may be hidden and small gesture, will surely have its unthinkable effect on the society at large as a pinch of yeast leavens the entire dough.

Prayer: *God most High and Boundless Wisdom, we are sad to hear about the sour transactions, went on between you and your people during their freedom-journey through the desert.*

181

Nonetheless, we are sorry for our own frequent, hardheaded conduct in our dealings with you. Getting angry with you, we start complaining, and even deviate our life either away from you or against you. Yet, we are grateful to know that with your constant mercy, you are patiently waiting for our return back to you. Kindly fill us with your powerful graces so that, as Jesus advises to see you and your action in renewed way, we may patiently wait for your providential and helpful touch in our tearful and fearful life. Amen.

Tuesday

Intimacy with God is possible only for those who love sinners
(Scriptural Passages: Ex. 33: 7-11, 34:
5-9, 28; Ps. 103; Matt. 13: 36-43)

We heard the Lord, identifying richly his true character to Moses, and saying: *The Lord, the Lord, a merciful and gracious God, slow to anger and rich in kindness and fidelity, continuing his kindness for a thousand generations, and forgiving wickedness and crime and sin.* Moses in response begged a favor from the Lord, namely the Lord should pardon the wickedness and sins of stiff-necked people; receive them as his own; and come along in their company. Plus to delight the Lord, we hear, Moses stayed on the mountain with the Lord for forty days and forty nights, without eating any food or drinking any water.

And as the Psalmist sings today, in order to secure justice and the rights of all the oppressed, the Lord, who is always kind, merciful, and forgiving, has made known to Moses his dreams about his people. And with the Lord's direction Moses also wrote the words of the covenant and the Ten Commandments.

The most breathtaking proclamation of Jesus, the Son of God, we hear in today's Gospel, is that he esteems any humans who listen and adhere to God's words of covenant and commands, which are found in the Scriptures, are the children of God's Kingdom. They are the ones Jesus names as 'the good seeds', planted by him in the world. All the others, in the eyes of Jesus, seem to be the children of the Evil One. And these are 'the weeds', planted by the Archenemy Devil.

Jesus' message today is about a permanent scenario of the world where from the beginning of time we find the constant warfare going on between the Good and the Evil. While in the OT we hear the words of God as 'be holy because I am Holy', Jesus was the One who taught us to be merciful, and to be perfect as our Heavenly Father is. From the day of his public ministry, he taught that, if we want to be the children of our Heavenly Father, we should love and pray for our enemies; because that's the right way to behave like our Father who *makes his sun rise on the bad and the good, and causes rain to fall on the just and the unjust.*

All of us undoubtedly accept the truth that humans, who are too unholy, cannot be friends with the All-Holy God. The distance between him and us is extraordinary; however, more than us, God longs to hold an unending friendship with us. The idea of friendship demands that something is shared between the two parties. Surprisingly, we find God showing and talking with Moses face-to-face. It is because, the compassionate God esteemed Moses as 'his intimate friend'.

There are indeed many among us lead in this world a life with God and his words as his intimate friends. Jesus fondly calls them the 'good seeds'. And the rest he names as 'the weeds'. Shockingly, he does not want those good seeds treat the weeds badly and reject or uproot them; instead, as he and his Father are compassionate and understanding toward the weakness of the weeds, he expects us to be patient, tolerate and above all, pray and wish for their conversion and salvation.

Prayer: *Lord who are holy with the holy, kind with the kind! In your Son's Light, we certainly notice ourselves unholy and incapable of attaining your perfection. You too tell us that we will be treated by you as your intimate friends, only when we treat with charity our fellowhumans, who may seem to us to live in the campus of the Devil. Kindly come and stay a while with us in the Garden. Inspire us to fulfill your Son's admonition to be merciful, as you are, toward our sinful neighbors. Amen.*

Wednesday

Let us glow with the Glory of God
(Scriptural Passages: Ex. 34: 29-
35; Ps. 99; Matt. 13: 44-46)

We read in today's first reading that whenever Moses entered the presence of the Lord to converse with him, he removed the veil until he came out again. On coming out, the children of Israel would notice the skin of Moses' face being radiant. Therefore he would again put the veil over his face until he went in to converse with the Lord. We can comprehend from these Scriptural words, that when Moses came down from the mountain, with an awesome inner spirit, being glowed with the fire of the Lord, he must have seemed almost ethereal. As the Psalmist would declare, every place, where Holy God is present, is qualified as his holy mountain. When we open our inner door and permit him to enter and stay in our heart, our inner spirit is glowed with his Glory and it is shown in our life's outward dimension.

This transformation of our outer look may seem to be miraculous but in human history we detect that such change comes over most humans as they encounter God "face to face" in some spiritual or religious experience or even in daily prayer. Indeed we venerate those people as saints, sages and mystics. These spiritually privileged people certainly should have felt a sense of what the kingdom of heaven will be like. Jesus, reminding about such human honour, ascertains in today's Gospel, how valuable and precious it is to seek and find and cherish such heavenly status even in our earthly lives.

First, Jesus labels this awesome heavenly realm as a hidden treasure which a person finds in a field and hides it again. Out of overwhelming joy he goes and sells all that he possesses and buys the field and owns that treasure. In his second parable, Jesus surprisingly names the same heavenly realm as a merchant who earnestly travels around the world seeking fine pearls; finally finding one costliest and finest pearl, he goes and sells all that he owns and buys that most precious pearl. By both images Jesus portrays two important truths about how humans, like saints and sages, achieve their mindblowing encounter with God and transform their inner and outer life radiant with the glow of God's glory.

First, as they recognise the hidden priceless treasure's what, where, when and how, they go after it with all their energy and wealth. They sell all; they are fully committed to possessing that valuable treasure. Second, as they start possessing the hidden treasure of God's realm, they in turn become like the heavenly kingdom, namely, as the New Testament Books declare, they turn out to be the

Abode of God, the Temple of his Spirit, the Body of Christ, and the Walking Tabernacle.

They don't stop there. As the merchant mentioned by Jesus, they persevere in pursuing as well as stabilizing the God's Kingdom within them by a disciplined life of cutting away all distractions; taking out all the riches they have accumulated in their life, such as property, money, popularity, social position and prestige, education and enrichment of all dimensions of life, boldly share them with the downtrodden, the poor, the socially-neglected and the weaklings in society.

When Moses came down from the mountain, Aaron and all the Israelites witnessed the change in his appearance. Likewise, when we move around and reach out our fellowhumans willingly and faithfully, as the Lord commands us to accomplish in their lives, our inner spirit would be glued to God's Holy Presence and consequently our outer appearance would be changed perceptibly. We may not recognize it, but surely our beneficiaries shall be observing it.

Prayer: *God the Holy, God the Strong! We admit our vulnerability of being insatiably appended to the things of earthly life, such as the material goods, the people, the relationships, the power, the emotions, the sensation of living; and because of which we lose the radiance of the Great Good. Jesus reminds us today, if we truly value heaven, we would trade all of these things for life in the kingdom of heaven. Grand us, we pray, the precious gift of grace to be detached from the worldly things as your saints and sages did. We need to let go all earthly, to be radiant heavenly. Amen.*

Thursday

We travel to Heaven onboard in Christ's Tent-on-the-Move
(Scriptural Passages: Ex. 40: 16-21, 34-
38; Ps. 84; Matt. 13: 47-53)

In my adolescent-spiritual life, one of my mentors advised me to pray consistently: *'Lord, make me fully conscious of your Presence in me as well as my presence in you'*. At the start, I could not understand fully what this prayer meant; but later gradually I could grasp its meaning and content. As the Lord Jesus underlines in the Gospel today, the Spirit of Jesus moved me from the Old Testament idea of the 'dwelling of God', as the Ark, the Tabernacle or the Temple, to a new perception, that Jesus is the dwelling of God, in him and through him my inner spirit too can turn out to be God's dwelling and I too can abide in his heart.

In Exodus we read that the Dwelling Tent, erected for God, consisted of an ark in which the two blocks of God's commandments were placed. We are also told that the cloud covered the Dwelling Tent, and the glory of the Lord filled that Dwelling. In the mind and heart of Moses and the Israelites we notice a strong belief of God's Presence and his Involvement in their day today life through his directives and admonitions.

Through Jesus' coming, we learned that the faith-filled view of God's Presence among Israelites as a personal, localized and law-binding one is a prefigurative symbol to Jesus himself who is 'God with us'. His Body is the Dwelling Place of God in physical, sacramental and ecclesial Presence in this world.

Because of our humanity is made in the image and likeness of God, we humans, like the Psalmist, continue to cry: *How lovely is your dwelling place, O Lord, mighty God! My soul yearns and pines for the courts of the Lord. My heart and my flesh cry out for the living God. I had rather one day in your courts than a thousand elsewhere.*

However, as the Lord stresses in today's Gospel, not all human creatures craving for such indwelling of God's Presence. Comparing the kingdom of God to a fishing net, Jesus points out that, as after fishing and hauling it shore, the net is filled with both good and bad fishes, God's Kingdom in this world is found with not only the just who are craving for God, but also the wicked who never care for God and his Presence. This fact of reality seems to the just too bad to hear as well as to tolerate. But Jesus exhorts the just to be patient and wait for the Day of his Second Coming. On that Day, Jesus assures, 'the angels will go out and separate the wicked from the righteous and throw them into the fiery furnace, where there will be wailing and grinding of teeth'.

Prayer: *Lord, Jesus teaches us to consider your dwelling place is not only our guiding law-and- love-binding light, but also it is our own body filled with strength and goodness. We know it is not in its fullness. Only at his second coming it gets its full stature. Until then, Jesus asks us to persevere patiently and to tolerate prayerfully the unjust. Kindly open our hearts to listen to your Son's words so that we may live a godly life in this world to inherit eternal mansion. Amen.*

Friday

Divine deeds done not by what we do but how we do with faith
(Scriptural Passages: Lev. 23: 1-37; Ps. 81; Matt. 13: 54-58)

In our human relationships, especially with our closest ones, there can be two kinds of second-parties, we would have come across. One group who think highly of us; and the other group, as the old slogan says, *Familiarity breeds contempt*, easily lose respect for us, and manytimes they don't care about what we say or do. Jesus was not exempted of such good and bad experiences in his relationships. In today's Gospel we see and hear his own kith and kins, his natives despising him; thinking little of him; not ready to believe him and his testimonies.

This is because of their close familiarity with him, they took him for granted; or consider him as one like them just typical Galilean. They had watched Jesus grew up from boyhood into adulthood; they knew well his father and mother well; they observed him begin his business as a carpenter. Unfortunately, they never encountered in him any outer signs of supernatural power. But when they heard so many miracles he was performing in his public ministry, according to the Gospel, they were covertly despising him and took offense at him. Namely, they came up against him and against his contemptible claim to be God in the flesh.

Our Scriptures declare to us that God's way of considering the others is not by outer appearance but by their inner warmth of faith and love. The same is fully true in looking at Jesus, who consistently demanded from others firm faith in him; and only for those who had such faith he performed miracles. Regarding his natives too, he could not do any great things and miracles in their midst because they did not have the faith he expected. Very sadly, due to their viewing at Jesus as someone like them, they lost sight of his true divine nature and the glory of God remaining in him; and thus they lost all the advantages of getting support and help from the Lord.

In continuation of what the Spirit underlines in the Gospel, the passage from the OT also reminds us how to deal with all our religious outer practices and rituals we perform for God. God, through Moses, gave specific instructions regarding festive practices they should do in his honor. And today the Psalmist also reminds us of statutes, ordinances, and decrees in the way we "Sing with joy to God our help" in the time and manner God ordered. God seems to reveal the fact that anything we physically perform in his Name or for his Glory, it must signify the mosaic of heavenly life of holiness even in this earthly situation, and more specifically, the Holy One living in the midst of us. If we attentively go through all OT words, we perceive how meticulous God is in whatever humans do for his sake.

In order to keep his Sovereignty in their mind, when his favorites perform outer religious practices, he orders them stubbornly to offer him only the firstfruits of their life, labor and their produce; and he demands some self-mortifications for their sins so that they never do or offer anything unholy to him who is All-Holy. In many of his precepts for the humans' religious practices, he prefers a lion's share of the offerings and produces must be shared with the needy and the poor as the true sacrifice to him. Such mindsetup of God is hidden in the long-listed precepts and rituals God has entrusted to his people through Moses.

Prayer: *God, King of the ages, through Jesus you tell us to respond to him as your Son, our Shepherd and our Way, not merely by our rationality but much more by our firm faith burning in our hearts. Whenever we gather together as your people to offer our thankful sacrifices, help us to remember all the salvific good things you, your Son and your Spirit are accomplishing in and around our life. Make us plainly and constantly believe that we are your people and there is only One who is worthy of Praise. And that is You and You alone. Amen.*

Saturday

Let me fight against Evil Kingdom; but let it start within me
(Scriptural Passages: Lev. 25: 1, 8-17; Ps. 67; Matt. 14: 1-12)

We recite in today's mass as the Gospel Acclamation, Jesus' words from his Sermon on the Mount: Blessed are they who are persecuted for the sake of righteousness for theirs is the Kingdom of heaven. These words truly connect all three readings of today, which take us to the apparent reality of our earthly life, tossed around between two different kingdoms. One, the Supernatural Kingdom, in which God is the only Sovereign as he declares in the first reading: *Do not deal unfairly, then; but stand in fear of your God. I, the Lord, am your God.* This kingdom is an eternal and universal kingdom, a kingdom of truth and life, a kingdom of holiness and grace, a kingdom of justice, love and peace. Two, the kingdom of the Evil One, that is based on mere natural resources of life and seeks to be satisfied with physical, emotional, and intellectual fullness and that too is to be achieved by any means- crooked, twisted, self-gratification, lies, and injustice and violence.

God eternally willed that more than any other creatures, we the humans must recognize his immanent Presence and his non-stop Interaction among us. As the Psalmist prays today, *God may have pity on us and bless us; may he let his face shine upon us. And thus God's way may be known upon earth; among all nations, his salvation. He rules the peoples in equity; the nations on the earth he guides. By making the earth yield its fruits, our God, has blessed us.*

We find God, as we hear in OT Books, choosing humans, freeing them from any sort of slavery of Satan, the supreme Liar, cherishes them as their beloved community or nation, and offers them many guiding

191

precepts to walk faithfully in his ways to reach their destiny of Full-fledged Kingdom of joy and peace. This is what we read in today's first reading. God prefers his people to consider earthly life with him is a festive moment. Therefore he wants them to celebrate it by so many festivals, including the jubilee celebrations.

We hear, for example, about the Day of Atonement, a special day of celebration. The trumpet resonated to prompt the people of the *liberty in the land for all its inhabitants.* It was esteemed as a time when all people should return home to their roots and family. On that day people must also willingly share with one another in equality all their riches, properties and products. Moreover, it was a time of fasting and forgiving. Totally that festivity was a time of expressing people's righteousness publicly and voluntarily in accordance to the words of the Sovereign God.

We read in today's Gospel about the bloody and cruel death of John the Baptizer who died for fearlessly proclaiming God's righteousness in front of a king, who was utterly enslaved by the Archenemy the Devil. In this event we see some unpleasantness and some mishandling of imperial power as in any natural kingdom; besides, we also find some righteous battle of power by truth, as it is consistent in the Kingdom of God. It was a horrible fight between worldly king's weakness and apparent innocence of Godly Prophet.

Prayer: *God, Heavenly King of the Universe! All of us are taken aback in hearing the fortitude and goodness of John the Baptizer, who lived as an apt Forerunner of Jesus, whom you made as our King on your behalf; and also he died to testify as a remarkable Prophet to the new insight into the sufferings and death of Jesus for the sake of righteousness. Father, kindly fill us with the gift of courage from your Spirit so that we can daringly* take more risks in our own life for the sake of righteousness of God's Kingdom though we may pay a costly price but at the end of the day we hope we will be rewarded as Jesus has promised. Amen.

WEEK - 18

Monday

We can be miracle-workers if our faith-
filled love for God is genuine
(Scriptural Passages: Num. 11: 4-15;
Ps. 81; Matt. 14: 13-21)

We hear in today's first reading, God's chosen people, while they were traveling in the desert, repeatedly complained to him through Moses whenever they lacked food, water and other basic needs. They cried for water to quench their thirst; he granted cool water from the rock; they pleaded for food; he fed them with bread; unsatisfied with vegetarian food, they begged for meat; and he gave it to them. Thus, the faithful God, with his eternal compassion, consistently fulfilled their needs with the help of his agents like Moses.

However, the people were immature and showed their ingratitude and faithlessness toward him. Moses tried his best to appease them; but they were hardheaded to listen any advice. Therefore, we find Moses feeling very desperate; and he cried to God: *Lord, I cannot carry all this people by myself, for they are too heavy for me. If this is*

the way you will deal with me, then please do me the favor of
killing me at once, so that I need no longer face this distress.
God's compassionate heart has been very much hurt. As
he exposed it to his people, he repeatedly lamented about
them, as we hear in the Psalm today: *My people heard not*
my voice, and Israel obeyed me not; so I gave them up to the
hardness of their hearts; they walked according to their own
counsels.

Gospel passage of today portrays that Jesus too acted
like his Father. When he saw a vast crowd following him
all the way to a deserted place and listening to his words
continuously, his heart was moved with pity for them. His
disciples were asking him: *This is a deserted place and it*
is already late; dismiss the crowds so that they can go to the
villages and buy food for themselves. Nevertheless, even
before people complained about their hunger, he took
action immediately and through his disciples, he fed those
hungry stomachs with his amazing miraculous blessing.

Whenever we complain to Jesus, during our life's
murky moments, about our inability to fulfill our basic
needs and desires, and about the needs of the poor people
around us, as the disciples did, his Spirit first enlightens
and strengthens us to approach such social struggles with
his loving, tender compassion and personal care. After
filling us with his riches, he always encourages us, as
he ordered his disciples, to offer some service to others,
even when our resources may seem scarce. He confirms
today when we do our bit, like his disciples of this Age,
our Father God, can work wonders through the ordinary
resources and limited gifts we've got.

Prayer: *Dear Father, Provider of our daily Bread! We are*
sorry we offend you whenever we impatiently appeal to you that
all our needs to be fulfilled instantly. Kindly do not give us up to
the hardness of our heart. Instead, enable us to walk according to

your Son's counsels, to be persevering in the midst of temptation, to be guided by compassion, and to pray to you humbly for help. If need be, make use of us as your agents in your providential actions to satisfy the needs of our fellowhumans. Amen.

Tuesday

*Uppermost-notch of our faith is to recognize
and accept Jesus, as he is*
(Scriptural Passages: Num. 12: 1-13;
Ps. 51; Matt. 14: 22-36)

Being followers of Christ, from the moment of our Baptism, we are committed to uphold true faith and trust in an invisible God and in Jesus of Nazareth as God's Son. As Paul would say, *we live by faith and not by sight.*

In the past, God demanded his fleshly human creatures to have faith in his spiritual interactions among them. In addition, he expected them to hold their respect and trust in those prophetic leaders and sages whom he chose and anointed to be his representatives. This is why, God detested any mistrust found in humans both against him and his chosen agents like Moses, as we hear in today's first reading. We find God so angry against Aaron and Miriam, because they unjustly spoke against Moses, who was by far the meekest man on the face of the earth. God too certified him as his servant and his prophet and attested about Moses: *Throughout my house he bears my trust, face to face I speak to him; he beholds my presence.*

No wonder then, God would be so stubborn in demanding the same faith and trust we must show to his beloved Son Jesus. Jesus too insisted the same from his followers: *You have faith in God; have faith also in me.*

Today's Gospel passage places before us the kind of Jesus we believe in.

First, we see Jesus, dismissing the crowd, went up on the mountain to pray alone and communed with the Father. He seemed to be a person of calm, deep, and silence, portraying himself as the beloved Son of God, drinking in the power and wisdom shared with his Father.

Second, we find the awesome sight of Jesus, walking calmly, and undisturbedly over the water of the Sea of Galilee that was swayed by strong winds and high waves. That event proves the tremendous power of Jesus who is the inheritor of God's entire creation in his Kingdom.

Third, when the disciples, being terrified by a strange figure, walking at a distance over the water, and cried out in fear of encountering a ghost, Jesus demonstrates his compassionate divinity, and sentiments of concern of humanity, by his consoling words and powerful action. To the fearful disciples he said: *Take courage, it is I; do not be afraid.* Then entering into their boat, he made the storm die down. And when Peter failed in his attempt of walking on the water to get closer to Jesus and began to sink due to his fear, to frightened Peter, Jesus said, *O you of little faith, why did you doubt?* and he stretched out his hand and caught him from sinking in the water.

Very interestingly, the Gospel Writer also included in this narration about how Jesus converted and elevated his followers from their little faith to its uppermost height. Jesus healed the disciples' fear-complex and animated them to proclaim the true identity of Jesus. Paying homage to him, they said: *Truly, you are the Son of God.* The same way, when the people of that area who saw and heard such remarkable actions of Jesus, we are told, they brought to him all those who were sick and begged him that they might touch only the tassel on his cloak, and as many as touched it were healed.

Prayer: *God, the Immortal, Invisible, only Wise! As the Psalmist prays, we entreat you to have mercy on us in your goodness. We are truly sorry for our little faith and blindfolded judgement toward you and your Son. With Peter we cry to you that we are sinking in muddy waters without faith and trust in your Son's persistent call to have faith in you and in him. Renew within us the steadfast spirit. With the touch of your Spirit we are certain we will jumpstart again our journey of faith with Jesus, who is truly the Son of the Living God. Amen.*

Wednesday

Genuine and wholistic faith persuades
Christ to offer all healings we wish
(Scriptural Passages: Num. 13: 1-2, 25 &
14: 1-35; Ps. 106; Matt. 15: 21-28)

Today's Gospel event draws our attention to the shocking faith of a pagan woman, demanding grace of healing for her demon-possessed daughter by recognizing Jesus as the Son of David and her Lord. Pointing out not only the greatness of her faith, but also reminding all of us who, like the Jews of his time, are leading a true demon-possessed life of discriminating and hating others on their caste and creed, race and status, Jesus cured the pagan girl, telling the mother: *O woman, great is your faith! Let it be done for you as you wish.*

Jesus wants to show to us, the awesome gift of faith is not a privilege of a few, nor is it the property of those who think that they are so good, but carrying outside of them a fake and nominal label of being righteous, and they even esteem themselves as perfect like God, since their belonging to a holy church or any social affiliations. In Jesus' time and before him, the chosen people of God were example of such twisted and abused faith-based life.

Like most of the human race, as the Psalmist highlights today, the Israelites were victims of the certain amnesia problem in remembering the marvelous deeds God did among them from the onset of their freedom-journey to the Promised Land. They had witnessed one miracle after another, as God used a series of plagues against the Egyptians followed by the actual parting of a sea to orchestrate their miraculous escape. In each case, God came through for them, as he demonstrated over and over again that he was with them and that He loved them. But their faith in him was fading, and they were grumbling and complaining and even getting angry with God and his Servant Moses.

We read in today's first reading, at the time of Israelites' entrance to the promised land, probably in order to test their faith, God directed them to send some leaders to go into the promised land for exploration. Regrettably, from the observation-report submitted by the leaders, as well as from the reactions the sojourners demonstrated, God found out that, instead of seeing him and his permanent powerful presence, people saw only the idea of worldly power, well-fortified armies with monster-like soldiers. Their trust in God was at stake and weakened; they seemed to have already forgotten his ever-present role in their midst. Hence, this time they paid a heavy price for turning their backs on God, who swore that none of these who started their journey from Egypt would enter into the promised land.

As we are only sojourners living and moving in this world, God prefers that we, with no fear, should not grumble against the Sovereign God who is both Good and doing Good only. Rather, we must focus our full attention to reaching our heavenly Father's home, where there will be no distinction, discrimination whatsoever. In the meantime, we are to persevere in our love for God, even when our prospects seem bleak, and to keep trying, even when our loving God may seem silent and distant.

Prayer: *God of power and mercy, your action precedes any human's fake religious action. We know also, you have designed our life and you too have scheduled each one's time go along with yours. Because as the wind blows, so is the move of God's Spirit in human life. But your Son assures us that if we hold the same sort of humble faith the pagan woman had, we will succeed like her in bringing forward your timetable of curing, sharing and filling our needs by repeating our request to you despite all resistance and dark clouds around us. Amen.*

Thursday

Any stony heart can be melted by Jesus, the Rock Star of Love
(Scriptural Passages: Num. 20: 1-13;
Ps. 95; Matt. 16: 13-23)

Today's Scriptural passages again exhort us to hold relentless and consistent faith and trust in the Lord. In addition we are demanded to express it through proper words and actions.

In today's Gospel event we hear Jesus asking his constant heartbeat-question to all his followers: *Who do you say that I am?* Peter immediately replied: *You are the Christ, the Son of the living God.* As Jesus himself explained, *For flesh and blood has not revealed this to you, but my heavenly Father,* Peter did not give this reply by his human faith and appreciation for Jesus. Rather it is God, who can make even the stones to shout out this revealed truth, has used him to deliver this revealed truth. Because we know from the Gospels, how miserably Peter failed God and Jesus by his unreliable, impetuous and hardheaded character. In today's Gospel we read how Jesus was irritated about Peter's weak and fragile personality and chided him, saying: *Get behind me, Satan! You are an obstacle to me. You are thinking not as God does, but as human beings do.*

One more mindblowing incident we observe in today's Gospel is the same weakling Peter, full of hardheadedness and impulsiveness, was selected by Jesus to carry on after him the responsibility of heading his Church. Jesus categorically ascertains: *Blessed are you, Simon son of Jonah. I say to you, you are Peter, and upon this rock I will build my Church, and the gates of the netherworld shall not prevail against it. I will give you the keys to the Kingdom of heaven. Whatever you bind on earth shall be bound in heaven; and whatever you loose on earth shall be loosed in heaven.* The question arises in our hearts: How is that possible? We know the Word from God: Nothing is impossible with God.

Through Biblical history, we can find how people of God hurt their Master in so many ways, all just for their cravings were not satisfied by him or his agents. The Promised Land meant nothing to them; they did not believe the Lord's word; they stayed muttering in their tents, they were deaf to the voice of the Lord. We hear in today's first reading one of those despicable conducts of the people. While they were sorely tired of the wandering in the widely dry desert, they complained loudly about their situation: *Wasn't it better in Egypt? At least there they had food and water. But here in the desert they experience hunger and thirst.* They made God and their leaders like

Moses terribly hurt. But God, with his compassionate heart, wanted them to increase their faith in his benevolence and greatness.

God also admonished them, as we hear in today's Psalm: *Oh, that today you would hear his voice: Harden not your hearts as at Meribah, as in the day of Massah in the desert, Where your fathers tested me; they tested me though they had seen my works.* Besides he also did a miracle of a hard rock, abundantly gushing forth pure water to quench people's thirst.

It is this all-loving God who invites us today to be converted from our own nature-made hardheadedness and hardheartedness to uphold strong faith and trust in the goodness and greatness of the Lord, especially in the amazing gentleness and powerfulness of Jesus, his beloved Son. Every time we hear the Scriptural verses, we are reminded of human strength and weakness, and human glory and fall, in particular when we come across the Biblical words like 'rock' and 'flesh'. We are glad to hear today about a rock becoming a water-source that was vital for survival, and a "human rock" becoming the foundation of the church. We are also warned by his Spirit telling us how the "flesh" indicates the limitations of human nature, unable to fully understand Jesus.

Prayer: *Benevolent God, we beg you not to let us fall into temptation of becoming a stumbling stone like Peter for not thinking in your holy way. We are indeed grateful that you keep faith in us even after we fail you many times. And you too perform your salvific work powerfully in and through us, though we are the imperfect human beings. As your Son demands from us every day, help us to keep trying to find and follow your truthful and life-giving way. Amen.*

Friday

In Jesus' Kingdom pain is gain and loss is profit
(Scriptural Passages: Deut. 4: 32-
40; Psalm 77; Matt. 16: 24-28)

We hear Jesus says in today's Gospel: *Whoever wishes to come after me must deny himself, take up his cross and follow.* It is indeed very hard to even hear his demand of denying ourselves and the worst is, to take up our crosses as he did, in truth and justice. At the same time we too are fully aware of God's Masterplan for us which is to live our life fully for him alone.

Due to such Masterplan of God we hear in OT the same kind of demand from our God through Moses. He instructs his chosen people to remember all his wondrous salvific deeds for their possession of life of freedom, prosperity, and longitude. The Psalmist today echoes the same expectation of God from his people and pledges to him that he would remember and meditate the wonderful things he had done for him and his people.

According to Moses, the sequel of people's remembrance of God's wonderful deeds to them must be accepting God's demand. And God's demand was very precise and concise: *This is why you must now know, and fix in your heart, that the Lord is God in the heavens above and on earth below, and that there is no other.* In order to express such spiritual connection with him, Moses adds: *You must keep his statutes and commandments which I enjoin on you today.* He too ends his exhortation with the promising words of prosperity: *So that you and your children after you may prosper, and that you may have long life on the land which the Lord, your God, is giving you forever.*

203

It is for attaining such remarkable goal, that Jesus expects us to follow his hard footsteps. To live fully means, as we understand in the light of the Scriptures, that we are called to go all the way without hesitation all the time, wholeheartedly loving God and our neighbors; totally surrendering ourselves with everything we possess, acquire and save in this world; and if it need be, to dispose everything, even our life, for the uplifting of his needy creatures and inspire them to follow God's Son. Thus God enlightens us how to celebrate our life fully and truly.

Prayer: God of Goodness and Graciousness! *Grant your grace to all of us, especially those who carry heavy crosses at this moment, to find in our faith and prayer a great source of strength from your Spirit, so that all our burdens become light and our yokes easy in walking the walk of Jesus toward our fuller life. Amen.*

Saturday

Even with our little faith, if it is total, we can do marvels
(Scriptural Passages: Deut. 6: 4-13; Ps. 18; Matt. 17: 14-20)

In today's Gospel we hear about a boy, who was suffering seriously from the illness of epilepsy. He was unable to discern between fire and water, often fell into both. There are too many of us like that sick person, failing in our discernment of the good and bad around us, and being succumbed to do many evil things for ourselves and for others. Such outrageous failing and falling can be cured only by what Jesus calls, the 'faith'. His disciples were incapable of healing the sick boy but Jesus cured him by his audacious faith in his Father's goodness and greatness; he also verified that also we, his disciples, can free ourselves and others from demons, by even with 'faith the size of a mustard seed'.

To explain little more about this powerful faith, God in today's first reading exhorts us to observe the first and the greatest commandment: *You shall love the Lord, your God, with all your heart, and with all your soul, and with all your strength.* He further explains what he means by the wholistic and total love we should hold toward him. He says, *Take care not to forget the Lord, who brought you out of the land of Egypt, that place of slavery. The Lord, your God, shall you fear; him shall you serve, and by his name shall you swear.* Plus he admonishes us to take to heart his love-commanding words, and to drill them into our children by speaking of them at home and abroad, whether we are busy or at rest.

That is how God wants us to uphold him and his love consistently, faithfully and sincerely. This action of love is nothing but our faith-module. As today's responsorial Psalm suggests, we are to relate intimately to God and love and praise him as our strength, our rock, our fortress, our deliverer. our rock of refuge, our shield, the horn of our salvation, our stronghold and what not!

In this exposition about the faith the size of mustard seed, let us remember Christ Jesus telling us to add him also in our loving list. *Have faith in God, also have faith in me.* This is because, according to God's plan, as Paul writes to Timothy: *Our Savior Jesus Christ has destroyed death and brought life to light through the Gospel.* Through this twofold faith, even be it the size of the mustard seed, if we say to this mountain, 'Move from here to there,' and it will move. And nothing is impossible for us.

Prayer: *God of Love and Truth, we sincerely admit that we will not ever be free from tragedy and hurt while we walk this earth, but one thing we are certain. We will never have to face* *that hurt alone. We are always in the arms of you, our Father and the bleeding Cross of Christ our Savior, and comforted by our loving Mother Mary and the numerous angels on earth. We entreat you, that the ordinary people who share their hurtful stories with us, may hear your Son in listening to ours, and together may our lives be healed from the clutches of demons who make us sick severely. Amen.*

WEEK - 19

Monday

In life and death let us fight the good fight
(Scriptural Passages: Deut. 10: 12-
22; Ps. 147; Matt. 17: 22-27)

After intense fasting and praying for forty days and forty
nights and meeting and talking with the Lord God, Moses
got from him not only the Ten Commandments but also
some inspiring messages on those commandments to be
delivered to the people. A portion of those messages is
what we hear in today's first reading. As *the heavens as
well as the earth and everything on it* belongs to God, the
Israelites must recognize the eternal truth that God is the
sole Sovereign Proprietor of them and therefore all their
possessions, including talents, heritage, and prospects
are only advanced to them as gifts. Their assignment is
nothing but to use it all as God designs according to his
will.

Moreover today's exhortation of God through Moses
to his people consists of not only the Command of God
to love him with their whole heart, mind, and soul, but
also an explanation of how that love must be expressed

in their life through being generous, merciful, kind and understanding to the strangers, aliens, widows, orphans and the needy because those socially backward are favorite sons and daughters of God. Everything God has permitted and shared with the people of God is simply to be considered as an opportunity to share and witness the goodness and greatness of God.

As a continuation of enunciating God's marvelous love-life program proclaimed in the past for God's children, Jesus brings home to us today in the Gospel about how our day-today earthly life is crowded with many complicated major as well as so many trivial conflicts and shows to us how to tackle them as he won.

In the first part of the Gospel, Jesus predicts for the second time about his death and resurrection. Every time Jesus spoke about his impending ignominious death, his disciples, either rebuked him or underwent terrible grief. To pacify their hurt-feelings, Jesus always included the awesome fact that *he would be raised on the third day.* He also chided them for their incapability of understanding him and his mission. However, the disciples did not fully comprehend it. They continued to live in that gloomy and disappointed mindset until the risen Lord appeared to them and bestowed on them his Power from on High.

Besides, in the Gospel we hear Jesus offering us a trivial incident of paying taxes that happens in our life. When it was told that Jesus and his team must pay the Temple tax, he put a simple question, *who should pay this tax, the foreigners or the subjects?* Though he, as God's Son, had no duty to pay the tax, he did it by getting the right amount miraculously out of a fish. Thus, today's Gospel teaches us that Jesus knew vividly his mission and he did not allow any trivial matters such as paying the temple tax divert him or his disciples from his salvific mission.

As we hear in today's Psalm,, all the Israelites esteemed themselves as an uppermost nation in the world because they assumed that God, with his crazy 'one-sided love', *has proclaimed his word, his statutes and his ordinances only to Israel. He has not done thus for any other nation; his ordinances he has not made known to them.*

We may perhaps hold the same feeling as we are a chosen race, a royal priesthood, a holy nation, and a people of his own. But we easily forget what Peter exhorts us about how we should proclaim such privilege in day today life. He writes: 'We should announce the praises of him who called us out of darkness into his wonderful light'.

Prayer: *Lord, God of mercy and fidelity! In the light of today's readings, we learn that in the midst of our lifesituations filled with both major and trivial conflicts, we must, like Jesus, must consider that for everything-most good but some not so, you hold a reason. And accepting them willingly, you want us tackle the bad conflicts according to Jesus' Way, go on praising you for all your wonders you do in our midst. Help us, Lord, to be full of faith and hope like Jesus, to experience the deliverance from all sufferings and attain Jesus' peace-filled joyful life in this world and in the world to come. Amen.*

Tuesday

Only the 'littleones' are eligible to attain abiding peace and joy
(Scriptural Passages: Deut. 31: 1-8;
Deut. 32: 3-12; Matt. 18: 15-20)

The responsorial canticle of today, taken from the Book of Deuteronomy, proclaims that God considered Israelites as his own portion and his hereditary share.

And this mindset of God was proven in his continuous and consistent deals with and for his people as faultless, right and compassionate. Though most of the Israelites believed such incredible greatness of God's relationship with them, being fragile in stable fidelity, in their critical lifesituations, they forgot it and got broken of hearts.

One such situation was at the moment they saw their Leader Moses reaching his final hour and telling them, he would not walk with them into the Promised Land. In today's first reading we observe the good-hearted personality of Moses. He, in faith and resignation to his friendly God, encouraged his people with outstanding words of encouragement. He told them: *It is the Lord, your God, who will cross before you; it is the LORD, your God, who marches with you. He will be with you and will never fail you or forsake you. So be brave and steadfast and do not fear or be dismayed.*

Matthew today takes us, who are dismayed and disoriented by all kinds of chores of life, to Jesus of Nazareth who encourages us with his charming words as we hear in Gospel Acclamation: *Take my yoke upon you and learn from me, for I am meek and humble of heart. My yoke is easy, my burden is light.* As an annex to such encouragement, we see Jesus in the Gospel reaching out to the little children endorses them as our rolemodel for getting our yoke easy and burden light. He advises us to be like little children, who tightly hold the hands of their parents or elders with full trust and hope, especially during their needs and fears. Thus he expects us, as Moses told his people, to hold a consistent vision of mighty God walking with us, staying with us and sharing with us.

Besides through a small parable about the lamb strayed and caught back by the shepherd, Jesus asserts that, if we develop within us the spirit of little ones, we will see our God is always vigilant and reach out to us, if we slide downhill, and when he finds us safe and sound, he will rejoice over us than those who are righteous already at his side.

Prayer: *Loving God, our hearts are aching, as Jesus and Sages like Moses, to see your strong but secret presence leading us onward through our difficult transitions to the new moments of joy and peace. We pray for the light of your Spirit to be showered on all of us who hold some power or responsibility of leadership in the families and in communities; so that we may realize that the power and authority we own is not finally taking us to the Promised Land, Heaven; rather it is only our childlike humility, simplicity, innocence and purity that will guarantee us to reach eternal life. Amen.*

Wednesday

*Only with fire of divine love we can reach
heaven despite any hurdles*
(Scriptural Passages: Deut. 34: 1-12;
Ps. 66; Matt. 17: 22-27)

As the Psalmist testifies today, when humans are solely and sincerely connect themselves to the Lord God, their soul is filled with fire; there will be a non-stop praising in their hearts and lips, proclaiming God's glory found in his marvelous deeds; and they will not only incessantly share their testimony of how God is compassionately dealing with them, but also stir others to join with them in praising the glory of the Lord.

I personally love to hear from the Bible that our Creator God delights to interpersonally relate to each one of us and relishes in sharing with us face-to-face his will as he interacted with humans, especially gentleman, like Moses, about whom Scripture says: *No prophet has arisen in Israel like Moses, whom the Lord knew face to face. He had no equal in all the signs and wonders the Lord sent him to perform and in the might and the terrifying power that Moses exhibited in the sight of all Israel.*

Knowing such godly experiences in Scriptures and tradition, many of us may think it is good to live alone without any other human beings. And that way we feel we will be at peace and enjoy untarnished peace and joy. Regrettably, that is not the way God and his Son exhort us. As the greatest divine Command of God admonishes, besides loving God wholeheartedly, we must hold a loving heart-felt relationship with our fellowhumans. Namely, we should establish and maintain loving relationship with our neighbors. Against such weird backdrop of inclusive Commandments, Jesus today teaches us that we should preserve our neighborly relationship despite its burdensome and irksome results.

Our daily experience shows every relationship with fellowhumans, either totally from the beginning till the end takes away our peace and happiness or atleast it may start well but gradually it may turn out to be bitter, malicious and even inimical. Even at those times, Jesus expects us to tolerate, to forgive, to pray, and to do good to our second party who behaves hostile. He also offers us a scheduled strategy of how to deal peacefully with those harmful persons. Above all, in order to highlight the importance of our forgiving deals with our neighbors, he includes in his exhortation some assertions about the magnanimous and awesome benefits that come out of our neighborly, interpersonal community actions.

We hear him say: One, our human neighborly gathering will be blessed with his dynamic presence:

Where two or three are gathered together in my name, there am I in the midst of them. Two, because of his presence in our human group or community, we will be empowered with certain heavenly dynamics: *Whatever you bind on earth shall be bound in heaven, and whatever you loose on earth shall be loosed in heaven.* Three, our prayer in neighborly gathering will be powerful to produce amazing results: *Amen, I say to you, if two of you agree on earth about anything for which they are to pray, it shall be granted to them by my heavenly Father.*

Prayer: *Father in heaven, today we hear in OT Scripture about the greatness of your servant Moses whom you allowed to live despite speaking with you face-to-face. But we are really shocked and surprised to hear one of the most pathetic, tragic events in which we see you didn't offer him a chance to enter into Promised Land with his people; instead he died outside the Promised Land, overlooking its loveliness. We too, many times overwhelm with sorrow, like Moses, facing so many unfulfilled and unaccomplished programs in our life. Yet, thanks to your Son's promise, we are able to get up and try to live our life in waiting and trusting. Kindly let us praise you consistently until our last breath and so enter heaven where we shall see you face to face. Amen.*

Thursday

Human fullness consists in crossing from hurt to forgiveness
(Scriptural Passages: Josh. 3: 7-17;
Ps. 114; Matt. 18: 21-19: 1)

Whenever I read the event, which we heard in today's first reading, I am reminded of Charles Bently's classic hymn, titled 'At the crossing over Jordan.' The whole hymn echoes the consistent heartbeats of Joshua and

God's people while they were crossing the Jordan River to the boundary of the Promised Land. The core-theme of the heartbeats of the people was nothing but their faith-filled hope in the Lord's continuous Presence with them: *At the Crossing God will be there; because we hear him say: Fear not, I am by your side.*

According to the first reading, God demonstrated his Presence among them through his miracles: *This is how you will know that there is a living God in your midst, who at your approach will dispossess the Canaanites. The Lord of the whole earth, touch the water of the Jordan, it will cease to flow; for the water flowing down from upstream will halt in a solid bank.* Thus the people crossed over opposite Jericho, walking through the dry ground of River. Being strengthened by God's wonderful deeds, people upheld firm faith in God and in his faithful and parental Presence in their midst, and simultaneously they put relentless hope in his promising words. As a matter fact, that was the undaunted and unbending expectation of the Lord from his people as he indicated them through Joshuah. As today's Psalm reports, *this is how the nation of Israel became God's sanctuary and his domain.*

Relating this OT event to today's Gospel about neighborly forgiveness, one preacher says that to forgive unlimitedly our fellowhumans for all their offenses is like that of walking into the cold deep waters of our own inner spirit with the Ark of the Covenant as the priests courageously step into the Jordan river and walked in frontline. One thing is certain. As the priests and the people carried with them the Ark of the Covenant as the symbol of their faith and hope in the mighty Presence of the Lord, any disciple of Christ cannot by themselves fight against their frigid mindset of unforgiveness in wading into their interior cold stream of personal sense of self-reverence, self-respect, and self-graced-acceptance, and so on.

It is possible only when we allow Jesus in our heart as our just and compassionate Giver of New Commandment of Love enthroned within us. We should go on singing the words of the composer Charles Bently, not just as a ritualistic habit, but from the start, through the process and to the end of our crossing the lifelong river of human relationships from this world to the Other World: *Let us put our trust in Jesus as we go.* When we near the river Jordan, with its rushing, swelling tide, we shall hear his gentle whisper, 'Fear not, I am by thy side; surely at the crossing over Jordan he'll be there.

Prayer: *Heavenly Father God, as your Son affirms, we truly believe that you do offer us your amazing forgiveness as much as we forgive our own fellow humans from our whole heart. You know well, we are trapped by the feelings of vengeance and retaliation when we suffer terribly pain and rejection from our neighbors. We pray earnestly for your grace to carry your Son and his Love in our heart always and to enjoy your eternal peace by forgiving our fellowhumans unceasingly as our Master exhorts. Amen.*

Friday

Epiphany of God is superbly triggered by
proper use of our sexual power
(Scriptural Passages: Josh. 24: 1-13; Ps. 136; Matt. 19: 3-12

We hear in today's first reading, about a community event of Israelites listening to the words of Joshua, who performed his leadership duty of listing out the historical and extraordinary deeds of the Creator God and inspiring people to be grateful to God, who acted compassionately as their Redeemer. Indeed, all those, who listened and believed sincerely to Joshua's words as those of God himself, got strengthened in their faith in God. They acknowledged God's unbroken and permanent Presence among them; and also his dauntless fidelity to them as his heritage and portion. Joshua's recounting of the history of the Israelites was the basis for their trusting in God. They realized well how remarkably God's reliable fidelity to his promises to them were fulfilled and such understanding inevitably gave them uncompromising hope that God would do so again.

In the same wavelength of marvelous relationship existed between God and his people, as we hear in today's Gospel, Jesus teaches his followers about how their connection with him and his Father to be upheld more fruitfully. He starts his expounding of our sublime relationship with Triune God in our daily walk of earthly life, saying: *Have you not read that the Creator from the beginning* ... He bases all his exposition and argument on one primal reality that all relationships and structures in this world are not produced by human beings; rather, it is the sole enterprise of the Creative God. Nonetheless Jesus never denies the important place of human choices in choosing, shaping, and forming those relationships and other structures. We are clearly warned many such human preferences, made out of their powerslot of intelligence and freedom, can lead them either to life or some don't.

From all details, which Jesus shares with us regarding the core dimension of humans' earthly life, namely the powerful option of sex and marriage, we understand more about God's Sovereign input in these choices than about our own. We are told the sole intent of God to create humans male and female is to fulfill his eminent dream of his human creatures, who, using their God-given gifts of freedom, intelligence, and the sense of justice and charity, begin to lead a life of integrity, fidelity and stability like himself.

Here are his dreams about humans' sexual life: *A man shall leave his father and mother and be joined to his wife, and the two shall become one flesh. They are no longer two, but one flesh. Therefore, what God has joined together, man must not separate.* If we go to Book of Genesis and read the rest of the story of human creation, we hear from God empowering his human creatures: *Be fertile and multiply; fill the earth and subdue it. Have dominion over the fish of the sea, the birds of the air, and all the living things that crawl on the earth.*

God has demonstrated himself from the beginning of time his goodness and greatness, as the Psalmist sings today, through his enduring mercy; out of such eternal mercy, God has been performing among his people marvelous deeds of liberation from darkness and perils of life; and granting them power to realize their dream of possessing a prosperous environment to be peacefully settled in this world and the world to come. Undoubtedly, though God has never shown to us his glory face to face, he has been manifesting his goodness and greatness through so many men and women who are blessed with seeing and hearing him within them in the spirit of faith. He and his Son want that way to speak and to act among us.

In particular, we get the glimpse of his eternal fidelity and love only through how our forebears, like our parents and grandparents, and friends, have been living their married life in love and fidelity, in joy and sorrow and in sickness and health and in prosperity and poverty. Also, many of our elders, widows, widowers, and singles, are testifying to the divine eternal sacrificial love for humanity through their sacrificing of even the legitimate pleasures for the sake of God's salvific actionplan. And only through their covenantal commitments, they made us fully understand the eternal covenant he made with us.

Prayer: *Lord, God of our forebears! Today we remember you thankfully, that you created us as a sign of your power and you are devoted to us as a Father; and very importantly you have elected so many of your human creatures to show your goodness and greatness through their faith and thus you brought us to proper knowledge of you; and through their hope you enabled us to be open to your unbroken promises. God of love, this is how you expect us to proclaim and transmit your Son's Gospel values and your salvific deeds to our new generation. Please grant us the courage to do the best we can to narrate your eternal stories through our covenantal life that is permeated by our physical, sexual and social life. Amen.*

Saturday

Success in life depends on how we are connected to God as little child
(Scriptural Passages: Josh. 24: 14-19; Ps. 16; Matt. 19: 13-15)

As a matter of Biblical fact, God demands from us a decision of faith only after he has accomplished his salvific deeds among us from the day of Abraham upto this day through his Son and his Church. The choice we make today, about our tomorrow's life, requires a firm decision whether we integrate it into the history of God's salvation.

This is what we are instructed through today's first reading. First we hear Joshua proclaiming his and his family's implacable covenant with the Lord saying: *As for me and my household, we will serve the Lord*. Then reminding about God's continued benevolent deeds in the past for their sake, he exhorted the entire gathering of people, *Fear the Lord and serve him completely and sincerely. Cast out the gods your fathers served beyond the River and in Egypt, and serve the Lord*. And the people promised Joshua, *We will serve the LORD, our God, and obey his voice*.

History portrays how God fulfilled his promises of bringing safely his people to the Land which was prosperous and plentiful in its resources and of protecting them as their powerful Guardian day in and day out. As a reciprocal fidelity and obedience to their covenant with God, many of his people sincerely preserved their faith in him; his name became part of their history; and his covenant turned into their inheritance. Hence their hearts were continuously singing with the Psalmist: *You are my inheritance, O Lord. Keep me, O God, for in you I take refuge. O Lord, you are my allotted portion and my cup, you it is who hold fast my lot*.

Having become the new chosen people of God by our Baptismal promises, we are expected to do the same reciprocal covenantal response both in our attitude and action. In today's Gospel, ordering the disciples to bring the children to him, our Master points out to us that we too should get closer to God, with a spontaneous and pure heart and try to behave like children trusting him wholeheartedly and taking him in our life as our priority. This is because, as he underlines, *God's Kingdom belongs only to such as these*.

Childlike spirit of trust is the basic need to continue in our covenantal life with God. Let us remember that the Psalmist, who sings God as his inheritance, also repeatedly exposes in his other Psalms his genuine attitude of being a child to God the Father: 'Lord, I have given up my pride and turned away from my arrogance. I am not concerned with great matters or with subjects too difficult for me. Instead, I am content and at peace. As a child lies quietly in its mother's arms, so my heart is quiet within me.'

Prayer: *Almighty God, while we are grateful to you, we pledge you that today and every day we will choose you as our partner and the meaning and joy of our life. Like the chosen people of New Age, we too promise you that we will serve you, our God, and obey your voice. Please help us to lead our daily life with a serious, definite sense of personal responsibility towards you; and our following you may be clear and simple, pure and spontaneous like that of a child. Amen.*

WEEK - 20

Monday

*in our imperfect walking with him God
still holds our hands tight*
(Scriptural Passages: Judges 2: 11-
24; Ps. 106; Matt. 19: 16-22)

As the maxim says 'History Repeats', in the community
life of Israelites we discover people hurting their God
repeatedly despite his benevolence expressed in their day
today life toward their welfare. This is what we hear in
today's first reading: *The children of Israel offended the Lord
by serving the Baals. Abandoning the Lord, the God of their
fathers, who led them out of the land of Egypt, they followed
the other gods of the various nations around them, and by
their worship of these gods provoked the Lord.* We also know
that even when God, out of his mercy, raised up judges
to deliver them from the power of their despoilers, the
stubbornhearted people did not listen to their judges,
but continued to worship other gods; and they never
relinquished their evil practices.

This detailed portray of the transactions between
God and his chosen people were the unwarranted cyclic

happenings in the sad story of humanity: People's sins always brought to them sorrow and oppression; the pain and slavery they encountered induced them to cry to God for mercy; and God with his immense compassion replied by sending his liberating leaders; and when people were liberated, they enjoyed a new period of peace and freedom, but very sadly the same period of glory and prosperity occasioned people forget God and fall into the sins of injustice and sensuality.

This gratuitous cycle has been recurrently mentioned in the Bible. As the Psalmist today testifies, because those people became defiled by their works, and wanton in their crimes, the good Lord grew angry with his people, and abhorred them whom he had been envisaging as his inheritance. Despite many times he rescued them from their inimical perils, they embittered him with their counsels. However, being a compassionate Father, when they cried for help, he had regard for their affliction and fulfilled their impending needs.

The history of the chosen people repeats cyclically for centuries in our lives too. For some real but unexplainable reason every one of us finds success more difficult to handle than failure. This is why, Jesus teaches his disciples in today's Gospel a splendid way of living our life. First he wants us to esteem God as our Father, who is, as we hear today from him, 'the only One who is good'. He also exhorts us as he did to the young man in the Gospel: 'If you want to be perfect and good as the heavenly Father, detach yourself totally from the earthly dreams and material possessions. Become poor in spirit and follow me swimming against the current of materialism and satanic mammon'.

Jesus' way may sound radical and weird but his true followers believe it as the only realistic and levelheaded way not to enter into the wrong cyclic way that takes us to hellish life. We are being led deeply into the mystery of the kingdom where actions are not judged by worldly wisdom but by the instincts of faith.

Prayer: *Lord, we confess that we are often careless to your Son's way of abandonment of worldly goods and frequently desert you, misusing your beautiful gifts. Yet, you hear our continuous cries of pain and affliction, caused by our sinfulness and come to our rescue. We are indeed very grateful to you for your enduring patience and for your readiness to turn our sorrow into a moment of purification and new life. We pledge today to give ourselves fully that you may transform us totally. Amen.*

Tuesday

Dreams natural but impossible for us are
possible and achievable for God
(Scriptural Passages: Judges 6: 11-
19; Ps. 85; Matt. 19: 23-30)

Today's first reading narrates the encounter happening between Gideon and God's Messenger. Interestingly, in that holy encounter we find Gideon behaving exactly how we the modern civilized people do in our dealings with the Lord. Hearing the Angel's greetings, *The Lord is with you, O champion*, Gideon puts to him two legitimate questions: One, *My Lord, if the Lord is with us, why has all this happened to us?* Two, *Where are his wondrous deeds of which our fathers told us when they said, 'Did not the Lord bring us up from Egypt?*

Not to our surprise, God's Messenger responded in his usual way. Not bothering about the questions asked, he ordered: *Go with the strength you have and save Israel from the power of Midian. It is I who send you.* As any other holy persons, sages and prophets, Gideon expressed his inability to lead and save Israel with his lowest background. But the Lord insists through his Angel: *I shall be with you.* Being requested again by Gideon, the Angel performed a miraculous deed in front of him and confirmed the Lord's promising words are valid.

We hear in today's Gospel Jesus cautioning his disciples with a stunning statement: *Amen, I say to you, it will be hard for one who is rich to enter the Kingdom of heaven. It is easier for a camel to pass through the eye of a needle than for one who is rich to enter the Kingdom of God.* At the same time he emphasizes that those who follow him would be getting the greatest and the richest blessings. To answer the legitimate question of Peter, Jesus clearly listed out his definite promises of richness and prosperity to those who decide firmly to follow his Gospel values sincerely and faithfully.

His main richest promise is: Among his followers, the ones, who are last in their walk of life, will be made first; Regarding this richest promise, Jesus tells that after their earthly life in the new age, the lowly people will inherit the eternal life, namely in the otherworld, when Jesus is seated on his throne of glory, they will also be seated on the glorious thrones of judgement. Plus, even while they were moving in this earthly physical life, they, who have given up worldly riches- houses or brothers or sisters or father or mother or children or lands for the sake of his name, will receive a hundred times more. Very sadly, Jesus uttered his curse about those, who esteem self-righteously and blindfolded themselves as the first, will be thrown down as the last.

Prayer: *God, who bring salvation to the lowly people! Though you are Almighty, immensely holy, out of your merciful love and concern for human beings you permit them to have* *dialogue with you in full freedom, especially you have been very fond of conversing with your faith-filled agents and leaders like Gideon. Lord, we promise that, pleasing you and serving you will be our one and only concern and desire in life. Please help us to seek you and your Kingdom above all else. We give to you, dear Lord, our whole being so that what you have destined for us may be completed as you desire. Amen.*

Wednesday

*Wide-opening of our inner eye sees God's
deals are just and the best*
(Scriptural Passages: Judges 9: 6-15; Ps. 21; Matt. 20: 1-16)

In continuation of the richest promise of Jesus '*the last will be first, and the first will be last*', as we heard in yesterday's Gospel, he confirms it in today's Gospel passage through a parable. We are stunned to hear him repeatedly exhorting us about our ultimate inheriting of God's Kingdom and its fruits of eternal joy and peace. Through riddles and parables he underlines to attain our final rewards is entirely belonging to God's justice and mercy. God the Father have the ultimate authority either to make the last to be first or the first to be last. He is the sole Sovereign and powerful, and just and compassionate Proprietor to employ us in his Kingdom as well as to contribute the wages as he wills. Hence Jesus advises us to be careful in dealing with the earthly positions and material possessions.

Jesus demands all his followers to be and behave like the Psalmist, who held an unassailable mindset to recognize the interactions of the Creator in every phase of lifesituation, especially in climbing up the social ladder and getting a high position in life. That means, we should remember and recognize gratefully God as our Planner, Designer, and Provider, when we are coveting all educational qualifications, professional skills and with that background getting a super position in the society. King David's words in the Psalm demonstrate this truth. He sings: *Lord, in your strength I am glad; every heart-desire of mine has been granted such as your life filled with goodly blessings, lengthy life, your glory shared through your victories, golden crown on my head, majesty and splendor you conferred upon me. You made me a blessing forever, and you gladdened me with the joy of your face.*

In our Scriptures we find God elevating humans as the leaders of his people, suchlike David. We know, after David, only a few leaders were faithful to God, as victorious Gideon, who possessed a faith-filled daring heart to refuse the people's entreaties to become their ruler, saying *I will not rule over you, nor shall my son rule over you. The Lord must rule over you.* Following Gideon's death, regrettably Abimelech, one of his seventy sons, because of his hankering for kingship, murdered all his siblings except one, Jotham, who seemed to be God-fearing person like his father Gideon.

The parable we hear today in the first reading was used by Jotham to remind people the faith-filled leadership of Gideon, which was based on Godly values. Namely, at every step of human life, from conception to resurrection, the sole Sovereign Master and Landowner is none other than our God. He advised them, not to choose wicked Abimelech, rather to choose and anoint their leader in good faith and be ready to settle under the umbrella of the virtues of his father. Otherwise, he also prophesied, they would face disgraceful outcome of their bad choice.

Prayer: *Lord, our Sovereign God! We fully believe, your ways are not our ways, and that you hold power to search our hearts and find who we are in front of you. Grant we pray that wherever we hold places of authority or control over others, we may respond with compassion and concern and may remember that the strong can afford to be humble and like yourself to share with them our life and its richness. Kindly Father, as your Son promised, on the day of his glory, reward us not according to our deeds but according to your grace. Amen.*

Thursday

Surprisingly, Pearly Gate is wide open
for all but only a few enter it
(Scriptural Passages: Judges 11: 29-
39; Ps. 40; Matt. 22: 1-14)

Today's reading, from Judges, narrates the very sacred but dreadfully sad story of the Jewish warrior Jephthah who, being blessed by the Spirit of the Lord, began his journey with his troupe to wage war against the hostile Ammonites. At that time he made a vow to the Lord. He said: *Lord, if you deliver the Ammonites into my power, whoever comes out of the doors of my house to meet me, when I return in triumph from the Ammonites, shall belong to the Lord. I shall offer him up as a burnt offering.*

As Jephthah prayed with his vow, we are told the Lord delivered the enemies into his power. When Jephthah returned victoriously to his house, he saw first his daughter, his only child, who came forth in front of his chariot, playing the tambourines and dancing. When he saw her, he was so much stressed at this unfortunate event and the girl encouraged him to fulfill the vow he made to

God. After two months of mourning her virginity, she let his dad do to her as he had vowed.

When we read such story in the Bible, some of us may wonder how cruel and egocentric God seems to be in his dealings, as we see him in Scriptures expecting from humans some bloody ransoms and burnt offerings. However, silencing our inner hot-beats, we hear him in today's Psalm, saying loud through David's song-beats: *Sacrifice or oblation you wished not, but ears open to obedience you gave me. Burnt offerings or sin-offerings you sought not; then said I, "Behold I come." "In the written scroll it is prescribed for me. To do your will, O my God, is my delight, and your law is within my heart!" Here I am, Lord; I come to do your will.* What sort of offerings God demands from us: to do his will; to make the Lord our trust; and not to turn to idolatry or to those who stray after falsehood.

In addition, we get from Jesus some valid reasons, in today's Gospel parable, for God's such deeds of stern justice. Parable exposes to us the eternal fact of how God keeps open wide the doors of his Salvific Eternal Banquet Hall to every human being. In his covenantal interactions with humanity, he always appreciates the amazing fidelity and love of his faithful servants, who surrender themselves to his will with gratitude as the only sacrifice they can offer to please him. And this undeniable commitment is the specific condition, he proposes through his Son, to enter into his Banquet Hall of joy and peace.

The parable also indicates how most of humans fail to offer their reciprocal response to God's eternal call. Many offend him rejecting his invitation with flimsy excuses, and preferring to material and earthly affairs. And Jesus cautions us, as the king was enraged and sent his troops, destroyed those disobedient to him and burned their city, our Just God also will treat those of us who don't care about the Sovereign Lord's salvific invitation.

Plus, we see the king in the parable making his attendants to bind hands and feet of one of those invited guests and to cast him into the darkness outside, where there will be wailing and grinding of teeth. This is because that guest didn't follow the code of wearing wedding garment. Through this incident Jesus teaches us that according to God's salvific will, even accepting his invitation if we don't fulfill his spiritual, moral, and social ordinances and precepts in this world, we will not be blessed with participating heavenly blissful Banquet. Thus Jesus underscores that out of all humans, whom the merciful God invites to enjoy his heavenly Bliss, some are fortunate to attain it but many would be cursed and the Pearly Gate will not be open to them.

Prayer: *Lord, today we promise sincerely to live to do your will. Purify our hearts and guide our conscience through Scripture and through the wisdom of church tradition. Place your spirit within us. Grant all of us, who participate your Son's Eucharistic meal, foreshadowing ritually our Eternal Banquet, the grace of singing your kindness until the day when you clothe us in a wedding garment forever. Amen.*

Friday

We can win the Evil only by obeying
God's integrated love- Command
(Scriptural Passages: Ruth 1: 1, 3-6, 14-
16, 22; Ps. 146; Matt. 22: 34-40)

We read in today's Gospel, the all-knowing God's Son Jesus, summarizing all divine commandments into two, adds surprisingly the most unthinkable fervor and flavor to our Law-binding Christian life. As he places the command of loving God with all our heart, with all our soul, and with all our mind, he exhorts us the love, we should have for God, must be with our whole being; namely, loving him with a passion, not as a duty and fear; our love should be passionate one that is willing even to die for that love. In sum, our love for God should be without any limit.

Such unlimited love for God is therefore, in Jesus' eye, our primary concern in earthly life. Only then, he asks us to love our fellowhumans not only as we love ourselves but also as we love God. It is because he knows well how we find it hard to love our fellowhumans as he loved us. He taught us to love our neighbors, with sincerity, with no discrimination whatsoever, without any biased attitude, even if they seem to be unjust and inimical. That is why he placed first the command of loving God; and from such Godly love, the true love of our neighbors will automatically flow.

He too insisted that if we love God with our whole being, our neighborly love would surely become easier; and we would begin to love our neighbors wholeheartedly, truly and perfectly. As St. Bernard has said: *What we love we shall grow to resemble.* Those of us who sincerely keep up to the 'integrated Love'-Command of God, never fail to praise the Lord, remembering with the Psalmist, the factual truths about the immense love of God who *keeps faith forever, secures justice for the oppressed, gives food to the hungry. He sets captives free; he gives sight to the blind; he raises up those who were bowed down; loves the just; protects strangers; and he sustains the orphans and the widows.*

As an example for such human integrated love of God and neighbor, we find in the life of a lady, named Ruth, who is mentioned in today's Old Testament Reading. She was born in the Moabite community, who were considered as enemies by the Jews of that time. She got married to a Jewish man whose sudden death made her as a young widow. However, she demonstrated her deep love for the God of her Jewish in-laws who were from Bethlehem of Judah.

Naomi, her mother-in-law, who also lost her husband and her sons, planned to leave Moab, due to the impending famine in that area, to her native town Bethlehem. She permitted her two widowed daughters-in-law to stay at Moab with its people and their god. While one daughter-in-law accepted to stay at Moab, Ruth said to her mother-in-law: *Do not ask me to abandon or forsake you! For wherever you go, I will go, wherever you lodge I will lodge, your people shall be my people, and your God my God.* So Naomi returned to Bethlehem with the Moabite daughter-in-law, Ruth.

Prayer: *God our Father, we beg you to make us love you with our whole being, so that as the Psalmist and the Widow Ruth discovered your greatness and compassion, we too may hear the cry of the poor and the needy around us; and loving them wholeheartedly we may perform many good things to uplift them. Lord, if only what we pray were to turn into reality, what a revolution they would cause! It is for such love-based fire of revolution our Master Jesus called us to ignite in this world. We know how dangerous thing the true love is; it can lead only to the cross. But we know it can also lead to Easter morning. Amen.*

Saturday

Modernday Pharisees are the Spoilers
of the Glory of God's Church
(Scriptural Passages: Ruth 2 and 4; Ps. 128; Matt. 23: 1-12)

Every one of us, in our human life of womb-to-tomb, must unavoidably go through many transitions in all its dimensions. Though those transitional periods are natural and expected ones, while a few are delightful, many others are very painful, such as separations, rejections, sickness and humiliating deaths and exterminating burials or cremations. While we are troubled with giving meaning to those dreadful transitions, our Bible helps us with God's solid directions. Specifically, in today's Scriptural readings we get some of those directions.

Today's first reading brings before us the young widow Ruth, who in all her life's changes, placed her faith and trust in the God whom she came to know from her mother-in-law Naomi. Despite Ruth's 'foreign' identity, her faith in the true God, as well as her humble commitment to show her love to God through her neighborly love, influenced the men of the soil, like Boaz, accepting her warmly and by encouraging her, he made her happy and peaceful in her transition time.

We hear him saying to her: *I have had a complete account of what you have done for your mother-in-law after your husband's death; you have left your father and your mother and the land of your birth, and have come to a people whom you did not know previously.* Thus, Ruth, in accordance with the true God's values, being humble and obedient, showed love, honor and respect to her mother-in-law, rather than doing things self-gratifying. For such faith-filled humble loving life, as the Biblical history portrays, she is included in the genealogy of Jesus as the mother of Obed, who was the father of Jesse, the father of David. It is from this clan was born our Redeemer, Jesus.

Today's Psalm narrates the same kind of successful lifestory of many humans who walk in God's ways with fear, blended with love and fidelity. The Psalmist lists out the benefits they enjoy in this world: *They shall be blessed and favored in eating the abundant fruit of their handiwork; their spouses shall be like a fruitful vine in the recesses of their homes; their children like olive plants around their table. They also will see the prosperity of Jerusalem all the days of their life.*

In today's Gospel, Jesus calls us to be humble. *The greatest among you must be your servant. Whoever exalts himself will be humbled; but whoever humbles himself will be exalted.* Plus, he adds two important dimensions of that the spirit of humility. One, its origin and basis and end should be our faith in God as the only Father, Christ as the only Master, and Jesus as the only Teacher.

Two, its practicing style should be not as that of the Pharisees of his time, rather all our undertakings, such as preaching, teaching, and outward social and religious performances, should not be showcases nor promotional ads nor mere powerplays and games. We should be what we are; behave as servants to the just Proprietor God; and do what we can within our limited capacity but do them as best as we can. The rest we should place on the lap of Christ. He will take care of its successful ending.

Like the passionate death of Christ, our ending of earthly life, becoming dust unto dust, though very painful experience, must turn out to be disinterested time of surrendering and of handing over to our Master all that we leave behind. This needs a firm and continued conviction that God is the Sovereign Provider of all gifts. Additionally, as Jesus, Psalmist, and Ruth, we are obliged to posit our faith in God, who would bring forth something good from the lifetime losses. That is, as the Scriptures say, a resurrected and fulfilled, blissful life.

Prayer: *Our Father of immeasurable majesty, as human beings, our earthly life is always in transition with lot of shocking changes. However, being followers of Jesus, we believe that since we are journeying in this world with Christ at our side, we discover more fully who God is calling us to be. Hence we are moving on through transitions, not only separating ourselves from the past, but also bridging it with the future of our final ending with sharing Jesus' resurrection and fullness. Father, we are thankful to you and we plead to preserve us staying with you determinedly and with humility, holding Jesus' loving and bleeding hands tightly wherever we are stationed in our life's journey. Amen.*

WEEK - 21

Monday

God is delighted seeing we are delighted in Him
(Scriptural Passages: 1 Thess. 1: 1-5, 11-
12; Ps. 149; Matt. 23: 13-22)

The Psalmist today proclaims the eternal truth that *the Good Lord takes delight in his people.* Explaining the primary meaning of God delighting in us one online preacher writes: *What God delights in about us is that we delight in him.* In other words, God is delighted whenever we try to find delight in him and in his values.

Today's Psalm uncovers the list of those in whom God delights: Those are the ones who praise God together with the assembly of God's faithful; who recognize and glad in the Supremacy of God as their Maker; who as little children, rejoice in God as their sole King; who admire at his constant love for humans, especially embellishing the lowly with victory; and who consider overwhelmingly that their glory consists only in loudly praising, thanking and singing about God's greatness and goodness as their life's priority.

In this same spirit of the Psalmist, Jesus is portrayed in the Gospels and in Apostles' preaching, as the First Human, who cherished as his heartbeat, food, and water in focusing his entire life on only being delighted in God. Jesus, who made himself as little mouthless lamb in his plan of being delighted in God, was elevated by God the Father as a Good Shepherd to his followers. As our Shepherd, he declared: *My sheep hear my voice; I know them, and they follow me.* He relates himself to us as a Good Shepherd and considers us as his faithful flock.

Therefore he expects us follow him wherever he goes by hearing his voice, and knowing him as he knows us. His words may be very harsh and sometimes hurting us as we hear in today's Gospel. One thing we are sure. Our merciful Master never fails to bless us if we follow him with sincere dedication to his values, but he will be surely hurt, if those of us, who were ordained by him to be his proxy-leaders in his kingdom, disobey him and scandalize his flock by their hardheadedness, bursting with fake supremacy and insincerity.

Paul, in today's first reading, joining with his other Christian leaders Silvanus and Timothy, identifies themselves, as sincere, and dedicated preachers of God and rolemodels as Jesus, to Christians at Thessalonica. Wishing those disciples of Jesus at Thessalonica, he first appreciates them gratefully remembering their dedicated life, that is blended with steadfast faith and good deeds: *In every place your faith in God has gone forth, so that we have no need to say anything. For they themselves openly declare about us what sort of reception we had among you, and how you turned to God from idols to serve the living and true God and to await his Son from heaven.*

With the same grateful heart Paul confirms about the ceaseless prayer of him and other leaders for their

Christian brethren. He feels very grateful for knowing how his Christian brothers and sisters were loved by God, and how they were chosen by him. And he adds: *We give thanks to God always for all of you, remembering you in our prayers, unceasingly calling to mind your work of faith and labor of love and endurance in hope.* He also claims the uniqueness of the remarkable Gospel ministry, he and his coworkers perform: *For our Gospel did not come to you in word alone, but also in power and in the Holy Spirit and with much conviction. You know what sort of people we were among you for your sake.*

Prayer: *God of justice and Truth, we thank you for giving us Jesus who is endowed with great and truthful shepherding personality and with redeeming power. Kindly pour out your graces in all of us, mainly in those who are gifted with leadership, so that we may walk behind Jesus following his Gospel-steps; and that we may serve you every moment of our earthly life with firm hope and love of Jesus until his second coming from heaven, who has the ability to deliver us from the coming curses and to be blessed with heavenly joy. Amen.*

Tuesday

*Let us not lose the efficacy of God's Word
by our double-standard life*
(Scriptural Passages: 1 Thess. 2:1-3a, 14-
17; Ps. 96; Matt. 23:23-26)

The word of God is living and effective, able to discern reflections and thoughts of the heart. These are the heartrending words, taken from the Letter to Hebrews, which we recited today as Gospel Acclamation. They are the splendid summary of the messages we heard in today's Liturgy of the Word.

In the Responsorial Psalm we hear about the elements consisting in the lively and effective interactions of God through his Word and his Spirit. As Psalmist confesses, God probes and knows about all our whoabout, whatabout, and whereabout and he understands our thoughts from afar; He scrutinizes our journeys and our rest and he is familiar with all our ways; even before a word is on our tongue, he knows the whole of it. Above all, behind us and before us he encompasses us in and rests his hand upon us.

For benefitting all blessings and not curses from the proclaiming as well as living the magnificent words of God, Jesus in today's Gospel offers his two splendid guidelines in the form of listing out curses for those who don't observe those guidelines. His guidelines are: 1. While paying the tithes to God, we should not neglect God's laws of judgement, mercy and fidelity. 2. While we perform the ritual cleanings of outside-environment for the sake of holy presence of God, we should also attend seriously to clean our inner spirit that is filled with plunder and self-indulgence.

Keeping in mind our Master's guidelines, Paul, in his First Letter to Thessalonians, meaningfully renames God's Word as the Gospel of God. And appreciating how his Christian brothers and sisters at Thessalonica received this amazing Gospel of God, preached by him and by his ministers, he highlights that though he and his team had suffered and insolently treated in the past, they drew courage through God to proclaim to them the Gospel of God with much enthusiasm.

It is very important to be noted that Paul and his companions were never self-centered, nor insincere in their words and deeds to the spirit of the Gospel of God. He writes: *Our exhortation was not from delusion or impure* motives, nor did it work through deception. But as we were judged worthy by God to be entrusted with the Gospel, that is how we speak, not as trying to please men, but rather God, who judges our hearts. Nor, indeed, did we ever appear with flattering speech, as you know, or with a pretext for greed—God is witness—nor did we seek praise from men, either from you or from others.

Prayer: *Truthful and Trustworthy God, as Christians, we believe that you chose us in Christ to be holy as you are holy and to share in your divine glory by following and proclaiming your Gospel. But too often, we are tempted to neglect the weightier matters of the law of charity and wrongly satisfied with external works and practices, done without charity. As we have decided today to follow your Son and to stand firm and hold fast to his teachings, we pray that your grace may bring consolation and eternal comfort to our hearts; and let your grace enable us to do good works of charity and to proclaim sincerely and faithfully the Gospel of salvation to our brothers and sisters. Amen.*

Wednesday

Brightened by God's words human spirit
sees God's light everywhere
(Scriptural Passages: 1 Thess. 2: 9-13;
Ps. 139; Matt. 23: 27-32)

We learn from the lives of sages and saints that, when human hearts are touched deeply by the merciful grace of God, some miraculous transformation occurs in their life. To begin with, they suddenly feel that their inner eyes are open wide and see through their past and present life looks so shabby and ugly as our Lord provokes us today in the Gospel with his surgical words: *You are like whitewashed tombs, which appear beautiful on the outside, but inside are full of dead men's bones and every kind of filth. Even so, on the outside you appear righteous, but inside you are filled with hypocrisy and evildoing.*

As an inevitable followup of such powerful scathy surgery of the two-edged Word of God, those inner-eye-opened persons start repenting for their evil deeds and beg for God's mercy. In addition, they continue to confess to the Lord with heart-jolted wonder and heart-felt gratitude as we hear in today's responsorial Psalm: *Lord, You have searched me and you know me. Where can I go from your spirit? From your presence where can I flee? You are there everywhere, guiding me and holding me fast. Even the darkness shall hide me, since I am with you, I feel night shall be my light, for you darkness itself is not dark, and night shines as the day.*

Surprisingly, these transformed people are truly perfected, as John writes in his first Letter: *Whoever keeps the word of Christ, the love of God is truly perfected in him.* And they turn out to be the beloved sons and daughters of God, join the company of Jesus' witnesses, as Saul who was transformed to be Paul the Apostle. The posteffect of sudden conversion in his life was marvelous. His entire teachings and advices to us in his Letters are simply his own experiences and undertakings effected by the conversion. After his conversion, he walked in a manner worthy of the God who called him into his Kingdom and glory.

In today's first reading Paul exposes to his Christians how his converted and consecrated heart and life was truly perfected in charity by God's Word. He writes: *Despite our toil and drudgery, working night and day in order not to burden any of you, we proclaimed to you the Gospel of God...*As he testifies today, he behaved toward the believers devoutly and justly and blamelessly. As a father treats his children, he treated each one of them exhorting and encouraging them and insisting that they walk in a manner worthy of the God who calls them into his Kingdom and glory.

Prayer: *Immensely delightful and lightful God, we are ashamed to observe ourselves behaving hypocritic as the religious elders of Jesus' time. We see them in us being extremely religious only in outward appearances and rituals, but always fail to lead a life of integrity as your Son expects from us. Renewed by your remarkable two-edged Words, we want to come out from our life of whitewashed tomb. Help us Lord to reexamine our daily life in a deeper manner, and change our double-standard actions so that we may build our life-structure on the solid foundation of your Word and start doing only lightful and delightful deeds as you and your Son expect. Amen.*

Thursday

Those who are awakened by the Word,
are blessed with real prosperity
(Scriptural Passages: 1 Thess. 3: 7-13;
Ps. 90; Matt. 24: 42-51)

Jesus prophetically advises his disciples in today's Gospel: *Stay awake! For you do not know on which day your Lord will come.* And he provides them two exemplary persons for knowing how we should stay awake. One is the 'staying awake' of a master of the house who knew the hour of night when the thief was coming. And the other is a servant to whom the master had entrusted the duty of taking care of his household before he went out. That servant was very faithful in fulfilling the duties his master gave him until he returned on an unexpected day.

Jesus wants his disciples to behave, like both the prudent master and the faithful servant, during their days in this world. He says to them: *So too, you also must be prepared, for at an hour you do not expect, the Son of Man will come.* He too warns them about bad result if they don't actively stay awake. *The Son of Man will come on an unexpected day and at an unknown hour and will severely punish the imprudent and unfaithful disciples and assign him a place with the hypocrites, where there will be wailing and grinding of teeth.*

Paul in his Letter today prays for his Christians that they may actively and fruitfully stay awake in their day today life. *May the Lord make you increase and abound in love for one another and for all, just as we have for you, so as to strengthen your hearts, to be blameless in holiness before our God and Father at the coming of our Lord Jesus with all his holy ones.*

Besides, points out that his deep love and affection for his fellow-Christians originates from the immense love and affection he possessed in God and his Son. He also shows how with him and his associate leaders they should continue faithfully and prudently staying awake to meet the Lord at his second coming. He insists that every action and suffering, that he and his associate ministers endure in their ministries, must be closely connected to the Day of the Lord's Coming; and by showing their longing toward seeing the Church-members in person, he writes: *We have been reassured about you, brothers and sisters, in our every distress and affliction, through your faith. For we now live, if you stand firm in the Lord. What thanksgiving, then, can we render to God for you, for all the joy we feel on your account before our God?*

The Psalmist today proclaims very plainly that, despite God's miraculous and glorious creation of humanity is evident, we should never forget its frailty and limitations.

He emphasizes that not only God has the superpower to turn us back to dust but also his time is not our time; while a thousand years in his sight are as yesterday, now that it is past, as a watch of the night. Therefore, during our short-lived life over this earth, the Psalmist encourages us to ask the Creator to grant us the wisdom of heart to number our days aright; to beg the Lord to return soon to us. And in the meantime he asks to petition to God to prosper the work of our hands and to fill us with his love so that we are able to sing for joy.

Prayer: *God our beginning and end, being reborn in your mighty grace we firmly believe that despite our many deficiencies, we possess the capacity you shared with us to be and do good works. Gratefully acknowledging it, we earnestly pray that we may be enlightened by you to reflect daily on whether we are leading our life under your grace to its fullest and also grant us an uninterrupted, stirred spirit to be prudent and faithful servants until your Son arrives. Amen.*

Friday

We can enter into heaven only by our
unstained baptismal identity
(Scriptural Passages: 1 Thess. 4:1-8; Ps. 97; Matt. 25: 1-13)

Gospels, especially Matthew's, repeatedly quote the Lord's words: *Many are called, but few are chosen*. Matthew explains very vividly this saying of Jesus through many Parables. One of them we hear in today's Gospel Parable of the Ten Virgins. When Jesus, our Bridegroom, arrives to take all his discipled souls as his beloved brides, according to his Father's designed schedule, some of us would be entering with him to his Eternal Chamber, but some others who come late will not get that golden chance. While those latecomers, knocking at his door, crying: *Lord, Lord, open the door for us,* the only reason he would give them for not opening it is: *Amen, I say to you, I do not know you.*

The legitimate question arises: Why would the Lord disown those foolish virgins? They were not wicked nor indecent, just foolish! They really did nothing seriously evil, not even mildly wrong. They simply began to fall asleep! They failed to bring proper supplies and so they were not ready at the precise moment of the Lord's return. And the Lord's valid answer to our question has been offered by him throughout his three years' preaching: His main demand from his disciples is, not merely to begin our journey to heaven with so much excitement and thrill but also we need to be alert, never miss our enthusiasm even a single moment in our service to him; and always to keep our eyes open.

From the beginning of creation God expected all his human creatures to be justones and as the Psalmist today sings, *only those who are just in the eyes of God enjoy the true happiness of God. As God's entire creations proclaim his justice and glory, his human creatures should rejoice in the Lord through their voluntary justice-based life. Consequently light dawns for the just; and gladness, for the upright of heart.* God showers abundantly awesome safety, security, and deliverance from the wicked.

In such peaceful environment, just people, like the wise virgins, keep their lamps of their inner spirit burning and when the Bridegroom appears to them on an unexpected moment, they will be joyfully taken by the Lord into his Chamber of eternal bliss.

Moreover, while we are waiting for the Lord, we should not be like the Christians in Thessalonica, whom

Paul cautioned through his Letters, about their slip into habits of improper activity, even into blatant wickedness. The primary and goal-oriented instruction given to early Christians by Paul and his coworkers who had received it through the Lord Jesus was: *God's will for us is nothing but our holiness in this earthly life. God did not call us to impurity but to holiness.* This means, we should abstain from immorality and especially those of us who enter into married life, must not exploit their spousal relationship by lustful passion but in holiness and honor. This is the only way to conduct ourselves to please God.

Prayer: *God of justice and joy, through your words you make us understand well our life's goal is to please you by fulfilling your will that we must attain your holiness. At the end of our earthly time you will send your Son to reward us for our chivalrous life of waiting actively for him. We are fully aware of the fact that just being baptized as Church member does not in itself guarantee our being ready to welcome the Lord. Hence we entreat you to grant us the grace of patiently enduring our daily hardships in safeguarding the light, your Spirit has bestowed in our human spirit, and keeping it burning bright until our Bridegroom's arrival. Amen.*

Saturday

To get divine interests let us invest our gifts on love of needy humans
(Scriptural Passages: 1 Thess. 4: 9-11; Ps. 97; Matt. 25:14-30)

We read once again in Matthew's Gospel another parable that portrays our judgement Day Happenings. This Parable of the Talents ends with a paradox of

Jesus: *To everyone who has, more will be given and he will grow rich; but from the one who has not, even what he has will be taken away.* In the light of God's Spirit, we get a beautiful and relevant explanation of this paradoxical and seemingly uncompassionate saying of Jesus. God's gifts, like an automobile or a computer, must be used to remain in good condition; non-use of them leads to stagnation, sticky parts and clogged valves.

In the same manner, physical and spiritual life quickly degenerates in isolation and dark confinement. Also, the wrong use of life, gifts, automobiles and computers also destroys them, perhaps more quickly than non-use. Today's Gospel and other readings enable us to balance and integrate these factors in the use of our talents. Like the one who received one talent, many of us get into jealousy and frustration in comparing and contrasting our status with others.

This is because we easily forget the Scriptural truth that God, out of his goodness and wisdom, blesses us according to each one's abilities. We should firmly believe that the Lord our Creator rules the earth with justice. The Responsorial Psalm of this day exposes to us the powerful and continual reigning of God over us with fairness; day in and day out he comes to rule us with justice; working wonders he brings salvation to us; like all his other creations we also must ring out our joy at his eternal presence among us.

Paul, in today's first reading, knowing such spiritual problems among his Christians at Thessalonica, recommends to them three things: First he wants them to remember God's command to love one another with fraternal charity; and advises them to always aspire to live a life of tranquility and forgiving, despite our neighbors being more prosperous, more helpful, more generous, or more scandalous, intriguing, selfish. Second, he urges them to work with their own hands in developing themselves and their talents as best as they can. Thirdly, they should mind their own affairs and be settled in God's providence.

Indeed, in our past we would have done many good works with the talents we inherited by birth and developed them by our hard efforts. Perhaps, we might not have accomplished them with the best of our hearts leaning on God's goodness. But now, this day, the only day is in our hands; it is the proper time we can develop our hearts pleasing to the Lord better and best maximum possible by spending every moment and step of our life and doing possible ordinary things in an extraordinary way for the greater glory of God.

Prayer: *Lord, Giver of all our gifts, we thank you sincerely for the abundant gifts you share with us. Grant us the hearts to appreciate, develop, and use and share them for the growth and welfare of our fellowhumans. Because in the light of your Son's words we comprehend that if we don't move forward or are not productive, then we go backwards. Amen.*

WEEK - 22

Monday

*Faith makes us leap into darkness; hope
keeps our inner light burning*
(Scriptural Passages: 1 Thess. 4: 13-
18; Ps. 96; Lk. 4: 16-30)

From the beginning of human life on earth till now, the God's Archenemy Satan controls the good portion of humanity with his unjust and untruthful social systems, with the support of human persons who are very easily enslaved to him. Hence the Anawim, the good-willed people, continue to cry aloud to God with faith, like the Psalmist: *The Lord comes to judge the earth. He shall rule the world with justice and the peoples with his constancy.* Only these people poor in spirit, encountering God's presence in them and in all creations, can sing prophetically with joy and gratitude as their ambitious dream: *Let us tell his glory among the nations; among all peoples, his wondrous deeds. For great is the Lord and highly to be praised; awesome is he, beyond all gods.*

Today in Luke's Gospel we hear Jesus proclaiming his excellent Gospel Manifesto, quoting from Prophet

Isaiah, plainly promising that the perpetual dreams of humble-hearted humans would be fulfilled by his life and ministry. He announced that he came to alleviate human unjust misery- spiritual and physical. He assured he would establish a social system of justice, love, truth and peace. And in fact we see him during his public ministry as a healer, consoler and forgiver.

But along with his positive promises, he confirmed through his very life and death, such establishment of God's kingdom of justice and love can be possible only by countless broken-bodies and bloodsheds, starting from his own. It all started on the first day of his proclamation as we hear in the Gospel. When people heard his manifesto, all were filled with rage. They got up, drove him out of the town, and led him to the brow of the hill on which their town was built, so that they might hurl him off the cliff.

However, it is our well-founded belief, which Apostles and Saints taught us, that Jesus rose from the dead, and lives among us in his resurrected Spirit. He enables us to listen to all his directions for establishing his just system within us; he also urges us to hold his sense of service focusing on people in greatest need, regardless of their background or social standing. He encourages us to endure patiently in the times when people around us are upset, irritated and angry against us as he faced. All he asks is that we receive him on his own terms, which the people of Nazareth refused to do. He is always close at hand and even our sufferings, whatever form they take, can bring us close to him.

If we want to perform all those acts of justice, compassion and truth willingly as Jesus demands us, we need to maintain an unwavering hope and belief, as Paul today advises us, that one day Jesus would be back in glory and power; and we, both living and dead, will be caught up in the clouds together with them to meet the Lord in the air; and so we will be with the Lord forever. Plus, we will be reunited with our deceased relatives and friends. Let us then, as Paul exhorts us, encourage one another with these hope-filled words.

Prayer: *Life-giving God, we thank you for anointing your Son through your Spirit to be the truthful way for the poor people, who are able to be liberated from all our evils and to attain your fullest life. Knowing your Son's personal interactions with us, we firmly and joyfully hope that we will always be with you. The only thing we request from you is your continual grace to accompany us in walking the walk of Christ to wherever he takes us in this world in order to bring glad tidings to the poor. Amen.*

Tuesday

Colossal authority of Jesus can never let us be bound by demons
(Scriptural Passages: 1 Thess. 5: 1-6,
9-11; Ps. 27; Lk. 4: 31-37)

When Jesus was teaching people, as we hear in today's Gospel, they were astonished at his teaching because he spoke with authority. He wanted to prove to them that he held authority not only in teaching but also in casting out the unclean spirits. We find him victorious over the demon, which was possessing and troubling a man; by casting it out from him, and without allowing it to do any harm to the man, he demonstrated his heavenly authority.

According to Scriptures, demons are fallen angels who retain their spiritual powers. As the holy angels, demons have natural powers of communication and influence upon us and upon our world. They have turned from God and now they want to turn us to their evil side. But the good news is, as Jesus demonstrated his power against all evil demons, today he remains with us as guardian against those demonic temptations, if we persistently abide in him.

This awesome news of Jesus spread everywhere in the surrounding region. Even after two millennia as those people of Jesus' time were thunderstruck by his teaching, we wonder about the fact a human being rose up in the name of God and the world was converted, turned around, turned upside-down. Perhaps the demons of evil may strangle us and enslave us consciously or unconsciously. We are not afraid of such sudden attack of the devil, because God's Son is always in us and among us with an amazing authority he demonstrated while he was alive in Palestine.

Moreover, he has elevated us in our spirit to sing with the Psalmist daily: *The LORD is my light and my salvation; he is my life's refuge; whom should I fear? Only one thing I ask of the Lord; this I seek: To dwell in the house of the Lord all the days of my life and gaze on the loveliness of the Lord and contemplate his temple.* While we state such faith-filled seeking of our Fatherly God, we also, with hope-filled heart, declare: *I believe that I shall see the bounty of the Lord in the land of the living. I am waiting for him with courage.*

In addition, as Paul underlines in his Letter today, we are remade and renewed by the same Miracle-worker as children of light and children of the day; we are not of the night or of darkness of Satan. Our Christian faith assures us that God has destined us not for wrath but for obtaining salvation through our Lord Jesus Christ. Yes, this is what we are. This is what we dream about ourselves. We move around with an innovative serenity and peace to take the challenges of life and the sudden return of Jesus anytime and anywhere.

Prayer: *Creative God, help us, we pray, to continue in this frame of faith-filled life; on the strength of our faith in the words of the savior, aid us to relish the joy of detaching ourselves from the grasp of the enslaving powers of our modern age to become disciples of the freedom of the Gospel. we too request you to bestow your graces upon us to lead a life, in which, cost what it may, we may be artisans of peace; without despair but without gullibility, we may bear witness to hope, and to a future that is genuinely possible; despite our divisions, and the world's separatisms, we may gather around one Word and one Bread. Amen.*

Wednesday

All prayers get efficacious only by faith, hope and love in God
(Scriptural Passages: Col. 1: 1-8; Ps. 52; Lk. 4: 38-44)

In today's Gospel passage we read about healing miracles of Jesus. One, he does in his personal relationship environment as he healed Peter's mother-in-law for all that Peter was to him; two, as a community gift to all those who held strong faith in him, Jesus laid his hands on all the sick with various diseases, who were brought to him by those who had faith in him and cured them all. But all this did not happen easily or for all. We observe in those events of healings two basic requisites needed for Jesus' healings.

First, Jesus, in his tight daily schedule of caregiving ministries, was found taking some hours off for prayer. He made his way to a lonely place. There was still much to be done, but he needed time to pray quietly. This is because,

Jesus knew well that his powerful services to people could not be fruitful without his Father's intimate connections in prayer and meditations.

Second, we find among the relatives and community members of the sick and the needy, an amazing environment of caring for each other as they had interceded with Jesus for their healings. This endorses the practice of praying for one another with open heart reaching outward to all God's friends.

Their daily prayer had become efficacious first by their deep sense of gratitude and trust in God. Most of us are prone to be pessimists with an inclination of not trusting in God's mercy but lead an individualistic secular life to be overanxiously concerned and try out and figure out how to accomplish things ourselves. But the Bible emphatically points out that God wants everything beneficial for us and that he works all things only that are beneficial for us, and so there is no need to worry.

The Psalmist offers us today his personal understanding of how such trust in God should play an important part in everyone's life. *I will thank you always for what you have done, and proclaim the goodness of your name before your faithful ones. I trust in the mercy of God for ever.* He means that an attitude of gratitude is much more satisfying than a murmuring and annoying one; to a great extent, when it brings us more connected to God.

The second source of those miraculous events would be, as Paul reminds us today in his Letter, a mindset of being filled with hope. In his regular prayer of thanksgiving to God for his Church members, Paul appreciates, not only their faith in Christ Jesus and their love for all the holy ones, but also their hope reserved for them in heaven. It is a hope that has borne fruit and has continued to grow in human minds as it has everywhere.

When we are strong in charity towards each other, we certainly become people of unreserved hopes. This hope, born of love, is the resource, out of which miracles are worked and heaven is dreamed.

Prayer: *Lord God, make us be conscious of your Son's healing presence among us all day long, every day. Let us not be reluctant to leave our little cave of self to go out and meet Jesus who is the Shepherd of our souls. By abiding always in Jesus' presence, we may take strong commitment of defeating our selfishness in some small thing every day for the benefit of others' healings. And that is how Jesus expected us to get our own wholistic healings. Amen.*

Thursday

A life, well-pleasing God, makes us
empowered to do greater things
(Scriptural Passages: Col. 1: 9-14; Ps. 98; Lk. 5: 1-11)

Generally, we begin to feel often depressed and going downhill and sometimes as if we are already in the ditch. But as the disciples committed to Christ, we are not supposed to be in that unwanted mental and spiritual stage continuously. Besides, with our human weakness we can never rise up by ourselves from those critical situations and walk with peace and joy. This is why the Word of God today commands us to believe wholeheartedly, with the Psalmist, God's Masterplan of salvation can never fail and always wins. The Spirit proclaims through the Psalm the eternal fact that God the Creator has never kept his salvation hidden within himself or only within his clout; rather, *he has made his salvation known: in the sight of the nations he has revealed his justice. All the ends of the earth have seen the salvation by our God.*

God also demonstrated his miraculous deeds of salvation through his Son Jesus, who, as today's Gospel proclaims, made his Apostles bewildered at the miraculous catch of fish happened at his word; and encouraged them and us ascertaining that the same Godly salvific power is within us, by which we would have dominion over the living creatures for our abundant nourishment.

He too prophesied that we can empower our weak and needy fellowhumans to walk in the path of salvation by saying: *Do not be afraid; from now on you will be catching men.* As the wholistic aim of saving humanity, Jesus not only transformed the disciples' unsuccessful night's toil by giving them an abundant catch of fish, but also he claimed that he had the Godly power to elevate even sinful and weak disciples like Peter to capture humans into the nets of God's salvific kingdom.

In this regard, we hear from Paul today recording the multiple fruits and benefits of salvation with which God has filled all of us as Christ's disciples. With prayerful wishes the Apostle writes about some remarkable and positive changes occurring from our connection with Christ: We are filled with the knowledge of God's will through all spiritual wisdom and understanding to walk in a manner worthy of the Lord; we can be fully pleasing God; we can bear fruit in every good work; and we can grow in the knowledge of God; we can be strengthened with every power, in accord with his glorious might for all endurance and patience; we are made fit to share in the inheritance of the holy ones in light.

Prayer: *Lord, God of power and might, we hear from you in today's Scriptures that our salvation is gained mostly by our* normal activities, such as employment, study, health-care, eating and drinking, family life and certainly in our hardships and toils. However we are also told such thing is possible only if they are performed in faith and trust in your grace. We beseech you, that all of us be made strong with all the strength that comes from your Son's sharing of his glorious power, and that we may be prepared to endure everything with patience, while joyfully giving thanks to you, who have enabled us to share in the inheritance of the saints in the light. Amen.

Friday

Our continuous stay with Divine
Bridegroom brings us fulness of life
(Scriptural Passages: Col. 1: 15-20; Ps. 100; Lk. 5: 33-39)

Psalmist today invites the entire humanity to *come with joy into the presence of the Lord.* He asks us to serve the Lord with gladness and gratitude. This is because, as the Psalmist contends, *our Lord is God, who is the one who created us, and who tends us as his flock.* Moreover, *our God's goodness, kindness and faithfulness stay forever.*

Our Christian belief is, such a remarkable and unfathomable glory of God is dwelt among us as 'Emmauel' in the person of Jesus of Nazareth, who lived, died and rose from the tomb, all for oursake. Quoting from a liturgical hymn, prevalent in early Church, Paul writes in his Letter today: *The risen Lord Jesus is the image of the invisible God; he is before all things, and in him all things hold together. In him all the fullness of God was pleased to dwell, and through him God was pleased to reconcile to himself all things, whether on earth or in heaven, by making peace through the blood of his cross.*

In addition, Apostle highlights that we are blessed to be as the members of the risen Jesus' Body. As the body's organs, veins and bones are physically connected to the head, so is every one of us in the Church intrinsically and spiritually and mystically connected to Jesus, the Head of the Church. We are so happy to know that we continue to be present and to move our being in the Godly Presence of Jesus.

Since we are closely connected to Jesus' amazing Godly presence, we hear him in today's Gospel, advising us to move and have our being in complete joy. He too identifies himself as our Bridegroom and ourselves his wedding guests, literally, 'sons of the bridal chamber.' He urges us to be joyful and never hold any guilt-feelings until we are intimately connected to him. Besides he encourages us not to be afraid of progressing and renewing ourselves from our stagnant, static past to a lively newness *as a new wine in new wineskins*. Otherwise, according to our Lord, *the old fabric will never match the texture and color of the new.*

Prayer: *Father in heaven, we tell you with sincerity of heart that we don't want to be people of a rigid mindset and to put your grace under human control, rigidly maintained. We desire to work with the new wine of your presence in new ways, having some continuity with the old ways, but we will go beyond them. We pray today for a greater openness to your Son's Spirit who always brings us your divine energy so that we can promptly take some more new steps in our relationship with you as long as you permit us to survive in our voyage to eternity. Amen.*

Saturday

Serving the poor and the needy is integral part of Sabbath Duty
(Scriptural Passages: Col. 1: 21-23; Ps. 54; Lk. 6: 1-5)

Jesus, as he has been a holy and courageous Galilean, identifies himself in today's Gospel, as *the Son of Man is Lord of the Sabbath.* Let us remember the third commandment of God on "Sabbath Day Rest". God promulgated the Sabbath Day to be a time to remember and celebrate his goodness and the greatness of his work, both in creation and redemption; a day set apart for the benefit of his people, that is, to give them rest, to give them time and opportunity to worship him and him alone.

Against this backdrop, Jesus acknowledges himself *the Son of God, yesterday, today and forever.* As he is the Second Person of the Triune God, any commandment pertaining to divine worship refers to him also. He also claims, by today's Gospel statement, his personal redemptive role of renewing and enhancing God's Commandments, which are inscribed in OT. Jesus' faithful disciples, like Paul, never forget this truth and therefore they felt that God through Jesus has been blessing them abundantly with his salvation. Because of such experience, they proclaimed the wholistic Gospel in its integrity.

We hear from Paul today in his Letter about our present glorious situation: *You once were alienated and hostile in mind because of evil deeds; God has now reconciled you in the fleshly Body of Christ through his death.* This implies our focus in our religious life should be on the hope of Jesus' Gospel that reconciles us to God, and not merely its refusal of our evil deeds. Paul also indicates that if we have been offered ourselves as holy and without blemish through the Blood of Christ, we should also be craving for sharing that liberating message with others.

With Paul, if we wholeheartedly recognize Jesus as our Lord and Savior, we will dare enough to accept fully the factual truth of '*I am what I am*'. This humility and honesty would make our hearts sing, as all sages in God's kingdom would declare daily with the Psalmist, saying: *God is my helper; the Lord sustains my life.*

Plus, we will make the best use of any religious ritualistic practices, prescribed by God, by worshiping him in spirit and in truth, offering a living sacrifice of praise and thanksgiving every day, especially on the Sabbath Day, by patiently suffering the effects of earthly life but never degrade God's worship by ignoring and never-caring the needs of our fellowhumans in their hunger, thirst and other welfare needs.

This is the only way to glorify God and to present ourselves through Jesus to the Father, as his children, holy, free of reproach and blame. Otherwise, with our pride and foolishness we will go on making our human abilities and our produces as absolute ones; and perhaps, one day we may end up in considering even our religious faith as mere relativism as the modern pharisaical humanists proclaim.

Prayer: *Lord God, we are so sad to find today's world being bereaved of many catastrophes and our hearts are overcast with seeing tremendous miseries existing around us. We earnestly pray to you to increase our awareness of what 'good' we can do to alleviate the sufferings; and how we can identify and assist, as Jesus teaches us, when human needs take priority over the ungodly traditions, rules, regulations, and policies. We too entreat you to grant us the graces of mercy, wisdom, and leadership to promote the changes as need of the day. Amen.*

WEEK - 23

Monday

For sinfully-withered persons the only hope of glory is Christ
(Scriptural Passages: Col. 1: 24-2: 3; Ps. 62; Lk. 6: 6-11)

Paul, in today's first reading, with his intimate spiritual experience of Christ, writes: *it is Christ in you, the hope for glory*. Christ would be personally encountered as our hope of glory among us, only when we become fully alive as God's children. Unfortunately, because we are blinded by evil feelings of envy and other evil spirits, most of us lose the chance of the precious gift of hope of glory from God.

We are accustomed to behave like the Pharisees of Jesus' time. Whenever Jesus was performing any healing miracles to the sick and the needy, we find the Scribes and Pharisees reacting repeatedly with much intentional and calculated malice. We observe those religious leaders in today's Gospel, interested only in themselves and offended by Jesus getting in the way of their self-importance. Seeing Jesus becoming more popular and respected among people than those leaders they were filled with envy. It was this sin of envy directed them always to irrationality and foolishness and blinded them to think, say and do foolish things; they were unnecessarily furious against Jesus and conspired together how to destroy him.

In this context, Paul speaks to us in his Letter about how his heart was filled with the feelings of love for Jesus and for his disciples: *I rejoice in my sufferings for your sake, and in my flesh I am filling up what is lacking in the afflictions of Christ on behalf of his Body, which is the Church.* The Apostle understood well why he was allowed to survive in this world despite the hardships he experienced. He tells us that it was all because *he was a minister in accordance with God's stewardship given to him to bring to completion for his fellowhumans the word of God, the mystery hidden from ages and from generations past.*

This kind of well-balanced mindset, that is freed of evil feelings but saturated with sincere love, is possible for us, only if, as the Psalmist today sings, we keep our soul be at rest in God, from whom our hope comes. He must become our rock, our stronghold, our safety and glory.

Prayer: *Faithful and Truthful God, today you offer us an opportunity to look at our own lives and to examine how our feelings of envy and jealousy destroy our relationships in our family and community life. Lord, we really want to be free of the sins of pride, envy and jealousy. Help us to repent of these evils and to replace them with your mercy and love, so that we may be enabled to come together as God's family in love-based relationship with one another; and that every one of us may have all the richness of Christ, in whom all the treasures of wisdom and knowledge are hidden. Amen.*

Tuesday

Nailing our limitations to the cross Jesus
empowered us to triumph
(Scriptural Passages: Col. 2: 6-15; Ps. 145; Lk. 6: 12-19)

The Psalmist today encourages all creatures, mainly the humans, to extol God by singing: *Let all your works give you thanks, O LORD, and let your faithful ones bless you. Let them discourse of the glory of your Kingdom and speak of your power.* For such grandeur devotion to God, the Psalmist also gives the reasons that, *The Lord is gracious and merciful, slow to anger and of great kindness. The Lord is good to all and compassionate toward all his works.*

Undoubtedly, we, as disciples of Jesus, continue to experience the same greatness of God's immense mercy and love in what our Creator has done to us in our Baptism. As Paul exclaims in today's first reading, *thanks to the power of the God's Spirit, we are buried with Jesus in baptism, in which we are not only healed from all transgressions, but also raised with him through faith in his powerful mercy.*

According to Paul, God is the One who brings us to a new kind of resurrected life along with Jesus and makes us to share bodily in his fullness of the deity. Moreover, as we have received Christ the Lord in our life, we walk in him, we are rooted in him and we are built upon him and we are established in the faith, abounding in thanksgiving.

This gift of new life in Christ has caused, in weak and fragile humans, an amazing new power flowing from Christ. We hear in today's Gospel, a great crowd of Jesus' disciples and a large number of people came to hear him and to be healed of their diseases; and even those who were tormented by unclean spirits were cured. Everyone in the crowd encountered the power that came forth from him and healed them all. Astoundingly, it is from them Jesus selected his Apostles, not only to be with him and walk with him but also to go out on his behalf to witness to his Godly power and mercy by their own faith-filled life and ministry.

Gratefully we should recognize that, in our lifetime, we too have been chosen to share the most incredible status of being Jesus' apostles. As the miraculous power went out from Jesus, which cured all the sick, Jesus has been kind enough to share the same power with us, so that in our apostolic works we may bring new life of heavenly fullness to our fellowhumans by teaching, counseling, caregiving and healing ministries.

Prayer: *Gracious God, being renewed by frequently participating your life through Sacraments, especially daily Eucharist and prayers, we praise your name. We beg you to beautify the life of your humble children with ultimate victory. This is the glory of all your faithful ones. Amen.*

Wednesday

Blessedness of ascending life on earth
consists in seeking what is above
(Scriptural Passages: Col. 3: 1-11; Ps. 145; Lk. 6: 20-26)

Jesus proclaims in today's Gospel the manifesto of his dream-project of establishing God's Kingdom in this world. We hear him motivating his followers saying: *Rejoice and leap for joy on that day! Behold, your reward will be great in heaven.* He is very concise and precise in deliberating his byelaws for his Kingdom-Project. In accordance with his guidelines, if anyone wants to enter into his Kingdom and enjoy the blessedness of it, they are to be poor in spirit and in truth; to be hungry and thirsty for God's life; to mourn and weep for the human sinfulness; to be ready for being hated, rejected, and insulted on account of his Gospel.

The Beatitudes enumerated by Luke are absolutely the summary of Jesus' guidelines for achieving God's holiness. In this framework, we humans indeed are divided into two categories: One, belonging to the category of the blessed; the other, belonging to the category of the cursed. But we know well, Jesus Christ, who is the embodiment of God's wisdom and life in this world, does not simply canonize all the poor, the hungry, those who weep, and the persecuted, just as he does not simply demonize all the rich, the satiated, those who laugh and are praised. Rather, the distinction is deeper; it has to do with knowing what we put our trust in, and on what sort of foundation we are building the house of our life, whether it is on that which will fade away, or on that which will stay eternally.

Echoing Jesus' Kingdom-manifesto, Paul inspires us in his Letter today talking about the indwelling of God's Spirit within us; and encourages us that it is because of that Spirit, all Jesus' followers live a wholly-renewed life as citizens of God's Kingdom. Baptism has shaped us to be the members of the Family of Christ, who is the new Adam and according to God's image. Therefore we form the new human race, a race that transcends all distinctions of religion, culture, and class.

We must heed to Paul who advises us today to separate ourselves from old repulsive life to newly-enlightened life. He writes: *Now you must put them away your feelings of anger, fury, malice, slander, and obscene language. Stop lying to one another, since you have taken off the* old self with its practices and have put on the new self, which is being renewed, for knowledge, in the image of its Creator.

Through today's Psalm we are invited to keep always in mind, *God is compassionate and faithful toward us; and as grateful persons for such merciful God, we should daily bless and praise him;* plus, we are advised to discuss with one another, and speak loudly of the glorious splendor and power of God's Kingdom.

Prayer: *Compassionate and loving God, kindly shower your graces abundantly upon us so that we, faithfully obeying your Son's clarion call to holiness, may enter and stay permanently in your kingdom of holiness and being freed of immorality, we may run our earthly race as your sons and daughters, full of hope and immortality. Amen.*

Thursday

Christian's breathtaking identity is 'God's chosen one, holy and beloved'
(Scriptural Passages: Col. 3: 12-17; Ps. 150; Lk. 6: 27-38)

For many of us today's Gospel passage may seem to be the most difficult one to be attended to. This is because it advocates an idealistic life that is apparently impractical and unachievable. It is definitely so unrealistic, especially during this postmodern Age, where we are surrounded by great violence, terrorism, increasing litigation, and murder. We can atleast agree to obey the golden rule Jesus proposes: *Do to others as you would have them do to you.* But according to him, this golden maxim cannot just remain as wishful thinking, but it must be translated into deeds, such as: *Love your enemies, do good to those who hate you, bless those who curse you, and pray for those who mistreat you.*

Besides, Jesus tells us we should love wholeheartedly those, who do harm to us, not only without any harmful reactions but also do some benevolent proactions, that are seemingly foolish and reckless, such as *to the man who slaps you on one cheek, present the other cheek too; and to hand over tunic along with our cloak to the enemies.* Why did Jesus propose such superficially nonsensical and unrealistic values?

First, in his own life he exemplified and certified by practicing it fully in his very life, and thus he demonstrated, it is practical for any goodhearted and godly persons. Secondly, he offered us some valid reasons for such impossible but magnanimous deeds: *If we love those who love us, and if we do good to those who do good to us, what credit is that to us who name ourselves as your children and Jesus' disciples?* He points out that our Creator God is kind and merciful Father to the ungrateful and the wicked. Hence if we want to be God's children, then we must *be merciful, just as also our Father is merciful.* One more thing he includes that if we deal kindly and mercifully with our adversaries, *we will receive God's forgiveness abundantly and amazing gifts will be given to us by him in a good measure, packed together, shaken down, and overflowing.*

Apostle Paul today makes us remember about our inability of performing such gregarious and godly deed of loving our enemies; and exhorts us if we decide to obey Jesus' amazing command, we need to allow the word of Christ dwell in us richly and permit the peace of Christ control our hearts splendidly. He underscores this sort of unthinkable and undoable deeds of generosity and love are not beyond our power if we are convinced of our breathtaking identity of being God's chosen children, both holy and beloved in his eyes. Being enabled by the living Christ, who is already alive within us, our life with him certainly will empower us rich in love, kindness, patience and generosity and to obey Jesus' Command.

When our inner spirit is thus filled with heartfelt compassion, kindness, humility, gentleness, and patience; and by bearing with one another and forgiving one another, the peace of Christ will control our hearts; and as the grateful and faithful creatures of God, we will ceaselessly sing with the Psalmist: 'Let everything that breathes praise the Lord!'

Prayer: *All-loving God, today we are led to feel and touch upon the wounds and scars we carry within us due to the inimical actions of our adversaries. Your Spirit tells us now that these wounds can become the sources of our own holiness and happiness, if we let you transform them and our hearts will be filled with magnanimous love for everyone who has mistreated us. Help us, Father, with your powerful grace for surrendering to you all our feelings of anger or hate and replace those feelings with true charity as your Son demands from us. Amen.*

Friday

More the sins swarming, greater the graces abounding
(Scriptural Passages: 1 Tim. 1: 1-2, 12-14; Ps. 16; Lk. 6: 39-42)

The incredible Scriptural saying, 'More the sins swarming, greater the graces abounding' is a hysterical statement that has been hundred percent true with the principles of God's Kingdom, in which Jesus has officially accepted us. Starting from Peter and Mary Magdala, continuing in Saul who become Paul, upto this day, when millions of proven sinners like Augustine, ascended to heaven; all because of the abounding graces of the Triune God.

However, we should never misunderstand that if we continuously commit sins we can enjoy the abundant graces showered from on High. It is not that way the Spirit utters those amazing Scriptural words. They purely mean the immense compassion of God, enduring all humans' transgressions patiently and waiting for the sinners' return to him with their honest, humble and contrite of heart.

One example for such deed of God is Paul who deliberately, transparently, and humbly speaks today in his Letter about his sinfulness to one of his young disciple Timothy: *I was once a blasphemer and a persecutor and an arrogant man, but I have been mercifully treated because I acted out of ignorance in my unbelief. Indeed, the grace of our Lord has been abundant, along with the faith and love that are in Christ Jesus.*

This change or conversion of human heart, effected by the amazing grace of God, can be called as 'earthly resurrection' from the tomb of darkness and ugliness. If that resurrected person persists in climbing up the holy Mountain faithfully with Jesus, then that person, as Paul, would be dare enough to state: *I am grateful to him who has strengthened me, Christ Jesus our Lord, because he considered me trustworthy in appointing me to the ministry.*

If we go on ascending with Jesus fortunately, like that resurrected person, we will have the energy like that of the Psalmist to sing daily: *O Lord God! my allotted portion and my cup; you it is who hold fast my lot. I bless the Lord who counsels me; even in the night my heart exhorts me. I set the Lord ever before me; with him at my right hand I shall not be disturbed. You will show me the path to life, and fullness of joys in your presence.*

We, who are ascending with the resurrected Lord, would do one more amicable thing; and that is, as the Lord Jesus teaches in today's Gospel, we will be faithful disciple of Jesus, our Grand Teacher; being fully trained in his Spirit, we begin to live like our Teacher Jesus. Moreover, we won't behave like hypocrites, rather we would be forgiving and tolerating the sins our neighbors commit, as we acknowledge sincerely the heavy burden of blindfolded sinfulness we carry within ourselves.

Prayer: *Ever-forgiving God, Your Spirit calls us repeatedly to be converted interiorly to behold much deeper than our limitations and failures, to observe how you treat us, and to recognize the mercy you offer us despite our sins. We implore you to grant us your grace so that, being healed of our blindness, like Paul, you can use us to help others. Also, help us to lead a life of personal integrity, to recognize and face boldly all our life's challenges, and to learn from Jesus how to be sincere and compassionate teachers and guides like him for fellowhumans. Amen.*

Saturday

*From the heart filled with Jesus' words
we bear good and solid fruits*
(Scriptural Passages: 1 Tim. 1: 15-17; Ps. 113; Lk. 6: 43-49)

In today's Gospel passage Jesus makes use of two metaphors to point out how his disciples should lead a fruitful life in God's Kingdom. Contrasting the good fruits of good trees against the fruits of rotten trees, Jesus teaches us that *a good person out of the store of goodness in his heart produces good, but an evil person out of a store of evil produces evil.*

And by another metaphor of contrasting a solid and unshaken house that is deeply founded on rock with the shaky and destroyable house that is built on sandy ground, Jesus declares that his followers, who *calling him 'Lord, Lord', not only listen to his words, but also act on them, are like those who construct a house built on rock*; but his followers, who *call him 'Lord, Lord' and even listen to him but do not act according to his words, are the ones who built a house on the ground without a foundation. When the river burst against it, it collapsed at once and was completely destroyed.*

Apostle Paul was one among such countless humans, who built their life on the words of Jesus, the Rock. Today when we read the passage from his Letter, we are led to remember some of his peculiar commands to his readers. While he advises to imitate God as his beloved children (Eph. 5: 1), he gives his bold directive to *be imitators of me, as I am of Christ* (1 Cor. 11: 1). In today's Letter he explains brightly what element we should imitate from his life. Confessing his identity as 'the foremost sinner' he writes: *But for that reason I was mercifully treated, so that in me, as the foremost, Christ Jesus might display all his patience as an example for those who would come to believe in him for everlasting life.*

He places himself and his life before us as the captivating example, not only to give us his personal testimony about the merciful deeds of God in his life, as one trustworthy and deserving full acceptance; not only to share about his firm commitment to live according to God's words; but also more importantly to encourage us to identify ourselves as sinners, like him, to be fully aware of the merciful nature of God, who in Jesus is waiting for our return to him in order to grant us forgiveness and transformation as the Apostle relished.

Jesus and Paul stir us today and every day to lift up our hearts and voices all praises to God our Father as the Psalmist bids us: *Blessed be the name of the Lord both now and forever. High above all nations is the Lord; above the heavens is his glory. He raises up the lowly from the dust; from the dunghill he lifts up the poor.* This is how all the disciples who have been enriched and strengthened by Jesus who foretold: 'Whoever loves me will keep my word, and my Father will love him, and we will come to him'.

Prayer: *God of incredible patience, we sincerely admit our inability to save ourselves from our own foolishness, selfishness and sinfulness. And we too acknowledge our salvation is possible only by your unimaginable patience that manifested in Christ. Lord, you only can fill us with superabundance of love that can make us faithful and fruitful. Grant us therefore your marvelous love, Jesus' faith and Spirit's wisdom so that our entire life may bear good fruits of love like those of the good tree and whatever we build and develop in this world may be solid, valid and for eternal glory. Amen.*

WEEK - 24

Monday

*God's salvific plan is steered by ceaseless
communal prayer thru Christ*
(Scriptural Passages: 1 Tim. 2: 1-8; Ps. 28; Lk. 7: 1-10)

Through God's words and church's testimonies we know any religious prayer gets its full efficacy only by our stable faith and persistent hope in the goodness and power of the Lord. This is the truthful fact, declared by the Psalmist today. Lifting up his hands to God's Holy Place, he specifies his strong faith: *The Lord is my strength and my shield. In him my heart trusts, and I find help; and with my song I give him thanks.* He also expresses his relentless hope in the Lord's positive response to his prayer even before he encounters it: *Blessed be the Lord, for he has heard my prayer.*

In today's Gospel we hear the miraculous event in Jesus' life, spelling out what kind of effective prayer we should pray daily. The Gentile Centurion's prayer is an example of how a valuable qualityprayer should be. First, it is filled with strong faith in the healing power of Jesus; second, he makes petition to Jesus, not for his own self or friends belonging to his family or his culture; rather very stunningly, he prays for the health of his slave.

Also, the most important element of the Centurian's prayer, which even made Jesus astonished was: *Lord, do not trouble yourself, for I am not worthy to have you enter under my roof. Therefore, I did not consider myself worthy to come to you.* When Jesus heard these words, he was amazed at him and declared to his followers: *I tell you, not even in Israel have I found such faith." And the centurion's prayer was answered and his slave was healed.*

Paul in his Letter today brings home to us the importance of prayer in God's plan of salvation: From the beginning of creation, God willed all men and women to be saved and to know the truth and reach their destiny of eternal life. For such marvelous plan to be fulfilled, his Son Jesus gave himself as a ransom for all. In God's plan salvation becomes easier and more joyful, more respectful of human dignity, more attractive and effective for good, because salvation in Christ Jesus unites all men and women as members of one family with no discrimination whatsoever.

Moreover, in order to implement this heavenly plan of salvation successfully and effectively upto the final hours of the universe, Jesus chose many men and women, like Paul, as his coworkers in this plan of action. He wanted them to sacrifice their time, energy, comfort and even their very self for the sake of salvation of their fellowhumans.

On top of everything, following Jesus' teaching, Paul recommends his coworkers to pray wholeheartedly and ceaselessly to the Father for the salvation of themselves and of all humans. He also advises them to offer to God consistently their salvific heartbeats with supplications, prayers, petitions, and thanksgivings for the religious and social leaders and for all in authority.

Prayer: *God of saving Power and Might, we undoubtedly believe the fact that you expect us to join his team of prayer-angels. If at all you have permitted us to breathe some more years beyond our limitation, it is for accomplishing such duty of prayer. We pray today and daily in the words of the Apostle, that we may lead a quiet, tranquil and prayerful life in all devotion and dignity so that we may truly please you, our Savior, who wills every one of us to be saved and to come to knowledge of the truth about your Salvific Plan through Christ. Amen.*

Tuesday

We are born to attain to mature manhood,
to the full stature of Jesus
(Scriptural Passages: 1 Tim. 3: 1-13; Ps. 101; Lk. 7: 11-17)

From Acts of the Apostles and Letters of Paul, we know at the inception of the Church it was not considered as a formal institution or organization but it was esteemed as the 'Way' Christ proclaimed for the salvation of the entire humanity. Later on, as we hear from Paul, the fledgling church grew in the power and wisdom of the Spirit, some levels of formal leadership emerged in the church. The focus has turned to the roles of bishops, deacons, deaconesses and later on presbyters and widows. According to the signs of the time, the Spirit moved the church to develop herself as more organizational way of directing the community with efficient leaders, in the midst of so many social crises and evils, which threatened the Church.

However, Jesus never permitted in his kingdom anyone to hold such Godly power who was not fully filled with Jesus' Spirit and his Values. These Values are listed out by Paul today: *those leaders should be irreproachable, married only once, of even temper, self-controlled, modest, hospitable, not addicted to drink, a good manager of one's own household, holding fast to the divinely revealed faith with a clear conscience.*

Those values, expected from the Church leaders, have been continuously demanded by God from his human creatures. As today's responsorial Psalm proclaims, let us be fully convinced that God in Jesus always prefers to choose men and women as his coworkers in his kingdom only those, who personally pledge to him: *Lord, I will persevere in the way of integrity; I will walk with blameless heart; I will not set before my eyes any base thing; I will not slander my neighbor in secret; and I will not walk in this life as a person of haughty eyes and puffed up heart.*

All the Christian leadership-virtuous qualities, Paul enumerates today, have been found in Jesus, our Master. We can observe them in all his actions-ordinary or extraordinary, as we hear in today's Gospel. Despite his popularity among numerous crowd of followers, we see him attending to one single person who, as a widow, lost her son and was in tears. When *the Lord saw her, he was moved with pity for her and said to her, "Do not weep."* Touching the coffin he ordered the dead body of the widow's son saying: *Young man, I tell you, Arise.* The dead man sat up and began to speak. Jesus then entrusted the risen man to his mother and made her one of the happiest women ever lived in this world.

Thus Jesus testified to the crowd two goals, which he came to this world to fulfill: One, to attest to the healing presence of God the Father among his fellowhumans, who glorified God saying: "*God has visited his people.*" Two, to reveal his personal role entrusted by his Father. His compassionate deed stirred the crowd to exclaim: A *great prophet has arisen in our midst.*

Prayer: *Lord, our lamp, who lightens our darkness! The risen Lord reaches out to us with his compassion in all our lifesituations, be it a service-oriented status, or be it a leadership-execution or in any situation of grief and loss. When we are at our lowest and most vulnerable, his compassion is our support. Grant us through your Spirit the gift of undisputed hope and trust in Jesus as well as the generosity to be channels of compassion to our fellowhumans in their hour of need, to carry each other's burdens, as Jesus expects from us. Amen.*

Wednesday

*Children of wisdom pronounce judgement
only in Spirit and in Truth*
(Scriptural Passages: 1 Tim. 3: 14-16; Ps. 111; Lk. 7: 31-35)

In today's responsorial Psalm, we sang to our God: *How great are your works O Lord! You have made known to your people the power of your works, giving them the inheritance of the nations!*

What are those amazing works of God in our midst? God, choosing us as his favorite children, purified and liberated us from the darkness of sinful evils through his Son's Body and Blood and Words and he gathered us as the Church by Jesus' Spirit. Plus, the same God entrusted to us some unimaginable ministries and services for the whole world.

However, in order to make our human ministries be more valuable, effective and beneficial, God expects us to keep firmly in our heart the excellent identity of the Church we belong to. Paul in his Letter to Timothy today describes this excellent nature and function of our church. *Our church is the Church of the living God, his household or family which is the pillar and foundation of truth. And undeniably great is the mystery of devotion we encounter in this Church.* Its function is the tireless proclamation of the Christian message-*a message that is not a theory, but a mystery.*

To tell the truth, as every human family has its own history and story of its background and its exquisite traditional experiences, we the Catholic Church family has our own redemptive stories and God's deeds in our midst. But when we begin to proclaim such phenomenal church's mysteries, like humble and simple little children of God, those children outside of our Church, as the Lord Jesus talks about in today's Gospel, may be, out of prejudices or ignorance or arrogance, begin to disrespectfully criticize us. *'When we play the flute for them, but they won't dance; when we sing a dirge, they won't weep.*

This also is possible even among ourselves as church members. We divide ourselves from each other by race, by customs, by language, by opinions, by politics and even by the styles of faith, our reactions to the mysterious and magnanimous deeds of God can be, and it is true, blown out of proportion and distorted in our crazy mindset. As unfortunate result of such division, not most of the members of the church-family gain the true benefits from the mysteries we celebrate. Thus, some people can be so self-centered, that they are unable either to dance when someone plays a tune, or to mourn when someone sings a dirge. Jesus's Spirit warns us today to be aware of such devastating occurrences happen in our midst knowingly and unknowingly.

Prayer: *God of power and majesty! We admire incessantly how great your works are. In our household of church-family you make a remembrance of your abundant goodness. At the same time, Lord, we honestly admit we forget the eternal fact that every bit of our move and gain comes from your hands. You are the One who bestows food to those who fear you; you are forever mindful of your covenant and you have entrusted to us as one family the entire world as our inheritance. With contrite heart we request you to grant the spiritual stamina to keep you always in our mind and to interrelate ourselves with each other in true wisdom, love, and justice. Amen.*

Thursday

What sort of sinful person we may be, by
genuine faith we can be healed
(Scriptural Passages: 1 Tim. 4: 12-16; Ps. 111; Lk. 7: 36-50)

Psalmist declares in today's Psalm: *The fear of the LORD is the beginning of wisdom; prudent are all who live by it.* This 'fear of the Lord' is nothing but a conscious and even emotional outburst of humans towards God's rare-blended nature of both love and justice. If any human approaches him with such humble and sincere attitude of fear for receiving his just and compassionate support, God immediately grants their request.

That is what we hear from and through Jesus in today's Gospel. The event, narrated in the passage, is very much consoling to all of us who are burdened with our sins; but for others, who carry within them a fake self-righteous image, it would be disturbing and hurting. In that event we hear, a sinful woman in the city came to him, stood behind him at his feet weeping and began to bathe his feet with her tears. Then she wiped them with her hair, kissed them, and anointed them with the ointment. Appreciating her love and repentance, Jesus tells her personally 'your sins are forgiven'. But he forthrightly states in public to those who were prejudiced against his dealings with public sinners, like that woman: *I tell you, her many sins have been forgiven; hence, she has shown great love.* Besides, he prophetically said to all sinners in the world: *The one to whom little is forgiven, loves little.*

With this Godly inspiration, Paul includes today in his exhortation to his disciple Timothy a list of instructions about how the fear of the Lord with its endresult of wisdom should enlighten and enliven all his ministries. *Be diligent in these matters, be absorbed in them, so that your progress may be evident to everyone.* The quality of our Christian life is ultimately judged by the way we externally live our Christian calling, not just by what we say or the authority labels we attach to ourselves. What people can see outside of us, should also clearly reflect what is inside. We cannot, in any case, live a false life for very long.

We know in detail how Jesus lived and served as Servant of God in his short tenure of life. As we observe in the Gospel, Jesus can express stern and tough feeling against the self-righteous and proud, but towards the humble and repentant penitent he is tender and protective. Because Jesus based his entire life on God's generous initiative in loving and forgiving. We are all called by God in Jesus to minister to others as long as we live in this world.

According to God's words today, we are asked to minister towards one another, within the Gospel and authority of the church, with encouragement and esteem for the young, with tenderness for the repentant, with stern dedication to God's love in the case of the proud and the self-righteous. We should not judge others or allow ourselves to be judged merely on the matter of age, whether we are young or old, or on any other prejudicial stereotype for that matter – being a woman, handicapped, member of a religious or ethnic minority, sexual orientation or whatever.

Prayer: *Lord, you are faithful and just, reliable forever and ever. Your covenant and Gospel are always directing our lives. Amazingly your mercy endures forever. That is why Lord, despite our weakness and nastiness, you still love us and will not let us die but live forever proclaiming how good you are. Amen.*

Friday

Religious deeds are more for spiritual gain than material
(Scriptural Passages: 1 Tim. 6: 2-12; Ps. 49; Lk. 8: 1-3)

Though today's Gospel passage is too small to our eyes, it contains the most valuable message we need for Christian life. It tells us is that, only through certain experience of the living Jesus, touching our lives, healing us, forgiving us and transforming us, it is possible for us to follow him wherever he goes. We discover this truth, not only from the men and women, mentioned in today's Gospel, but also from most of the disciples who left everything and followed him.

Their following of Jesus was not just an emotional one that came out of incredible gratitude but it was the awful bond between Jesus and the disciples that went so much deeper. It was a bond created by the gift of grace and salvation. All these men and women had experienced a greater level of freedom from sin than they had ever experienced before. Grace changed their lives and, as a result, they were ready and willing to make Jesus the center of their lives.

These disciples were the littles ones, not only at the time of Jesus but also in the two thousand years old Church, to whom God has revealed the mysteries of the Kingdom. They were blessed to possess the Kingdom of heaven because they were poor in spirit. These holy men and women are a model of how human communities should be lived. They were serving Jesus in his tedious ministry of journeying from one town and village to another, preaching and proclaiming the good news of the Kingdom of God. In particular, as Luke brings to our notice several women provided necessary financial and other material helps for Jesus and his team out of their own resources.

Indeed, these selfless and serviceable holy men and women, as Paul underlines today, never made their religion as a means of material gain; rather, they felt in their life the joy of fulfillment in sacrificing all their savings and possessions toward Jesus' Gospel. They have pursued righteousness, devotion, faith, love, patience, and gentleness; competed well for the faith; and laid hold of eternal life, to which they were called.

In God's Kingdom there are always two roles to be performed by followers of Jesus for the Gospel ministry. Certainly these two roles are categorized not by gender. Among those holy men and women, some are chosen to be apostles whose function it is to proclaim the Gospel and establish the Kingdom by word and deed, by preaching and by the example of the communal and shared life they are leading. And others are called to play the role of disciples who are materially better off and who support the work of proclaiming the Gospel by providing for the material and other needs of the church. Both roles are complementary and both, taken together, form the evangelizing work of the Church. Let us follow the call of God and take any role he has offered us but do the best we can in that role until he takes us to his abode to reward us.

Prayer: *Lord, the Champion of the poor, your Son Jesus continues calling us to enlarge the territory of his mission of preaching and proclaiming the good news of God's Kingdom. He too expects us to lead a life of happiness in our mission to prove our deeper relationship with him. We also know this happiness will be doubled when we, who have enlarged our qualifications, talents, wealth and properties, must share them with those who have nothing left but their lives. Help us, Father, to walk with your Son daily in this perfectly-enlarged mission and receive your heavenly rewards. Amen.*

Saturday

Narrow-gate walk demands persistent perseverance with God's words
(Scriptural Passages: 1 Tim. 6: 13-16; Ps. 100; Lk. 8: 4-15)

Jesus has taught us about his Kingdom Values by his preaching and teaching, not only in plain words but also in parables. They contain many revelatory but mysterious truths he wanted to share with us. Regarding those parabolical teachings, Jesus gives us a shocking truth in today's Gospel, saying to his disciples: *Knowledge of the mysteries of the Kingdom of God has been granted to you; but to the rest, they are made known through parables so that they may look but not see, and hear but not understand.*

He considered every one of his disciples, chosen from his hearers, as his friends who belong to his inner circle. The revelatory truths, contained in his parables, as we hear in today's Gospel, are the sources of enlightening guidance to his disciples in their walk of life through his 'narrow gate' about which he commanded his loved ones belonging to his inner circle: *Enter through the narrow gate. For wide is the gate and broad is the road that leads to destruction, and many enter through it. But small is the gate and narrow the road that leads to life, and only a few find it.*

Walking through this narrow gate is not that easy, because we know by experience how our faith is put to the test and how we have to suffer for witnessing to God's words. It is about such difficult walking with, through and for those divine words, Jesus gave some valuable guidance in today's Gospel Parable of the Sower.

We may, as faithful disciples, start our journey through the narrow way listening attentively to God's words with good spirit, but as we proceed, the inner spirit of some of us, due to our carelessness, may become like the footpath where the valuable words of God are either trampled or sidestepped or the Devil comes and takes away from us; some more persons' inner spirit may be changed like rocky ground where the divine words may be received with joy but sooner they are withered due to dryness and lack of wetness, showered by the Spirit of Living Waters.

Furthermore, the inner spirit of so many among us may turn out to be like the field, filled with thorny bushes of anxieties and riches and pleasures of life, and as we go along, the divine words would be choked by and they fail to produce mature fruit. But there are some disciples in our midst, like saints and sages, preserving their inner spirit, as spiritually rich and fertile ground, not only begin their journey of discipleship willingly with generous and good heart but also persevere till the end bearing valid, solid and plentiful fruits.

The Spirit of God today moves Paul to advise us in his Letter that, if we want to be true disciples in Jesus' inner circle, we should lead a careful life as simple as possible and not fall prey to the evil trap of money; because he explains such horrible traps from the devil may entice us to drop away from Jesus' inner circle and lose our faithfulness to God. Adding to all this, Paul reminds us to persevere in our faithfulness to God and in our Christian righteousness, as we walk through the narrow path of the Gospel, is not in our ability; but any impossible is possible with us only because the God we serve is the blessed and only ruler, the King of kings and Lord of lords, who alone has immortality and dwells in unapproachable light.

Continuing the same view of how our fragile human life can become stronger and more faithful to God, the Psalmist invites us today to worship our Sovereign God joyfully day in and day out. He affirms that God made us; we belong to him; we are his people, his flock. God is the Lord, our Creator, our Shepherd. He is good and his kindness and faithfulness last forever with joyful singing, service, coming before him, thanksgiving, praise, and blessing.

Prayer: *God of love and majesty, thank you for letting us to be the friends of Jesus and offered us a place in his inner circle. We beg you to make us aware of our inner spirit's limitation tossed by worldly glamours and also make our interior life be open to your Spirit within us. Grant us your grace not to be choked by the anxieties and riches and pleasures of life; and help us to embrace the marvelously joyful promise of your divine words with a generous and good heart and bear good fruits for your glory and for universal salvation. Amen.*

WEEK - 25

Monday

More we spread our inner light, greater it will out-shine bright
(Scriptural Passages: Ezra 1:1-6; Ps. 126; Lk. 8:16-18)

Cyrus of Persia, we hear about in today's first reading, was a pagan king but he is esteemed by the historians as the figure more than a great man who founded an empire. Remembered as an ideal monarch, he was called the father of his people. While he conquered so many kingdoms with his brave and daring heroic capacities and enlarged his empire far and wide, he also maintained peace and tranquility in all those kingdoms, because of his great qualities such as tolerance and magnanimity.

Such a lovely person seemingly was very kind and respectful, whose spirit was stirred up by the Lord, as believers thought, not only to free the Israelites from captivity but also to rebuild the ruined Temple of Jerusalem. He also ordered those who resided already in that area to assist the freed Israelites in all possible means. In fact, all their neighbors aided them with silver vessels, with gold, with goods, with animals, and with valuable gifts, besides all that was freely offered.

The Israelites were very happy at such marvelous deeds of God done through king Cyprus. Today's Responsorial Psalm echoes the heartbeats of those God's children exclaiming the stunning greatness of God and expressing their gratitude toward him. They fully recognize and testify loudly that if we sow in tears of labors and hardships with faith, hope and love towards the Lord for the realization of our dreams, he will make us sing when we reap.

This is what the Lord Jesus expects his disciples to live each moment of our earthly life, which is intimidated by evils. As disciples of Jesus, through Baptism we have been entrusted with a shining light of the Spirit and we were exhorted by the priest we and our neighbors need to keep the flame burning brightly within us as the Lord stirred up the pagan king Cyrus.

Jesus says: *A lamp must go on a lampstand, to brighten the house.* We should in no way hide it within our inner sanctuary, rather it must be put outside and that too at a high level so that everyone of our neighbors see its shining. When it brightens their paths of life, not only they recognize God's greatness through the marvelous deeds of God in building up our Christian life but also they in turn spread the same light around them; and joining together we travel successfully with them toward our glorious destiny.

The most amazing grace Jesus has shared with us to make the same light of faith brightly shine outside of us through how we live, what we do and how we do it. According to his salvific plan, the light we possess may be a splendid instrument for our neighbors, especially for our family and community members to experience the same shining light.

Prayer: *God of greatness and goodness, kindly relight the flame of our baptism today. Help us to be aware of your presence stirring up in our hearts. We desire to run this world-race like your Kingdom's champions. May your light be always with us to guide us to eternal life in that kingdom. Grant us also your magnificent grace to carry that shining light into the nook and corner of the world we live in and share it with others, so that they too enter into your light and see brightly all your marvelous deeds and live until they reach heaven, where you live and reign for ever and ever. Amen.*

Tuesday

*Christian Macrofamily, bonded not by
natural blood but by Jesus' Blood*
(Scriptural Passages: Ezra 6:7-8, 12, 14-20; Lk. 8:19-21)

My dad was a full-fledged traditional Catholic. In the years of my childhood he would be carrying me over his shoulder whenever we travelled some miles to get public transport. In that walking whenever we crossed a Hindu temple or small shrine, he would tell me to close my eyes. His reason was my Catholic faith would be distorted or influenced by the devil living in those Hindu's sacred places. As my dad, almost all of us possess within us certain tribal heritage to judge any stranger as not child of God unless and until that person joins in our religious sect. But we hear from God in today's readings he never discriminates any humans because of their background of cast, creed and culture.

As any other race or tribe, Israelites found their God as true and genuine and surprisingly they assumed that he wanted a sacred place as his residence in this world.

His aim, according to them, was to meet with his people and devotees and share with them his revelatory truths. Besides, whenever they entered that Temple, as we hear in today's Responsorial Psalm, they were filled with sheer exultation and sang loudly: *Let us go rejoicing to the house of the Lord"!*

They indeed considered that temple as the symbol of their origin and destiny. Unfortunately when their inimical nations destroyed their temple and took them in exile, they were so much worried and hurt. They felt their religious and racial pride is broken to pieces. Such evil of being mistreated and trampled down happened in every age by cruel and hardheaded leaders. However, surprisingly in the narration we hear in today's first reading that, we find some pagan kings, like Cyrus and Darius and Artaxerxes, showed their humane character to respect the faith of their citizens and helped them to build up their Temple for their God. We admire at this sort of character and goodheartedness in those kings who should have certainly been God-fearing persons.

For God, the entire humanity is one and the same. All of them are his children. Humanity is nothing but God's macrofamily. In that family there is only one element, the fear of God, that divides the members into two groups. Those who are holding fear of God and live a life according to his will and those who have no fear of God and don't abide by his word. God's Son, therefore in today's Gospel, declares that, while millions of people are being framed or categorized as Gentiles or non-believers, God cherishes in his parental heart every human as his child and longs to see them leading a levelheaded life and acting with magnanimous spirit, like those pagan kings, in order to bring new hope and energy to his macrofamily.

288

The message implies that God's idea of family far surpasses our own natural expectations.

Since fear of God is the beginning of wisdom, God was always pleased by such good-willed people. And Jesus verifies this truth with his stunning words: *My mother and my brothers are those who hear the word of God and act on it.* How strange this would have seemed to those tribal people in which family blood ties and nationality-check-in were everything! According to Jesus' mindset, we, his disciples, should not demonstrate fidelity through buildings or sacrificial offerings or laws. Breathing and acting on the word of God is what should bind us to one another and makes us 'genuine family.'

Prayer: *We pray to you, Heavenly Father, grant us your light and strength, so that we can be released from the inner darkness of not understanding the mind of you and your Son, in our religious undertakings and accomplishments. Kindly enlighten and strengthen us to enter into your sacred command of showing our sincere neighborly affections for our fellowhumans with no prejudice whatsoever. Thus, as Jesus demands from us, please assist us to include ourselves in his macrofamily of brothers and sisters bonded, only by nothing but love. Amen.*

Wednesday

*Christian life begins with mercy, proceeds
thru mercy and ends in mercy*
(Scriptural Passages: Ezra 9: 5-9; Tobit 2-8; Lk. 9: 1-6)

We recited a beautiful prayer from the Book of Tobit, as our today's Meditative hymn, in which Tobit declares his overwhelming conviction that *God scourges us; but then shows his mercy; he casts us down to the depths of the nether* world; nonetheless, he lifts us up from the great abyss. His only expectation from us is such trust and hope in his mercy must be upheld by us always, especially even in our critical moments, when we are overwhelmed with physical and social sufferings of evil.

This astonishing faith of God's chosen ones has been testified invariably in every Book of Old Testament. From the book of Ezra today we hear one of those religious testimonies. After the Jews returned from Babylonic exile, in one of their evening sacrifices, Ezra, their religious leader, falling on his knees, cried out to God in the Temple that was renewed and dedicated. He humbly acknowledged that the cause for their past unfortunate exilic life of cruelty, captivity and disgrace was nothing but their own wicked deeds. But he also joyfully and gratefully attested they got back the deliverance and renewed life only because of God's astounding mercy.

With contrite and humble heart, Ezra deplored how his and his people's wicked deeds were heaped up above their heads and their guilt reaches up to heaven. Simultaneously with his upholding of the Jewish faith-filled conviction, we hear him crying out: *And now, but a short time ago, mercy came to us from the Lord, our God, who left us a remnant and gave us a stake in his holy place; thus our God has brightened our eyes and given us relief in our servitude.*

In today's Gospel, we see what an incredible way Master Jesus brought in to his Gospel-system of life the traditional heritage of above-mentioned faith in the enduring mercy of God. He orders and guides his coworkers in his Kingdom who are sent by him as preachers, teachers, and healers with a robust demand. He tells them to testify to his dream of God's Kingdom by their life of poverty, simplicity, no selfish strings-attached, and above all, total dependance and trust in the merciful

Fatherhood of God. It is this way Jesus expected his entire Church to proclaim to the whole humanity the Good News of God's uncompromising justice that is blended with enduring mercy.

Prayer: *God our Savior, we are certain if we follow your direction and your Son's command of fully depending on you alone, we would get a share of his power and authority as his Apostles were blessed with, to subdue all demons that disturb all of us in our family and community; he would also use us to heal the sick and join him in proclaiming his Gospel. Father, help us to follow your light and live your truth. Knowing well that in you we have been born again as sons and daughters of light, we may be your witnesses before all the world. Amen.*

Thursday

*Church is made of humans with renewed
and reshaped inner spirit*
(Scriptural Passages: Hag. 1:1-8; Ps. 149; Lk. 9:7-9)

God of Love manifested himself in Jesus as the source of salvation the dusty and vulnerable humans. This is how Jesus claimed his identity through a shocking statement as we hear in today's Gospel Acclamation. *I am the way and the truth and the life; no one comes to the Father except through me.* But in his time, so many of God's people and their leaders lived like King Herod, who, with his slovenly political and purely worldly attitude, as today's Gospel mentions, was puzzled to find another adversary was competing his leadership and power; but also he was curious to see and hear Jesus. We know, it was an idle curiosity that did not lead him to faith in the true identity of Christ. He was totally blind interiorly not to recognize

Jesus' background and greatness and only kept trying to see him but never believed him.

It is eternally true, as the Psalmist sings, *the Lord takes delight primarily in us, his people.* Namely, God will be pleased with all our external undertakings, religious offerings and practices we generate and organize, such as building sacred places, and conducting festive dancing and singing of his praises, if our inner spirit, first and foremost, is purified and rebuilt with truth, justice, mercy, and goodness. He ever shunned people, like Herod, who were whitewashed-sepulchers outside but unclean and darkened inside.

This is why, God told his chosen ones, as we read in today's first reading, not to rebuild his Temple. Through his Prophet, he highlighted his reason to his people: *The time has not yet come to rebuild the house of the Lord. Consider your ways!* He then explained in a figurative way that their life is full of injustice, pleasure-seeking, and never caring their neighbors. In addition he announced: *Go up into the hill country; bring timber, and build the house, that I may take pleasure in it and receive my glory, says the Lord.* Probably God wanted them to make reparation for their sins through climbing up the mountain, going through hardships and rebuild his Temple of glory.

Through God's bountiful grace and Jesus' Brokenbody and Bloodshed, we have been included as members of the Church as its living stones. Our church is indeed the Living Temple. God personally expects us to go on renovating and rebuilding his Church to become a holier, more stainless and brighter shining Abode for him. Most importantly he takes greatest pleasure and delights in our affiliation to the Church which is his Son's mystical Body and his own ever-living Abode in this universe.

As a matter of Biblical fact, we know how personal, meticulous, and cautious God has been to rebuild and enhance the demolished Jewish Temple. That Temple prefigures our Church, the Body of the risen Son, as the new temple not made by human hands and the defending wall of the New Jerusalem, built of living stones, shine with spiritual radiance and witness to your greatness in the sight of all nations.

Prayer: *Beloved Father, we confess the unmistakable truth, that despite we are your people, and members of Christ's Body, possessing within us many spiritual aspirations, we easily sink into materialism. Plus, we too are aware of the fact that if our religion is used for politics or for mere curiosity, it has nothing to do with authentic faith. What we truly seek is a faith that is practiced with love. Cast out from our hearts the darkness of sin and bring us to the light of Jesus Christ, who lives and reigns gloriously, not only with you and the Holy Spirit in heaven but also lives among us as the Way, the Truth and the Life in our earthly life, forever. Amen.*

Friday

Blessed are those who see redemptive power in their sufferings
(Scriptural Passages: Hag. 2:1-9; Ps. 43; Lk. 9:18-22)

The story of every human's life has many chapters and stages. God's eternal concern has been to make our life more joyful and more satisfactory in every stage of our life. God's first advice for living such life is recorded in today's first reading. Through Haggai, a Godly religious leader, God advises us to put our past memories to their proper use. Without dodging the issue of discouragement, Haggai asks the chosen people: *Who is left among you that saw this house in its former glory? How does it look to you now? Does it not seem like nothing in your eyes?* In other words, through him God advises us to hold the beautiful and positive memories about his goodness and graciousness, and his constant call to us to work at our holiness; plus he recommends not to forget his pledge to be with us always to pursuit of that call.

Our Creator's main instruction for our well-lived life is to go with its flow. No life remains monotonous for long. Sooner or later a severe trial strikes. We are well aware of this from human history and mainly in the social life of God's chosen people. For them, the entire existence came down in fiery ruins. The temple of "former glory" lay a heap of ashes and rubble. In that crisis through Haggai God repeated his valuable words of assurance: *Take courage! Wait for my mightiest action. One moment yet, a little while, and I will shake the heaven and the earth... and the treasuries of all nations will come in...Greater will be the future glory of this house.* By such enduring patience and trust in him we hear the stunning changes happening to your people: *The horrible exile purified the people, greatly reduced their material wealth and also greatly enhanced their spiritual ideals and hopes.*

In Jesus' first coming in our midst as our Master and Teacher, the world gladly recognized this new "moment" of God's magnanimous and stunning actions for our fulfilling life. Jesus made us fully understand God's Masterplan of our life's betterment and prosperous future. We hear him today in the Gospel foretelling about his passion and death. *The Son of Man must undergo great suffering, and be rejected by the elders, chief priests, and scribes, and be killed, and on the third day be raised.* He wanted us to learn from him how to destroy our death by our own physical death; to make every suffering and trial we face in this world as the effective tool and source for being renewed and becoming holier and worthier in front of our Creator. In sum, he expected us to be like him.

However, many of his Jesus' followers didn't have even the rudimentary knowledge about who he was. As the Gospel passage points out, Jesus was anxious to know how the people around him, especially his disciples thought of him. He could tolerate the ordinary people's wrong perception about him; but when he discovered his disciples still could not fully understand his unique personality and role he was doing, he was really upset. His question to Peter and his disciples was very crystal clear. *I ask you personally. Who do you say that I am?*

It is a fundamental question knocking at the door of every Christian; a question demanding from each one of us: adherence or denial; devotion or aloofness. If we boldly answer to him *Lord, you are both the Son of God and the Son of Man*, the Crucified Man and Resurrected Lord as well, then he turns toward us and tells us that we too have to keep going through the same Way of the Cross.

Hence, we need to respond to the loud and clear call of Jesus, inviting us to be his intimate friends and coworkers in his Vineyard, in the spirit of the Psalmist who sings today with his heartbeat of hope and fidelity. We should praise him, as our Savior and God; we should acknowledge him as our strength; we can boldly ask him to do justice and fight our fight in our battle with unjust and inhuman people. we also must plead with him to send forth his light and his fidelity, which certainly will lead us on and bring us to his Holy Mountain, his Dwelling place.

Prayer: *Faithful Father God, we promise you that we shall take every step of our Christian life in a very special friendly way. We love to grow in Jesus' amazing and chivalrous personality that contained along with his convictions about*

295

his heavenly connections, his readiness to embrace any kind of
sufferings or hardships or even death his human vulnerability and
weakness would bring to him. Help in this effort, dear Lord, to
hold firmly the truthful fact that out of the scorching trials of the
exile and the monotonous days afterwards, we hope to win our
eternal victory. Amen.

Saturday

*Living through Jesus' mysteries costs our
brokenbody and bloodshed*
(Scriptural Passages: Zec. 2:5-9, 14-
15a; Jer. 31: 10-13; Lk. 9: 43b-45)

We recite today the words of Jeremiah as the
Responsorial Psalm, In which we hear God pledging
that he who can scatter and punish us, will also gather
us together and guard us as a shepherd guards his flock;
he will turn our mourning into joy, and he will console
and gladden us after our sorrows. All Scriptures of world
religions present to us such numerous unthinkable and
unfathomable promises of God for the better and best life
of his human children.

We read extensively in the Bible about the eternal
truth that God our Creator, not only uttered his promises,
but also has never been tired of creating and recreating,
renewing and restoring his human creatures and their
systems. In today's first reading we discover this fact,
portrayed in the visions of the Prophet Zechariah. After
purifying the wickedness of Israel by scattering them in
exilic life, merciful God prophesized about his restoring
of not only his people but also the Temple-City Jerusalem
they had constructed. He says: *I am coming to dwell among*

you. I will be for Jerusalem an encircling wall of fire and I will be the glory in her midst. Many nations shall join themselves to me on that day, and they shall be my people.

However, for centuries, almost all of us born in this world, not understanding fully well all his promises and deeds, either avoided listening to him or ignored his words in our miseries. Even when he sent Jesus, the Word becoming flesh in order to confirm and clarify all his promises, humans who lived in Jesus' time couldn't recognize and accept his words.

Surprisingly, Jesus is quoted in today's Gospel saying: *While they were all amazed at his every deed, but they did not understand this saying.* All those promises Jesus voiced, and deeds he accomplished, couldn't be understood by his contemporaries as well as millions of people born till this day, because of the fulfillment of God's salvific plan. As stated by him, the event of the Son of Man being handed over to men was the salvific Masterplan of God and in order that that event to be fulfilled properly the death and resurrection of Jesus had to be hidden from humans.

As the New People of God, we, Christians, contend that the same marvelous restoring deeds God had done to us through his beloved Son Jesus. Keeping such a breathtaking restoration-work of God as the backdrop, God's Spirit advises us today, not to be too gloomy or pessimistic whenever we encounter both personal and social problems and afflictions in our day today life. Because, all the Prophets like Zechariah and the greatest Prophet Jesus and his Apostles emphasize, each sorrow of ours can be transformed into a reason for hope. But the saddest thing is we often think and behave like Jesus' disciples who failed to understand the amazing attitude of Jesus winning his victory over evils surmounting around him. He repeatedly reminded them and also tells us today that the hope for resurrection must also face the stern reality of death.

What about us when we face the reality of suffering and death in our own lives or the lives of those we love? We can often be confused at first; we hate to accept that suffering is most often inevitable but above all, very profitable and fruitful. Jesus asks us to look at how he endured all his trials and tribulations. It was only his unshakable vision and strong conviction about the glorious post-effects of his despicable earthly sufferings that sustained him through the bleakness of life, to reach his promised land.

Prayer: *God, our rock secure on which we build our life! We are so grateful that you never failed us and never left us in the darkness of blissful ignorance. Millions of disciples like us were enlightened by your Son and through his Spirit and his Church; and we are blessed with proper understanding of all your words of promises and instructions. And we daily try to express our sentiments of gratitude to you by participating in your Son's Eucharistic Sacrament. We beg of you, dear God! that those of our neighbors around the world, who are still moving in darkness and ignorance of your marvelous words and deeds, may be enlightened soon and join us in our pilgrimage to eternity. Amen.*

WEEK - 26

Monday

Acquiring the heart of a child is the secret
of entering God's Kingdom
(Scriptural Passages: Zec. 8:1-8; Pa. 102; Lk. 9: 46-50)

Today's Gospel Acclamation *'The Son of Man came to serve and to give his life as a ransom for many'* proclaims a clear portrayal of how Jesus brought God's salvation to humanity. He was so humble to be serve and so generous to sacrifice his life for fulfilling his Father's will of saving humanity. In nutshell we can say that Jesus of Nazareth behaved and ended his life like a true child of God. Jesus always echoed his Father's dream of filling his kingdom with childlike people. God the Father's magnificent dream about his human creatures, especially his chosen people, was to create their earthly dwelling as a new city like Jerusalem. That is what today's first reading talks about how God anxiously gave his promises to rebuild Jerusalem which was once demolished by enemies.

God promised through Zechariah: *I will return to Zion, and I will dwell within Jerusalem; Jerusalem shall be called the faithful city.* In that God-dwelling city, safety and security were well-guaranteed by the Lord. Even if this seemed impossible in the eyes of the remnant of this people, the Lord again promised, *I will rescue my people from foreign lands and I will bring them back to dwell within Jerusalem. They shall be my people, and I will be their God, with faithfulness and justice.* While his promises of rebuilding Temple and city being fulfilled, we find him rebuilding the Israelites' inner spirit that had been broken in exile, by instilling in them a childlike relentless hope and firm trust in his goodness and greatness.

This is why, as we hear today from the Psalmist, God's chosen ones were loudly singing: *The Lord will build up Zion again, and appear in all his glory. When he has regarded the prayer of the destitute, and not despised their prayer.* Also, they made pledge to God that, not only they will glorify his name, but also they would make sure that their children shall abide, and their posterity shall continue living in his presence.

Jesus, as his Father, had the same concern for the hectic future of his disciples in their journey with him in this world. He knew as weak and fragile humans, their inner spirit of pride and selfishness would be bothering them in coveting high positions in his kingdom as well as in preserving the supremacy of their religious identity. Hence as we hear him in today's Gospel, he shared with them a valuable and powerful strategy in tackling their future problems, namely 'be like little children and be humble to become great'.

And he also planned out his Salvific Kingdom project to be continuously implemented only by childlike humans. We observe this truth especially in today's Gospel event. We notice Jesus being surrounded by his grownup adults, who were not levelheaded and who, being filled with pride, craved and fought to covet 'number one' status in life. When he found out that among themselves they were arguing vehemently about which of them was the greatest, he took a child by his side and said: *Whoever receives this child in my name receives me, and whoever receives me receives the one who sent me.*

In the mind of Jesus children were the pledge of the future, the source of happiness and hope, and the teachers of true value and lasting treasures. Children truly take up where adults stop. While God planned to build up new heaven and new earth, so many grownups didn't accept nor recognize his Masterplan of salvation or perhaps accepted it with a yawn. On the contrary, childlike people received all that God in Jesus spoke to them about new life and get the most out of it. The story of such human dealings with God continue till this day. Those childlike people are indeed the living models for all of us in our dealings with God spiritually.

Prayer: *God, our protector, and sign of salvation, your humble and gentle Son Jesus has declared that whoever receives a little child in your name receives you, and you promised your kingdom to those who are like children. We sincerely pray let pride may not reign in our hearts, Father, rather may your mercy melt our proud hearts so that we may invest every bit of ours in trusting you and in going with the flow of your Masterplan of salvation we may long to see something new in life and chase for it to attain it with firm hope in your mercy and love. Amen.*

Tuesday

Let our church-life testify to the world that God is present with us
(Scriptural Passages: Zec. 8:20-23; Ps. 87; Lk. 9: 51-56)

Today's Gospel passage starts with the solemn introduction of Luke for his detailed portrayal of Jesus' climatic days at Jerusalem. It at once marks off all that to be followed as a winding-up of Jesus' earthly ministry, not just his passion, death and burial, even resurrection, but also his ascension. The expression, Luke uses, "that Jesus should be received up," is simply the rendering of one Greek word, which signifies "ascension." The beauty and excellence of this introduction consists in the words: *To face all those upcoming dark days and bright days of his life, Jesus resolutely determined to journey to Jerusalem, which was the place where his life's vision and mission would be fulfilled.*

Jesus was totally focused on hastening to his ultimate destination where he will be lifted up Heavenly Heights, through the means of being lifted up on the Cross. Therefore he never bothered about what was happening on the way, like the people of Samaria not welcoming him to go through their territory; and his disciples were angry and wanted him to call down fire from heaven to consume those people. But he rebuked only them for such revenging.

We know Jesus throughout his life repeated his dream of life frequently as: *The Son of Man came to serve and to give his life as a ransom for many.* He was resolute to realize that dream namely, he would not permit anything or anybody on any human and natural terms and motivations to obstruct and meddle with it. The one and only reason for such crazy holding on the part of Jesus was, he saw through his climatic life's happenings his fellowhumans would get a marvelous future. He was fully convinced that his Father's motif, to send him to encounter such dreadful earthly life, was nothing but the entire humanity to be saved and gathered together in his newly planned Jerusalem-the Spiritual Realm of God in this world.

He learned this fact from all the Prophets had spoken and read in the OT Scriptures. They had consistently highlighted God's Masterplan of restoring and rebuilding his New Jerusalem for which God himself chose the

Jewish Temple City Jerusalem as a model and prefigure. We hear about this again in today's first reading: The Lord of hosts says through Zechariah: *Many peoples, speaking different tongues and strong nations shall come to seek the Lord of hosts in Jerusalem and to implore the favor of the Lord, shouting out: Let us go with you, for we have heard that God is with you.*

With the Psalmist, those Jews who were religiously and spiritually committed to God and his Law, were treasuring their unique connection to Jerusalem with pride, and singing day in and day out: *Glorious things are said of you, O city of God that was founded on the holy mountains the Lord loved.* Indeed every nation, where Jews were residing, praised them because their birth place was Jerusalem where their God dwelt as his home.

Prayer: *Lord, our foundation and our refuge, this amazing prophecy of God indeed was fulfilled in the Church, which Jesus and his Apostles established on earth as the New City of God. They accomplished it through their bloodshed and death. We are so blessed that you permanently and actively is present among us and does marvelous deeds in many ways. One among them is the Eucharist we celebrate. Please help us to gain as much grace as possible by participating fittingly in the Eucharist so that as Jesus, we also may resolutely journey toward our heavenly home sweet home. Amen.*

Wednesday

We are no longer alien but citizens of heaven, our homeland
(Scriptural Passages: Neh. 2:1-8; Ps. 137; Lk. 9: 57-62)

It is historical and sociological fact that only those refugees and immigrants who left their native place because of some impending problems, know the greatness of their homeland, more than the natives who still reside in their native land. Today's first reading bring before us a God-fearing Jewish refugee, Nehemiah, who was presumably doing fine in Persia, with a very responsible position. But we find him longing to return to his homeland. For him, this was a particular longing to rebuild his dignity of living among his own people, rather than in exile as an alien.

In many Psalms such longings can be heard. Particularly in today's Responsorial Psalm we hear their loud nostalgic cries about their native Land. *By the streams of Babylon we sat and wept when we remembered Zion.* Though their jailors asked of those exiled Jews to sing for them the songs of Zion, they retorted: *How could we sing a song of the Lord in a foreign land? If I forget you, Jerusalem, may my right hand be forgotten!* They also verify their inner bitterness saying: *May my tongue cleave to my palate if I remember you not, if I place not Jerusalem ahead of my joy.*

More than all those arguments, Jesus shares with us today the eminent fact of our heavenly citizenship. The Spirit of Jesus through today's Gospel urges all of us, his disciples, to esteem the Kingdom of God, as our birthplace, where we were reborn and revived through Baptismal call of Jesus. As professed Christians and members of the Body of Christ, we hold dual citizenship: Besides our earthly citizenship, we have been granted a heavenly citizenship.

Echoing Jesus' heartbeats, his Apostles declare in their Scriptural writings, that we are citizens of heaven; it is pretty clear, we are expected to hold heavenly citizenship in the highest esteem; perhaps, just at face value, we can see that one is temporal and the other is eternal. These two worlds are only present realities and are intimately connected to our daily lives, not to mention the fact that what we do in this life has a significant and eternal impact on our next life in heaven.

Therefore, as Apostles held within them a firm hope of the future life of eternity, Jesus' Spirit makes us possess a stunning make-believe that we are currently 'seated with Christ in Heavenly places'. This means, we are to keep hold of the spiritual fact that we are in fact already in heaven with resurrected and ascended Christ at the right hand of God and now we have to see all earthly engagements from a heavenly vantagepoint.

In line with such expectation, we hear Jesus advising those who want to follow him. First, as Jesus had nowhere to rest his head, we, his disciples, should have no material ambition whatsoever for our future but just have him as our shelter and possession, so that, like Apostles we should claim: *I consider all things so much rubbish that I may gain Christ and be found in him.* Second, once we are on Jesus' side, we need to detach as much as possible from all our human relationships and things we possess because, *no one who sets a hand to the plow and looks to what was left behind is fit for the Kingdom of God.*

Discipleship in God's Kingdom is a marriage to Bridegroom Jesus, who demands from us as his lifepartner: *Unless you give up all you possess, you cannot be my disciple.* At the same time, he promises connecting us to our future life at Homeland: *If you leave everything to follow me, you will have it all returned a hundredfold and will inherit eternal life.*

Prayer: *God of eternal bliss, as you underline in OT that we are in this world for only a moment, visitors and strangers in the land as our ancestors were before us. Our days on earth are like a passing shadow, gone so soon without a trace. Our Christian hope dreams of our eternal life connected with your Son having been started already. Help us with your grace to live* *as true citizens of heaven, so that seeking first your kingdom and live according to your will, we may enjoy all our hearts thirst and hunger being fulfilled in this world and world to come. Amen*

Thursday

*Hush, let us walk rejoicing, for today is
the only day to glorify God*
(Scriptural Passages: Neh. 8:1-4, 5-6,
7-12; Ps. 19; Lk. 10: 1-12)

There's a sense of urgency in today's readings, calling on people to choose their basic purpose in life on the basis of God's Law, which is, as we recite with the Psalmist, perfect, refreshing the soul, trustworthy, and rejoicing the heart.

In today's OT reading we find Ezra reading out of the same Book of the Law, which the Lord prescribed for Israel. From daybreak until midday all God's people listened attentively to the book. At the end, he opened the scroll so that all the people might see it; and he blessed the Lord; and all the people, their hands raised high, answered: "Amen, amen!" Very religiously, he tried to prepare his people by renewing the covenant of Israel, based on God's written law. At that moment both the past and the future of people's relationship with their God was revisited and refreshed. Such ritualistic sharing of God's words brought fullness of joy and they celebrated it. As Ezra directed, they stopped crying in contrition but started rejoicing in the Lord with rich foods and drink sweet drinks; plus they allotted portions to those who had nothing prepared. All because that day was considered holy to the Lord.

Expounding the urgency of waiting for God's Coming, Jesus in the Gospel predicts that human hopes would soon be fulfilled in the reign of God. With this salvific mission in mind, Jesus chose his Apostles and countless disciples as those seventy two disciples, and sent them out to announce that God is near. He too expected them to depend only on God's power and not with any material possessions.

Facing choices in life for God and his values, we may look for more time to think and decide. Unfortunately Jesus highlighted frequently how risky, precarious and unpredictable our earthly life is; God will come any time we may not expect, like a thief breaking into our homes. We have experienced such times when we can have no time for reflection and we need to choose instantly, such as whether to accept open-heart surgery when we find that our arteries are blocked. We may have time later to correct mistakes, or on the contrary some decisions are fixed in stone, unchangeable. For the rest of life, possibly for eternity, we must live with the consequences.

The God of love did not intend his Law as a burden but as an authentic and joyful help to living. When Ezra saw the people in tears of repentance, he urged them in a friendly tone not to be gloomy; rather he urged joy in their everyday life, and proposed a faithful lifestyle to last into the future. The intention of Jesus also was the same when he sent his disciples to continue his apostolic mission. His main advice for those missionaries included: 1. *Have complete dependence on God. 2. Be cool, don't be afraid of being like lambs among wolves, because my power is within you. 3. Be a peace-lover and peacemaker. Wherever you go, whomever you meet wish them 'peace'. 4. Heal their sickness and all their maladies. 5. And then only proclaim to them: The Kingdom of God is at hand for you.*

Indeed by Baptism he has called all of us actively participate in his salvific mission within our lifesituations. Our world, our families, our personal ego, they all need God's salvation of justice, peace, love and joy. Whoever serves Christ in this way pleases God. Let us, then, make it our aim to work for peace and to strengthen one another. Let us do the best we can as Jesus demands from us.

Prayer: *Lord God, source and origin of our salvation, we sincerely thanking you for calling us to be Son's disciples and being sent into this world of darkness and tears, to bring joy to their hearts through preaching your words. Grant us to respond to your Word always 'Amen, Amen', as your children; thereby we may make our daily life proclaiming your glory and then one day we may praise you without ceasing in heaven. Amen.*

Friday

God's mighty deeds to us testify to his
Heart of justice and compassion
(Scriptural Passages: Bar. 1:15-22; Ps. 79; Lk. 10:13-16)

As Gospel Acclamation, we recite today a verse from Psalm 95: *If today you hear his voice, harden not your hearts.* Many may wonder what content God's Voice contains. From the Book of Baroch, today we hear a summarized version of the content of God's Voice, but only a part of it. It is about God's justice that cannot be compromised due to his amazing holiness. Moreover, it is echoed in the contrite prayer of God's people during their miserable lifesituation in the Babylonian captivity. They cried out: *Justice is with the Lord, our God; like our ancestors, we have sinned in the Lord's sight and disobeyed him. For we did not heed the voice of the Lord, our God, in all the words of the prophets whom he sent us, but each one of us went off after the devices of his own wicked heart, and did evil in the sight of the Lord.*

In today's Responsorial Psalm we hear about the second portion of the content of God's Voice. It is all about his extravagant mercy. And that too is exposed in the outcry of his people hurt and broken by their own sins. They begged him to show his immense mercy on them: *We have become the reproach of our neighbors, the scorn and derision of those around us. O Lord, how long? Will you be angry forever? Will your jealousy burn like fire? Remember not against us the iniquities of the past; may your compassion quickly come to us, for we are brought very low. For the glory of your Name, deliver us and pardon our sins for your name's sake.*

According to our Christian faith, we claim that Christ Jesus is the sumtotal of Gods' words of justice and mercy, uttered from the day of creation. As Prophet Isaiah foretold, *completing and shortening his words in righteousness, God will make a shortened word in the whole earth.* Church recognizes those prophetic words are pointing out to our Lord Jesus, who was the Word Incarnate, in whose life and saying, the volumes of God's words spoken over the centuries. Expounding those Prophetic words, Saint Cyprian wrote: *When the word of God, that is, our Lord Jesus Christ, came to all of us, bringing together the learned and the unlearned, and he made a compendium of his precepts, so that his pupils' memories should not be burdened by the heavenly teaching but might quickly learn what was necessary for a simple faith.*

Against this backdrop, we need to review Jesus' words of woes, which we hear in today's Gospel. We hear these woes from Jesus, when he was sending his disciples to proclaim to the people that he is the compendium of God's words of justice and mercy and that salvation for all will be possible only through him. He had already faced some horrible bitter experiences of rejection and aversion from people residing in certain cities of Palestine. With that hurt feeling, carried in his gentle and humble heart, he cautions as well as encourages his disciples saying, don't worry about the rejections you will face. Plus, he also empowers them with his foretelling: *Those people who do not receive you and your message of the Gospel are cursed in reality. Whoever listens to you listens to me. Whoever rejects you rejects me. And whoever rejects me rejects the one who sent me.*

Prayer: *God of goodness and graciousness, we gratefully acknowledge that Jesus is your Voice Incarnate through whom ultimately and totally you spoke to us. We too know well that he is not satisfied with only redeeming us with his blood, but also he continues to pray for us before you, his Father. Through his prayer we earnestly request you that just as you and your Son are one, so too we may be part of that same unity. Amen.*

Saturday

God expects those repent of their sins to turn ten times more to seek him
(Scriptural Passages: Bar. 4:5-12, 27-29; Ps. 69; Lk. 10:17-24)

Today's Gospel passage narrates a happiest event in the lives of both Jesus and his disciples. Due to the limited time and place, God designed for him to move around in this world, Jesus selected seventy two of his disciples and sent them to proclaim his Gospel in towns of Palestine, where he had not visited yet. Coming back from their evangelical trip, we find the faces of those disciples, glittering with joy and they were happily sharing with their

Master their breathtaking experiences they encountered during their ministry. They bragged about even the demons were subject to them because of Jesus' name.

Keeping his happiness within him, Jesus revealed to the disciples about his vision of the Archenemy Satan falling like lightening from the sky; and positively appreciated the heavenly power he offered to his disciples had been successfully utilized. Besides, in his level-headed style, he cautioned them not to rejoice because the spirits are subdued by them, but he exhorted them to rejoice more for their names were written in heaven.

At that very moment he rejoiced overwhelmingly in the Holy Spirit and imparted heartly to his disciples some remarkable insights regarding their participation in his Gospel ministry. First, he openly praised his heavenly Father for his benevolent act of revealing to them the hidden truths of his Kingdom that were exclusively handed over by the Father only to him. Through this praising prayer Jesus reminded them how heavenly Father and he love them and cherish them as one in their Trinitarian Family.

Second, Jesus underscored this privilege of knowing the mysteries of God is granted only to those followers of Jesus who live 'childlike life', like their Master. He was fully convinced and inebriated with the spirit of the Psalmist who sings: *"See, you lowly ones, and be glad; you who seek God, may your hearts revive! For the Lord hears the poor, and his own who are in bonds he spurns not.*

Third, he confirmed about the greatness of the honor God endowed his disciples saying: *Blessed are the eyes that see what you see.* We notice in human history thousands of well-educated and sophisticated persons such as prophets and kings, have been earnestly desiring to hear and see God's revelations, but their longing was not fulfilled;

unbelievably God has revealed those mysteries only to the childlike, humble and simple. The Spirit of God enables us to discover a perennial fact that while almost all his revelations start with exposing our human limitation, sinfulness and sloppiness, they always end with his positive encouraging hope-filled messages.

As we find in today's first reading, this truth, had been already foretold by God through Prophets, like Baruch. After feeling sorry about their sinful attitudes and actions against God, the Israelites were exhorted by God in a Fatherly way: 'Do not fear. Call out to me! Turn now ten times the more to seek me; for he who has brought disaster upon you will, in saving you, bring you back enduring joy.'

Prayer: *In a most astonishing way, God of truth and goodness, your Son Jesus, not only revealed the divine mysteries, but also being overwhelmed with love for us, he chose us as his disciples, empowered us with his strength and his fearlessness to join with you and him to fight against the evil force of Satan. We are indeed so pleased with you because through your Son we have been chosen to serve you. Lord, help us with your grace to be anointed by your Holy Spirit, so that we may take pride to act as your unprofitable but faithful servants in your Kingdom. Amen.*

WEEK - 27

Monday

Compassionate deeds are the hallmark of our Christian faith
(Scriptural Passages: Jonah. 1: 1–2:2,
11; Jonah 2: 3-8; Lk. 10: 25-37)

Our God, in whom we live, move and have our being, longs to see us to be and act in him, for him and cooperate with him in fulfilling his Masterplan of salvation of humanity. We know millions of men and women in world history ignoring and being careless to fulfill his longing and flying away from him.

One among them was Prophet Jonah, who, as we hear in today's first reading, was fleeing away from the Lord and his call to preach and convert the Gentiles. But we know our God's greatness and goodness. Once he chooses humans to be his cooperators, he would do maximum to get them through his successful deeds of goodness and battles against wickedness.

As Jonah was diverging away from God's call to go to Nineveh, God arranged, in his own method of implementing his holy 'conspiracy', an unprecedented event occurring in his travel. In order to save the entire crowd of passengers in the ship from the terrible storm, he was singled out by lots cast by them as the cause of God's anger. Realizing his mistake of being disobedient to God, he voluntarily accepted to be thrown out of the ship.

While Jonah was inside the belly of that fish, he cried out a heartrending but relentless hope-filled prayer to God, which we read today as Responsorial Psalm. The interesting thing about this prayer is that while Jonah cried out for God's help to deliver him from his unwanted situation staying in fish's belly, he envisioned firmly that God granted already his request.

Not only he expresses his desperate condition but also includes his persistent confidence in God's goodness. He prays: *Lord, you will rescue my life from the pit; out of my distress I called to the Lord, and he answered me; From the midst of the nether world I cried for help, and you heard my voice. I am banished from your sight! yet would I again look upon your holy temple. When my soul fainted within me, I remembered the Lord. My prayer reached you in your holy temple.* Amazingly, for such humble repentance and staunch resolve to surrender to the divine call, God rewarded Jonah by saving him from the belly of a large fish which had swallowed him and had kept him inside the belly for three days and nights.

There have been millions of God's little ones, who have surrendered to him and became his servants and joined with him in his salvific deeds. Either they fought as chivalrous soldiers in winning wars against any agents of evil or they served as good Samaritans, as one about whom we hear in today's Jesus' parable. They have brought healing and renewed life to those needy and vulnerable victims suffered by cruel and unjust agents of Satan.

We witness in Jesus' Parable that, while the hearts of faithful religious persons, such as the priest and the

Levite, were stony and merciless, only the heart of the socially-scorned Samaritan was moved with compassion. According to our Master, this Samaritan becomes the exemplar of living the great commandment of love. Through such mindblowing Parable, Jesus has portrayed that the main identification of being Christian consists not much in faithful observance of external religious practices, but more in being and doing compassionate deeds to those struggle in walking and crossing the 'bloody path' that is in-between heavenly Jerusalem and earthly Jericho.

Prayer: *Lord of immense compassion, we truly confess our sin of lacking compassion toward those whom we differ from and about whom we feel repugnant due to our baseless and wrong judgement. We promise now, not behaving like Jonah, the priest and the Levite, we shall be compassionate to those, ignored by us. We request your grace of love so that we may become their true neighbors as the good Samaritan, as Jesus points out today. Amen.*

Tuesday

*Let us possess the rare-blend Godliness
of just prayer and merciful acts*
(Scriptural Passages: Jon. 3:1-10; Ps. 130; Lk. 10: 38-42)

Before getting into pathway of God's Kingdom, we must be convincingly grasping in our mind that the God, who was introduced to us by Jesus, is simply a Life, which is a rare-blend of Justice and Mercy. The Psalmist today sings about such conviction, emerging from his heart. Out of the depths of sufferings and defilements, despite the fact that they are the outcome of the immeasurable justice, pronounced by the Lord, the Psalmist cries out to him: *"If you, O Lord, mark iniquities, who can stand?* Yet, knowing well his God is immensely compassionate, the Psalmist cries out to him: *Let Israel wait for the Lord, for with the Lord is kindness and with him is plenteous redemption And he will redeem Israel from all their iniquities.*

Regrettably not all humans, mostly well-educated and sophisticated persons, can tolerate and digest the concept of Rare-blend Life of God. Look at Prophet Jonah's life as we hear in this week. He was a man of action, not always prudent or praiseworthy action either. When told to preach repentance in Nineveh, his reaction was to head off westward, as far as possible from where he was told to go. This is because his choice of actions was not in contemplation of God's love. And even through him God proclaimed the same rare-blend of love-life for the Gentiles at Nineveh. Repentance meant more than the ritual acts of sackcloth and ashes. All persons were required to "turn from their evil ways." This means, God expected from the people both ritual and moral repentance.

Jesus never failed to insist and testify to the breathtaking the Rare-blend Life of God. The Gospel event today brings home to us the same rarity of God's personality. At first time when we hear the passage, it may seem unfair. In this Bethany event we see Martha working hard at preparing the meal for Jesus and his friends, whereas Mary is just sitting there at the feet of Jesus and listening to his admirable talk. So, Martha complains to Jesus. And interestingly, Jesus seemingly humbles Martha but praises Mary. But if we read the same passage again keenly, we would discover the classic Gospel truth, that both Martha and Mary were fulfilling each one's unique role at that moment. While Mary was listening to the life-giving words of Jesus, Martha was busy in observing the same living word of Jesus by her loving hospitality.

Jesus was not opposed in principle to people working hard in the service of others. Just before the narration of this Bethany event, Luke has included Jesus' Parable of Good Samaritan, which we heard yesterday. In that parable Jesus was praising neighborly compassion and active love. Even before that narration of the Parable, Luke brings home to us the mindsetup of Jesus and the manifesto of his Gospel, namely God's twofold command of love-wholehearted love of God and wholehearted love of neighbor. From this context we can understand that Jesus' Gospel cannot separate both the spirit of Mary and the spirit of Martha anytime or anywhere.

Christian spirituality is a rare-blend of divine and human love; of God's Word and human's deeds; of contemplation and action. As Thomas Merton would say, *our Christian life is nothing but contemplation in action or action in contemplation.* This is exactly what our Master instructs us today. Anything we perform in our love for other people as family and social actions and as religious practices, they have to be based on, started from, continued through and accomplished with God's living words.

Prayer: *Most of the time in life, God of justice and mercy, because of our impending problems in this world, we ask you like the Psalmist to listen to us and be attentive to our voice in supplication. On the contrary, Lord, you demand us first to listen to you as Mary sat at the feet of Jesus listening his words of enlightenment and guidance. And then surely you invite us to do all that we can in proclaiming your glory and work for your universal salvation-project. Pour out your Spirit within us to transform us into the stature of your Son as a humble servant in your Kingdom Amen.*

Wednesday

Quality-Prayer is communal, forgiving, above all, trust-bound
(Scriptural Passages: Jon. 4: 1-11; Ps. 86; Lk. 11: 1-4)

In today's Gospel we hear one of Jesus' disciples, requesting his Master on behalf of other disciples, including you and me: *Lord, teach us to pray.* Surely, as John the Baptist had instructed his disciples, all of us as good Catholics have been taught about prayer by our parents, catechists, and from spiritual authors. Today through the Scriptural readings the Spirit of Jesus reminds us and reshapes our approach to our daily habit of prayer.

First he wants us to stop thinking our prayer quota is over with participating in daily mass. All the Gospel writers portray Jesus usually spending intense time in contemplative prayer communing with his Father choosing some particular places and hours. Jesus was praying, as Paul would say, 'ceaselessly'. Jesus esteemed his interior spirit as the most relevant place for prayer and every one of his heartbeats was attuned to prayer.

Secondly he offers us a formula for how our prayer mode, style and content should be. This we fondly call 'the Lord's Prayer'. His main advice is, as his prayer's first half spells out, all our prayers should spring from a basic desire that our whole human world may be transformed, as our heavenly Father desires, and according his salvific Masterplan. And in the second half of the Lord's Prayer Jesus goes on to name some basic gifts and aids we really need: The forgiveness of our sins, sustenance for the day, and God's help when our faith is put to the test.

If we keenly go through Jesus' remarkable formula for our genuine prayer, we discover his only basic concern is we should never pray only for our individual welfare and heavenly reward. We must by all means include with ourselves the entire human family, be they strangers, unknown, inimical, and wicked. They too are God's children, our brothers and sisters. Besides, we should always pray with the heart of the Psalmist, who sings with his uncompromising heart of fidelity and faith in God's eternal mercy: *Lord, you are merciful and gracious. For you, O Lord, are good and forgiving, abounding in kindness to all who call upon you.*

Moreover, we should never feel like Prophet Jonah, about whom we hear in today's first reading. Though he knew in his heart that God is "merciful and gracious, slow to anger and rich in kindness", surprisingly he never wanted to include that good news in his preaching. The reason was, he was afraid that God might show mercy to those alleged 'wretched Gentiles' and include them into the super race of chosen ones. But God looked differently. He acted out accordingly and made the selfish Prophet realize his mistake and performed miraculous deeds of salvation for those pagans.

Many a time, while we beg God's mercy toward our sinfulness, we never care for the need of forgiveness in the life of our neighbors. This is why, the Lord included in his Prayer a splendid petition of forgiveness, not just for our sins but also for other fellowhumans. *Forgive us our sins as we forgive those who sin against us.* The great surprise here is not only God wanted him to forgive other people's sins but much more so he gets from us a pledge, as a requirement for our sins to be forgiven, that we in turn must forgive others.

Prayer: *Abba, Father in heaven, our hearts try to pray ceaselessly in accordance with the precious formula your Son has offered. In those prayerful heartbeats we always think only about our sins and their forgiveness from you. Deplorably many* *times we forget the sinfulness of other humans exactly the same or even less, as that of ours, must be included in our request for the merciful forgiveness of our own. Kindly grant us the merciful mindset to offer forgiveness for sinful fellowhumans, so that we may get your loving response to all our petitions we place before you. Amen.*

Thursday

Our prayer is granted, not because of our worthiness but by the merit of our persistence
(Scriptural Passages: Mal. 3: 13-20b; Ps. 1; Lk. 11: 5-13)

From the time of creation, till the Age of enlightenment, humans were in their entire life relating to God, the Supreme Being, allegedly out of fear and ignorance. But afterwards, continuing till this day, majority of them, being controlled by the power of knowledge, either denied or ignored the existence of God, lead this earthly life as any other creatures, except handling it little more sophisticatedly and philanthropically. They never bother about their beginning nor its end; plus accepting badness and goodness of humanity belonged to them by their nature; and blessings and curses are the intrinsic dimensions of their life.

In contrast, today's first reading tell us that our life's beginning and end are in the hands of God, the Creator; our life from its onset is closely connected to our end; if it is lived justly and rightly it will end in its extended glory, which will be rewarded by the Supreme Being. In order to get such glory at the end of our earthly life, we are supposed to be pleasing God in all our deeds which are being enlisted in God's Record Book of Life in heaven.

If such goal is to be fulfilled, God advises through his Prophet to lead our daily life in serving the Almighty with fear of the Lord and trust in him; with humility and innocence; and with no evils at all

Most of us, who meditate every day with God's words, are surely trying our best to please the Lord in serving him in Christian standard. However, as humans, due to our inborn ignorance, weakness, and limitation in understanding fully God and his marvelous plan and deeds in our life's past, present as well as future, we are prone to either defy him by our thoughts and words both interiorly and exteriorly.

This happens mostly at times when God seems to be silent, at distant and sometimes absent even. At those moments many of us may complain with anger, discouragement and frustration saying: 'It is vain to serve God. It is very sad to notice only the evildoers are prospering. And we ask ourselves: What do we profit by keeping his commandments and performing all our religious practices in his name?'

Perceiving this pitiable human plight, our God today confirms to us through his Prophet Malachi, that he is listening to us attentively those who fear and trust him; he has already written our names in his Book of Life; we are his own special possession; he will have compassion on us. And when he comes to take us to his home, we will clearly see the distinction between the just and the wicked; to the wicked he will appear like the blazing fire whereas to us who persevere in our fear and trust in him he will be like the sun of justice with its healing rays.

Such kind of prophetic promises God continuously has offered to us. We can hear so many God's people testifying to the fulfillment of God's promises in their life, as today the Psalmist sings: *Blessed are they who hope in the Lord.* Jesus reemphasizes in today's Gospel the validity of the same benevolent prophecies of his Father, saying: *Ask God, your heavenly Parent and your loving friend to fulfill your need and it will be given you; search for his heavenly treasures and you will find; knock at his pearls gate and the door will be opened for you.*

In this regard, Jesus also offers us through two small parables a valuable tip for getting what the Father has promised. Trusting in God's parental love and friendly concern, Jesus exhorts us we must keep on praying with persistence and perseverance. As the Spirit of God inspires us, let us first open our heart and mind to God in trust and perseverance as he continuously knocking at our inner heart.

Prayer: *Father of orphans, wealth of the poor, with the Psalmist we firmly believe that you watch over the way of the just, but the way of the wicked vanishes. You never judge us as human persons worthy or unworthy; because we, humans, are esteemed creations in your hands; rather, you look at only our ways of living. As your Son teaches us, you don't give to us what we request on the basis of our worthiness, but rather on the merit of our persistence. Kindly open our mind to see that the door to your blessings is always open to all who ask and who seek, so that we may live our life in such a way that others see your love at work in us with your abundant blessings, which also are available to everyone around us. Amen.*

Friday

By God's merciful justice we are both purified and glorified
(Scriptural Passages: Joel 1:13-15, 2:1-2; Ps. 9; Lk. 11: 15-26)

From the Bible we know there was a deep-rooted faith among the Israelites, who professed that 'ultimately

God will transform the universe for the better'. They indeed trusted that the transforming love of God would ultimately prevail. As the Psalmist sings today, the good-willed Israelites never ceased to hope that *God will judge the world with justice; he will judge the peoples with his truth.* And their Prophets, like Joel, whom we heard in today's first reading, acknowledged and ignited that faith.

While the chosen people were waiting for such God's transforming arrival, Jesus came and proclaimed God has already arrived and he was in their midst. In order to prove his contention, he performed many miracles, especially casting evil demons from his fellowhumans. Certainly Jesus was occasionally pointing out to the ultimate 'Big Bang' event to be occurred when he would come second time with his glory and power and restore the natural earthly environment as new heaven and new earth.

However his main thrust was, whenever people are liberated from the control of evil spirits, it is a sure sign that the loving power of Emmanuel, God with us, is at work. Hence he focused all his deeds and words to exhort his followers to be alert, to be cautious and to be vigilant for two kinds of his coming: First he would come to us individually, besides in his Sacraments, when we die. Second, he will come to us socially when the entire universe would meet the Big bang event.

As any parent, elder or friend, Jesus cautioned us, and continues to caution us whenever we take some new steps for life's bright future. Jesus, as our Prophetic Master does this in each step and moment of Christian life for achieving our ultimate destiny. This is why, at the end of today's Gospel passage he warns us, especially those of us who try our best to fulfill his Gospel demands, not to be complacent and to be fully satisfied with our accomplishments.

Only at this moment we should be very much cautious. We hear him say: *When the unclean spirit has gone out of a person, and finds our inner spirit swept and put in order, it goes and brings seven other spirits more evil than itself, and they enter and live there; and the last state of that person is worse than the first.* He simply underlines that we should persevere consistently in our religious practices, devotions and above all, in our performing good works to make our neighbors' life encounter God's salvation.

Prayer: *King of glory, Lord of power and might, your justice is unthinkably marvelous and exquisite. It exists in your essence because you are immensely holy and truthful. You can never tolerate in and around you any evil or falsehood. Hence you are as just as good. We beg you to share with us your wisdom and power through which we may surrender to your justice and always remain under your merciful shelter. Amen.*

Saturday

*Undoubtedly we are blessed only by hearing
and observing God's words*
(Scriptural Passages: Joel 4:12-21; Ps. 97; Lk. 11: 27-28)

Naturally so many men and women who followed Jesus and listened to his encouraging and inspiring words would have been thrilled and filled with overwhelming awe and joy. We hear in today's Gospel about one such Jesus' fan, crying out words of spontaneous praise for Mary, Jesus' Mother, who bore him in her womb and nursed him. But Jesus replied to that fan: *Rather, blessed are they who hear the word of God and keep it!* At the first time of reading of this tiny little passage, we may be surprised to hear such a response from our Master regarding his Mother.

But when we start reflecting deeper on his words, we would be genuinely loving and respecting Mother Mary more and more. In that process of reflecting about her whole life through God's words and Church Tradition, we know well that her heart, as the Psalmist sings, never ceased to rejoice in the Lord, esteeming him as her king. Together with God's creations-earth and heaven, she saw his glory and filled with the firm hope that the light of God will dawn for the just and the upright.

By the mystery-filled reply of Jesus, we should not misunderstand that he rejected the enthusiastic praise that ordinary woman dedicated to his Mother. Rather, it was the best compliment he could make of his own Mother. He acknowledged that Mary had been more blessed than any human born in this world, because she had been good and faithful in keeping the word of God. Her amazing humility and resignation to God's will ushered awesome historical events: A Redeemer would be born and live among us as God the Emmanuel, and through his death and resurrection he would bring salvation to the entire humanity. If Mary had not said to God's words, *behold the handmaid of the Lord, be it done to me according to your word*, neither Mary nor we would have been blessed by God.

Secondly, we find Jesus offering us, through this Gospel incident, the most phenomenal lesson regarding our Christian life. He instructs us that we must rethink our entire existence in the light of God's words, and evaluate our loyalty to family, country, race and even our church, if the Lord is to be our refuge and our stronghold. Our blessedness, namely the true and genuine happiness, which we would be enjoying in heaven after death, can be our possession even in this world, if we relate ourselves with each other on the basis of God's words.

This lesson is echoed in the preaching of Prophet Joel, as we hear in today's first reading. Through all of his rich symbolic expressions, Joel bids us to urgently rethink the heart and source of all our relationships. And he advises that the life of all the created universe must be re-consecrated to God in the valley of decision. In other words, the days offered to us by the Creator to breathe in this world are short but very precious because this is the period when we make very big decision to be or not to be with God and try to hear him keenly and obey his words sincerely.

In order to live according to this remarkable lesson, Jesus points out today to our Mother Mary, as our role model, she went beyond her own physical closeness to her Son Jesus in loving God in the neighbors. Let us listen again this day to God's word and act on it with new faith and confidence, and reach out with new bonds of love to our faith-family across the world, as close to us as brothers and sisters. As the Psalmist sings today, this is the only way any just woman or man can truly rejoice.

Prayer: *Lord, true light and source of all light, in order to be witnesses to the universal family of your kingdom, your Son wants us, being blessed by hearing and observing your words, uttered through him, to hold a close and personal family relationship with him, and also to be family with those beyond our immediate family relationships. We pray intently to bestow your power and wisdom to abide by his words, so that we may be more likely to set things right, both in our own lives and in the world around us that we encounter daily. Amen.*

WEEK - 28

Monday

Let us listen to Jesus in his words and encounter him in our life
(Scriptural Passages: Rom. 1: 1-7; Ps. 98; Lk. 11: 29-32)

In today's meditative Psalm the Spirit proclaims that our God has made known his Masterplan of salvation for us through his continuous wonderous deeds among us. He too revealed to us vividly his amazing justice, kindness and faithfulness. All those unimaginable but most necessary to our life have ultimately taken their climax in the words and life-deeds of our Master Jesus.

It is only through him we come to know the true goal of our life. Paul reminds us today in his Letter about that goal. According to his conviction, every one of us is called by God to be a saint by belonging to Jesus Christ. And therefore our every day's life is to be aimed at becoming holy as Jesus and attaining his perfection as best as we can.

Definitely, in that process most of us look at him for his guidance and direction at times when we face some occasions to make serious decisions. And therefore we wish fervently and pray incessantly that God would give us a sign from heaven as a way of making the right choices. Trusting his goodness and greatness we too promise him we would rely upon those signs to finalize our decisions to say either yes or no.

Surprisingly in today's Gospel our Master rebukes us for such behavior as he did to the crowd of people who certainly came to him for such signs in their life. He calls us 'an evil generation', plus he ascertains that no sign will be given to us. However, he never left us in that gloomy condition. He then offers a most remarkable advice: first he expects us to believe him fully as one wiser and greater than King Solomon, who is historically the wisest Leader. And amazingly, our Scriptures call Jesus 'the Wisdom'. And also Jesus states that God has already given to humanity many signs like Jonah. But he indicates that himself was the greatest sign among all the signs.

His main instruction is, in every decision we make for our life's betterment and happiness, we should look upto him as the sign and indicator, through the mysteries of his life, death and resurrection, and read and listen to his words of demands and admonitions. He assures us we will surely make the right and fruitful choices that would benefit not only to us personally but also to all our relatives and friends for attaining our ultimate goal of gaining his holiness and perfection. This is God's way and Jesus' way and should be also our way.

Prayer: *Lord God, our mighty king, as your Son points out today, we confess our inability that our ears hear but we don't listen, and our eyes are open, but we don't see your relationship and transactions with him. We too fail to absorb into our hearts Jesus' revelatory explanation about the reality of our life that needs the death of our selfishness for its newness and enhancement. Grant us your grace of enlivenment that moves* *us to conversion of our spirit and willingness to listen and follow Jesus' path of compassion and humility so that we may not only perceive the goodness all around us but also experience his resurrection both in this world and for the world to come. Amen.*

Tuesday

While we focus much on what is outside
God looks more into inside of us
(Scriptural Passages: Rom. 1: 16-25; Ps. 19; Lk. 11: 37-41)

The responsorial Psalm of today portrays very brightly how God's creations in the entire universe declare out-loudly the glory of their Creator God. And we, being the supreme handiworks of God, have to do the same but in a more distinct and sophisticated way. This is because we are endowed with power of God physically, intellectually and spiritually.

Agreeing with the Psalmist, Paul says, that ever since the creation of the world, God entrusted to all his creatures the role of proclaiming to us his invisible attributes of eternal power and divinity which can be easily understood and perceived by us. It is our Christian belief Jesus Christ is the Glory of God manifested among us. He also taught us as his remarkable Gospel through his life and teachings how outstandingly we can proclaim that glory in our earthly time of life.

It is this Gospel of Glory we must proclaim, as Paul writes, with no shame or any qualms. God's glory is nothing but the power of God for the salvation of every human who believes in the Gospel Jesus shared with us.

In the proclamation God's glory Paul reminds us to work for sharing the righteousness of God through our faith.

Lamentably, well-read humans, like the Pharisees of Jesus' time, although they knew God, they did not accord him glory as God or give him thanks. As we hear in today's Gospel, they became vain in their reasoning, and their senseless minds were darkened. As Jesus righty rebuked that,while claiming to be wise, they became fools. Instead of making God's glory to be shining in their inner sanctuary, they were keen on outer glory and praise of themselves and worshipping their self-image as god, they ignored any divine words coming out of the mouth of God, especially that of Jesus, God's Son.

We cannot be unwise as the Jesus' time-Pharisees, in paying attention only to take care of our outside appearance and not bothering about the unclean and disfigured status of our inner spirit. As the Scriptures teach us, we need the words of God, which are living and effective, in order to be able to discern our reflections and thoughts.

Prayer: *God of wisdom and truth, Jesus' Goodnews of correction today for us is that in our discipled life with him as your children, more than what we do cleaning outside of us as religious rituals and practices, we should concentrate first and foremost to clean our inner spirit, if it is filled with plunder and evil. Yes Father, he expects us not only to talk the talk but also to walk the walk with him. Kindly enliven our mind and heart not to become vain in our reasoning and darkening our mind but to follow his instruction carefully and faithfully and start to show the pure love of God on the outside in our daily life. Amen.*

Wednesday

True honor is that comes from God, not from humans
(Scriptural Passages: Rom. 2: 1-11; Ps. 62; Lk. 11: 42-46)

Expounding the how and why of God's judgement, Paul today plainly tells us that while God shows no partiality in his judgements, he indeed holds the power and right to judge and divide human creatures as the just and the wicked, according to the worthy status of each one's inner spirit.

The wicked are those who hold God's priceless kindness, forbearance, and patience in low esteem; those who possess stubbornness and impenitent heart. But the just are those who hold fear of God in their inner spirit and who uphold firmly at their every step of life that *all things work for good for those who love God, who are called according to his purpose.* With the spirit of the Psalmist, they ever maintain a strong faith in the *Lord as their rock and salvation, stronghold and refuge and never fail to sing hopefully 'Lord, you give back to everyone according to their works.' Thus, the soul of the just find true rest in him.*

Moreover, on the day of judgment, the just God will repay everyone according to their works: eternal life to the just ones but wrath and fury to those who selfishly disobey the truth and obey wickedness. While there will be glory, honor, and peace for everyone who does good, affliction and distress will come upon everyone who does evil.

All the above mentioned messages of Paul undoubtedly came from the Spirit of Jesus who was working in him through and through. The Apostle only echoes the heartbeats of the Lord about the Just Law of God as well as how many of us either abuse or misuse that sacred Law for their selfish motivations. We hear this truth loudly in today's Gospel. Jesus seems to be so vigorous in his message on God's Law that he spells them out with woes and curses against those who underrate or nullify the glorious Law of God.

Jesus insists on the value of freedom and the primacy of love, but also warns us against the excess of libertinism and individualism; against being torn between inner spirit and external actions, even in observing outward actions such as performing rituals and tithing and not doing justice and loving. He does not mount any campaign against the Jewish or Mosaic law. In fact, he observed it carefully and always had a sensible reason for departing from it.

The danger in concentrating and stressing obsessively the importance of outward performances lets humans to inventing more rules to control others; and by judging others' outward observances we begin to develop a fake self that brags we are holier than others. In this matter, Jesus adds a key word of advice: Before beginning to judge others we must first lift a finger to lighten their burden. Perhaps then we would become so aware of their good qualities, that negative attitudes would be silenced.

Jesus had a very different attitude to honor. He certainly did not seek it for himself and he did not encourage his disciples to seek honor for themselves. Rather than getting honor from others, he put the emphasis on giving honor or showing honor, the primary one to whom we give honor as being our God. Yes, Jesus assures us that in living in a way that brings honor to God, we will indeed receive honor from God, in the next life, if it is his will, even in this life.

Prayer: *Lord God, who are unchanging, always new, you have made Jesus Christ our wisdom and our virtue, our holiness and our freedom. It is your eternal will that we your children* *must honor your holy precepts, pronounced through Prophets and especially through Jesus. With you there is no favoritism. You want us to behave like you in our daily life with sincerity, integrity, in truth and honesty. Help us, Father, with your Spirit in purifying our inner self from deadly and sinful actions so that we may serve you the living God for ever. Amen.*

Thursday

At the end of the day God's mercy is our ultimate refuge
(Scriptural Passages: Rom. 3: 21-30; Ps. 130; Lk. 11: 47-54)

When one religious leader in the church retired from his position, out of his experience in life, he gave his final but splendid advice for his priests, saying: *Dear brother priests! Only one advice I give you. Kindly never stop holding on to your trust in the mercy of God!* All priests accepted warmly his advice because they knew from what background-mindset he was sharing his final message. They have heard his first exhortation as their leader about his motto: *You alone are the holy one.* They understood very well the intrinsic connection between the two speeches. They also knew well how during his amazing ministry among them he maintained his priestly holiness in the midst of his ups and downs, failures and successes. This is exactly what the Lord shares with us in today's scriptural passages.

Specifically, as King David sings in his Psalm, countless saints and sages almost in all ancient world religions, have been declaring endlessly that *with the Lord there is mercy, and fullness of redemption.* Their declaration is very personal, coming out of their daily experience in their contact with God. Such declaration gets its validity, sustainability and plausibility, as it has been frequent outcry to the Lord as they were in depth of sorrows, tears, darkened moments and inabilities. Their supplication includes their relentless holdings that *with God there is forgiveness; that with their own sinfulness they can never stand before his holy presence*; hence they continuously shout loud: *I trust in the Lord; my soul trusts in his word. My soul waits for the Lord.*

Jesus, as a faithful leader, tried his best to be the Way, the truth and the Life for us. He held it as his ultimate goal in this earthly life. Wherever he found double-dealings, life of lies and hardhearted attitude he was a fighter not simply tooth and nail, but in truth and fire. That is what we hear in today's Gospel. He throwed multiple and harsh woes on those boneheaded leaders and rebuked them for the misuse of their leadership-role. He said to them: *You have taken away the key of knowledge. You yourselves did not enter and you stopped those trying to enter.*

He also blamed them straightaway that instead being a path-walker of holiness, they behaved as devilish agents for paving and maintaining the wicked way that takes their people to perdition. While they were people-pleasers, preachers of material prosperity, and being show-case themselves, they made their people to observe only the outward and colorful practices of religion as an easy way of salvation. Jesus totally detested such cheapest and most shallow religion, which, according to him, makes the religion a bloody and distorted way that brings havoc to human generation being charged with their blood at the judgement seat of God.

In the light of testimonies of the Scriptures, Paul confirms today that there is no any connection between the gift of salvation promised and granted by God to humans with any of our meticulous observances of religious practices and regulations; rather, salvation is achieved only by our faith and trust in the mercy of God in Jesus Christ.

Prayer: *Almighty Father, and lavish Giver of the Light, so rich is your grace that you chose us through Jesus, your Word, to be children of light, and shared in us your likeness and image. This is all for us to bear the pledge of your glory. Unfortunately due to our downfall of sin, we have lost that original glory and now we are prone to be swathed in the darkness of erroneousness. With your grace, kindly help us to come out of this nightfall and being awakened we may stand always in the bright light of Jesus whom you sent us to be our truthful Way of eternal life. Amen.*

Friday

In the bright Son's Light we will rise up and ascend to Godly life
(Scriptural Passages: Rom. 4: 1-8; Ps. 32; Lk. 12: 1-7)

Through the responsorial Psalm today God's Spirit points out to us that if we want to be always happy persons, first we should become aware of all our sinful offenses against God and our neighbors, and at the same time, we must be fully conscious of God's continuous deals of mercy to us, humans. He forgives our sins; he never keeps in mind our transgressions; and therefore we should continuously acknowledge our guilt.

Whether we are still sinning or even we might have risen from sin-filled gloomy tomb, we should reckon plainly with the spirit of the Psalmist that we need to persevere in maintaining our relationship with the holy God; with the humble, contrite, and hopeful heart we should keep our hearts' beat of praying: *I turn to you, Lord, in time of trouble, and you fill me with the joy of salvation.*

Blessed is the one whose fault is taken away and whose sin is covered.

In our transaction with the God of Truth we should be cautiously just, pure and sincere of mind and heart and not as the Pharisees of Jesus' time against whom Jesus rebukes in today's Gospel as hypocrites, for their appearing to be one thing on the outside but being something else on the inside. When we honestly acknowledge our sins to God and never cover our guilts, we will be not only resurrected from the darkened tomb but also being gradually ascending to the High Above, where, according to our hope-filled faith, we are already with Jesus sitting at his righthand.

We too must be loyal to God like Abraham, about whom Paul refers in his today's Letter. Abraham, father of many peoples, observed the precepts of the Most High, and when tested, he was found loyal. Therefore, in Scriptures we read, God promised him with an oath that in his descendants the nations would be blessed. With Paul we need to agree the fact that, as the Scriptures declare the blessedness of the person to whom God credits righteousness apart from works, we are truly blessed because the Lord has forgiven our iniquities, even covered our sins out of his compassionate concern, and also he does not record our sins.

More than all the above-mentioned virtues, according to Jesus' words in the Gospel, if we want to be blessed and be always joyful and fearless, we should be fully depending on God and God alone. Jesus wants us not to be intimidated by Devil and his agents of evil. Because he states: *Are not five sparrows sold for two small coins? Yet not one of them has escaped the notice of God. Even the hairs of your head have all been counted. Do not be afraid. You are worth more than many sparrows.* This exhortation of Jesus on always-depending confidently and trustingly on God the Father, reminds the words of St. Teresa of Avila: 'Let nothing disturb you, Let nothing frighten you. All things are passing away: God never changes. Patience obtains all things. Whoever has God lacks nothing; God alone suffices.'

Prayer: *God, perfect light of the blessed, with our upright hearts we stand before you, being glad and rejoicing. This is because purely because of your immense benevolence of forgiving all our sinful, petty and pathetic doings which displease you. Father, bestow in us the confidence and trust which your Son had for you and expected us to maintain it. Then surely, possessing the divine gift of fear of God, we will rejoice in hope always even at the times of troubles. Amen.*

Saturday

We are saved only by love-based trust in God, not by law-based deeds
(Scriptural Passages: Rom. 4: 13, 16-18; Ps. 105; Lk. 12: 8-12)

Today's Psalm confirms that God remembers forever his covenant which he made binding for a thousand generations –which he entered into with Abraham. Because he remembered his holy word to his servant Abraham, he led forth his people with joy; with shouts of joy, his chosen ones.

Jesus reiterates in today's Gospel the same uncompromising eternal pronouncement of God about his way of bestowing the gift of salvation to us. Essentially he tells his disciples to have the unbending faith of Abraham. Going deeper into Jesus' words, we can spiritually feel how his Spirit endorses the fact of how our unique faith started from Abraham, continued through the faith-filled life of millions of God's children for centuries and ultimately elevated and enhanced by the replenished-faith life of Jesus Christ and his disciples.

Against this background, Jesus claims in the Gospel that everyone who acknowledges me before others the Son of Man will acknowledge before the angels of God. But whoever denies me before others will be denied before the angels of God. He too encourages his disciples with a significant promise that we should never be fretting over our weakness and limitation in accomplishing our Gospel-proclamation because the Holy Spirit, who comes through Father and the Son will teach us at that moment what we should communicate.

In today's first reading we hear from Paul highlighting God's benevolent deed done to Abraham, namely promising him that he and his descendants would inherit the world, and that way, elevating Abraham as our father in the faith. Why did he do that? The Scriptures underwrite, it is because Abraham *hoped against hope* that God, being immensely faithful and truthful, would do what he said. That amazing hope came out of his undisputed faith in the faithful God who made abundant promises to him and who is none other than One who grants life to the dead and brings into being what does not exist; plus, though Abraham didn't know how God would fulfill this deed of giving him descendants, while he and wife were old, but he relentlessly trusted him.

It is true that we cherish wholeheartedly and proclaim loudly the fact that "righteousness comes through faith". About this faith Paul underlines in one of his Letters that *only by the faith we profess in Jesus Christ we are made holy in God's sight. No observance of the law can achieve this.*

We should also keep in mind one important thing in the light of Jesus' Gospel, that our use of the term 'faith' does not exclude unbelievers; rather it includes uncircumcised heathens into the Body of Christ. Our Christian faith opens the door to any human with no discrimination whatsoever. This universal characteristic is a unique one for our Church. There may be opposition against such spirit of universalism of our faith, as Paul was challenged with.

The main reason for some church members to oppose it is surely certain kind of tribal fear threatening them by the new entrance of 'outsiders' or 'foreigners'. God, through his Son and his Apostles, teaches all of us to get rid of this fake fear and accept into our church everyone from any background because of the one basic fact that our universal church is built on God's amazing covenant that has been binding Jesus' disciples and followers together as one family for a thousand generations.

Prayer: *Father, Light and Salvation of all nations, as in earlier days of the Church, even now it wrestles in crucial ways with similar challenges of disunity, exclusiveness and discrimination. All in the name of our glorious and glowing faith. Pour out in us your spirit of justice and peace so that all of us, who gather around your altar of Bread and Word, may expand our vision of who constitutes our brothers and sisters and may our local churches become churches of many nations under One God in Jesus. Amen.*

WEEK - 29

Monday

In abundance of prosperity, only fools forget the Giver
(Scriptural Passages: Rom. 4: 20-
25; Lk. 1: 69-75; Lk. 12: 13-21)

Our Christian faith centers around a historical but
heavenly event, about which we recite today in Zechariah's
canticle as responsorial Psalm, that in Jesus' birth, we see
God himself coming to his people and setting them free;
he has raised up for us a mighty savior; And that was his
marvelous deed to fulfill the oath he swore to Abraham in
order to set us free from the hands of our enemies, so that
we can worship him without fear, holy and righteous in
his sight all the days of our life.

Every time we approach God to liberate us from
distress and discontentment, we hear him exhorting us
through his Son to pay more attention to the spiritual
possessions of love, peace and joy, truth and justice, than
to material and earthly possessions. He tells us the only
way to be freed of our psychological, emotional burdens is
to develop those inner resources, those spiritual strengths,

which enable us to appreciate his love for us and to trust in his care.

For this fruitful way of living, today Apostle Paul points out to us Abraham as a rolemodel, in whose life no distrust made him waver concerning God's promise, but he grew strong in his faith as he gave glory to him, being fully convinced that God was able to do what he had promised.

In this regard, we hear in today's Gospel Jesus cautioning us as he says: *Take care! Be on your guard against all kinds of greed; for one's life does not consist in the abundance of possessions,* such as riches, properties, human popularity and undisciplined possessiveness of other human beings. deliberately calls such covetous and greedy people as fools. In his Parable teaches us about how God the Father, though he is the Source of Prosperity, considers our earthly prosperity can divert us from the goal for which he shares his prosperity with us.

The rich man in this parable had such a bountiful harvest that he decided to tear down his old barns and build bigger ones so as to store the harvest. In that occasion of experiencing his overwhelming prosperity, he developed a hyper attitude and contentment and loses his sense of realizing the real fact that all his prosperity was bestowed by his Creator to whom he should be grateful; also he forgot that his life's enjoyment would shortly end and that all possessions he hoarded would never be used by him. Jesus expects us to clearly understand that material wealth is not evil in itself; but it has the ability to allure us, to trust and find full satisfaction in it, instead of trusting only God.

Prayer: *God of holiness and prosperity, help us to understand your Son's caution and instruction that growing rich either with wealth, friends, fame or success can become an* *obstacle to growing rich in your sight. And kindly enliven us through your Spirit so that, always keeping the proper priorities in life and to be purified in all of our desires, we can attend more and more to becoming spiritually rich toward you by using and availing the opportunities you offer us during our pilgrimage to our Home. Amen.*

Tuesday

The smart move in our life is
Faithfully doing our duties and hopefully
waiting for Jesus' coming
(Scriptural Passages: Rom. 5: 12-21; Ps. 40; Lk. 12: 35-38)

Generally, fragile humans as we are, we are threatened and frightened by the idea of dying and becoming a sort of being faded from the sight of our family and society and after a shortened memory we become a forgotten shadow. However, our Master Jesus, being fully aware of our disgraceful situation, enlivens us, as we hear in today's Gospel, through an encouraging positive message regarding our earthly life's end. Using an imagery, Jesus brings before us God, as Master, who returns back to his household from his long trip and us, as his vigilant servants, waiting patiently but actively fulfilling our household duties entrusted by him.

The most striking part of this parable is its twisted end. Jesus unexpectedly points out that when the Master returns, instead of the servants waiting on him, the Master waits on them. Jesus' words are: *The Master will gird himself, have them recline at table, and proceed to wait on them.* By that benevolent gesture, the Master makes them blessed. In fact, as unworthy servants, we don't deserve such excessive treatment; nevertheless, that is our God, introduced by Jesus. He is always a surprise giver and unthinkable lover. This is how Jesus wants us to rethink of the end of our life very positively and try to be faithful servants during the hectic time of far-away from our Home and until the Master comes to bless us with his heavenly reward us.

But so many of us, forgetting the above-mentioned Jesus' utterance about our life's goal, fail in fulfilling his direction to live our earthly life as that of God's faithful servants. This is why, as Paul writes in his Letter today, as when floodgates are opened, the water rushes forth with tremendous power carrying all before it, so with the spiritual power, which is God's grace won for us by Jesus Christ's death and resurrection. Paul proclaims: *Where sin increased, grace overflowed all the more, so that, as sin reigned in death, grace also might reign through justification for eternal life through Jesus Christ our Lord.*

With the Psalmist, we firmly believe that God's Son from the moment of his conception becoming human like us kept his entire earthly life as an *'one act of living sacrifice of obedience'* to do Father's will, offered to him and through that one righteous act, acquittal and life came to all of us and most of us were made righteous. We are crowded by so many modern technologies, scientific discoveries and cyber-magics. Undoubtedly modernity of our Age seems to be a wonderful thing. But, regrettably it may also making it difficult for us to be patient and wait obediently and hopefully for what is yet to come - something that will bring greater rewards than instant gratification can offer.

Prayer: *Loving and generous God, you are working with us and through us, and all around us, in helping us to grow into maturity in our relationship with you. We are very grateful also* for nurturing constantly and kindle our devotion through your Spirit. Please do help us to obey your Son's advice and act as your faithful servants in every lifesituation, praying ceaselessly to you wholeheartedly: Here I am, Lord; I come to do your will. Amen.

Wednesday

Raised by God from the death of sin, we
are steadily ascending to heaven
(Scriptural Passages: Rom. 6: 12-18; Ps. 124; Lk. 12: 39-48)

All of us have gone through our past life in which there was so much that needed to be done, including extra demands at home and at work. Such busy round of life, which can be very well spelt out by some old-fashioned British words, such as *life of 'Hurry-berry, Hurly-burly, and Hubbub*, drew us into a myriad of activities, all-important but all demanding more of our time and energy. So when we tried to do more, even our energies declined, and we experienced becoming seemingly like uprooted trees. But very surprisingly it is not so. Our life continues to be a 'hard job' as we grow older, to fulfill all our age-related issues, especially our ailing bodies, with some extra care and for many of us, carrying them singlehandedly.

It is at this juncture, our beloved God comes to our help with his sweetest messages and directions. Today he advises us through Paul to *present ourselves to God as raised from the dead to life and the parts of our mortal bodies to God as weapons for righteousness*. Namely, this God's call is nothing but changing our priorities and renewing of our inner strength through spiritual means.

In this context, today's Psalm also inspires that we need the totally trustful relation with God keeping our heartbeats sound loudly and perpetually: *Our help is in the name of the Lord.* Such confidence must be emerged, as the Psalmist states, from the belief in the evidential historical deeds God has performed, in our life, or in our family, or in our community. We should keep in mind firmly the fact that if God had not been with us, when hurdles and odds rose up against us, they would have swallowed us alive.

Jesus today cautions us in the Gospel, *You also must be prepared, for at an hour you do not expect, the Son of Man will come.*" We should not interpret this prophecy pointing out to our final days. But I feel honestly, it is mainly for our day-today life. He showers us his gifts of grace at his own time but at proper time so that we profit from all that we undergo or accomplish through this so-called 'hard job'. Constant attention to spiritual health is needed, not only because old tendencies tend to surface, but also because special moments of grace can come unexpectedly. For our God is always a surprise giver! We are directed to be fully and consciously engaged in the spiritual connections with God as his faithful and prudent servants and do the best and the most we can for his glory and for his plan of universal salvation.

Consequently as Jesus prophesied, not only we would be freed of his justice-demanding punishments but much more blessings will be poured on us. He will bestow us the fortune of possessing complete joy and true peace. This would happen even while we are either bedridden, homebound, disabled, or immovable. Let us never forget our Master's Golden Words specifically to us, his disciples: *Much will be required of us who have been entrusted with much, and still more will be demanded of us entrusted with more.*

Prayer: *Lord, our life and our salvation, thanks to you, as Paul underlines, that although we were once slaves of sin,* we started our baptismal journey with your Son and we have become obedient from the heart to the pattern of teaching, and freed from sin, we have become slaves of righteousness. But we are sorry we fail you occasionally in maintaining such marvelous righteousness. Grant us, Lord, the needed grace to liberate ourselves from the slavery of sin and get thereof all your heavenly rewards. Amen.

Thursday

Everything is rubbish, compared to the gain found in Christ
(Scriptural Passages: Rom. 6: 19-23; Ps. 1; Lk. 12: 49-53

There is a beautiful old saying: 'United We Stand, Divided We Fall'. Its core concept lies in working together with one heart and one mind in accomplishing victorious endeavors. But to work on their own instead of as a team, they are each doomed to fail and will all be defeated. Unfortunately if we go deeper into the human history, especially in our political and religious endeavors, we will be definitely convinced that humanity cannot exist in this world without divisions. First, because we are created that way being different externally from each other as different sizes of fingers.

Especially. as Paul underlines today, within our inner spirit, we are divided from each other due to the freedom we possess by choices we make, to become slaves either to God or to Satan. By birth all humans are born equally sharing the natural weakness to become slaves to sin of impurity and lawlessness, filled with hatred, discrimination and vengeance.

However, while so many continue to be as slaves to Satan, many among us, by our voluntary choice, turn out to be different from others by becoming slaves to God. Regarding those of us, who have become slaves to God, Paul says: *Now that you have been freed from sin and have become slaves of God, the benefit that you have leads to sanctification, and its end is eternal life. For the wages of sin is death, but the gift of God is eternal life in Christ Jesus our Lord.*

This sort of wars and conflicts are perennial and ageold from the day humans were created. There is an eternal war going on between the Good and the Bad; between God and Devil. Today's Psalm portrays a clear picture of the above-mentioned division among humans. According to him, humans are divided internally as the group of the just and the group of the wicked. The just are those who delight in the law of the Lord and meditate on his law day and night. The wicked are those who walk in sinful and impertinent way of life. Psalmist also confirms that while the group of the just will be like a tree planted near running water, which yields its fruit in due season, and whose leaves never fade, the wicked people will be like chaff which the wind drives away. Yes, the Lord watches over the way of the just, whereas the way of the wicked vanishes.

Jesus emphasizes today such division is not only possible but also it is for such war he came into this world to wage. *Do you think that I have come to establish peace on the earth? No, I tell you, but rather division.* Though division between good and evil is inevitable and justified by Jesus, he never tolerated with any division that comes out of our slavery to the devil. In our Scriptures we read the Spirit confirming that true peace and unity come only from God but all the fake, artificial and man-made divisions come from Satan who can never bear any genuine unity based on goodness.

Prayer: *God, the sovereign Lord of night and day, presenting to you consciously our physical, emotional, intellectual and social life as slaves to righteousness for sanctification; and as your Spirit today instructs us, we are ready to conform to our Baptismal submission through the power of Christ's Spirit to be freed from sin and have become more faithful slaves of God. This is because its end is eternal life. Help us, Father, in this journey to boldly differ from others whether they are blood-related or politically and even religiously related, and allow within us the blazing fire that Jesus has already set on, so that joining in his continuous war of justice, truth and love, we may inherit the glory of eternal life. Amen.*

Friday

*Our life reaches its peak of glory only by
sticking to God's commands*
(Scriptural Passages: Rom. 7: 18-25; Ps. 119; Lk. 12: 54-59

From the days of first human family, we know personally many kinds of wars and conflicts disturbing our own families and communities, and as a secondhand information we also see, hear and read in media every day about national wars, civil wars, cultural wars, and religious wars and so on. According to the sociologists, the main reasons for such struggles and clashes are three: Economic concerns exploded by globalization and technological progress; legitimate but more ambitious longing for autonomy and independence; and individualistic bloodthirst without proper guiding leadership.

In olden times, when there was a war, it was a human to human confrontation. Nowadays, it is much more terrifying, because a man in an office can push a button and kill millions of people and never see the human tragedy he has created. Worse still, twenty-four-seven, people bombard each other through social media. Yet, all want to live in a peaceful world and reach its pinnacle of success and glory. How is it possible?

St. Paul understood well about the roots of all those conflicts and wars. Today he cautions us with his exposition of his own personal earthly experiences. He was very sure any evil happening in his own life as well as in his relationships and contacts with his neighbors originates from the inner conflict existing in his inner self, namely a continuous conflict between the principle of good and the principle of evil. So he confesses to God and to us: *I do not do the good I want, but I do the evil I do not want. I discover the principle within me that when I want to do right, evil is at hand.*

Today Jesus offers some solution to our pitiable huma situation by his two questions: One, *You know how to interpret the appearance of the earth and the sky; why do you not know how to interpret the present time?* Two, *Why do you not judge for yourselves what is right?* Pointing out to the importance of our intellectual power in interpreting the appearance of the earth and the sky, he orders us forcefully to interpret with the same natural ability the present time namely the signs of the time.

Plus, he reminds us that we are endowed with the ability to know what is good and bad, and what is right and wrong. And when we sincerely judge ourselves, we will discover the solution for true way of peace. Jesus asks us to go deeper into all those human undertakings filled with only blood-thirsts and death-wishes and we will realize that the conflicts in the world have its origin in the conflict that goes on in every person's human heart.

Also the Psalmist today teaches us that in the midst of our life-conflicts the only solution for our peace and tranquility is to uphold the precepts of God as our standard. Listing out the reasons for his statement are that God's precepts are sources of wisdom and knowledge; they come out of the goodness and bountifulness of God. He also adds, he would never forget God's precepts, because it is through them God gives him life, moreover, they include God's merciful and compassionate promises.

Prayer: *Almighty Father, in the light your Spirit we learn today that it is true the internal conflict within us may take many forms. It can show itself through greed, hatred and thirst for power. Once we are able to resolve this inner conflict and enjoy inner peace, peace around us will be the natural result. Lord, we find it hard to heal ourselves. But we know who will help us to resolve our inner conflicts and give us inner peace. He is none other than your own beloved Son Jesus. As Paul, we cry: 'Miserable one that I am! Who will deliver me from this mortal body? Thanks be to God through Jesus Christ our Lord'. And we too beg you, kindly pave the way for us to reach Jesus in daylight and become the little ones to be able to understand and live by the mysteries of your kingdom. Amen.*

Saturday

Second chance in life is the most benevolent gift of God for us, sinners
(Scriptural Passages: Rom. 8: 1-11; Ps. 24; Lk. 13: 1-9)

The Parable of Fig Tree, narrated by Jesus today, is very applicable to the personal life of every one of us. In human history, such second chances or continuous escapes from others' malicious and unchristian conspiracies are certainly the outcome of the unthinkable compassionate deed of God in history.

The event, we hear in today's Gospel, is not anything new in one time and in one place occurring in this globe. We know how many times we have experienced and witnessed thousands of accidents and tragedies every day and in every corner of the world for centuries, such as natural disasters like tsunami, cyclone, tornado, earthquake, plagues, catastrophes in travelling by flight, train, car etc.; in which so many died; devastations by flash flood and drought. During these calamities, some die, others survive, like many of us, as of today.

God doesn't say we should not thank for such fortune. But he never encourages us to include in our prayer to him, as the Pharisee prayed, that we have been escaped from all these tragedies because of our good works or good qualities and so on. This is exactly our Master Jesus emphasizes today. He proclaims today first of all, that he never came here to judge us in any way; and secondly, that God our Father doesn't act impulsively or hastily in judging either to punish or to reward us. He sees not only what we have failed to do in the past but also what we are capable of doing in the future. He looks on us with generous and hopeful eyes. And that is the way we are to look at each other and, indeed, at every situation in life.

This is what today Paul underlines: *Now there is no condemnation for those who are in Christ Jesus. For the law of the spirit of life in Christ Jesus has freed you from the law of sin and death.* Most of us, especially who hold certain leadership at home or community, do not judge others, according to the Spirit Jesus has offered us but only according to our flesh. Paul defines 'Spirit' as life of love, purity and fidelity, while "flesh" for him indicates weakness and moral instability.

Jesus exhorts us therefore, we should never even think about such abominable doings; rather, he wants us to keep in mind how God and his Son deal with us in our wretched status of being born in sin and enslaved to the devil. And he expects us to uphold the factual truth, as Paul puts it today, that out of the mercy of God through his Son we have our new being and reborn in Godly Spirit and elevated from the fleshly lusts and horrors. We too have to keep in mind, God does not deny the importance and greatness of our human flesh. But we should be fully aware of its despicable behavior inducing us to live only in our flesh and disown all other heavenly things.

However, God instructs us, instead of setting our minds on the things of the flesh, we should set our minds on the things of the Spirit. And also we must associate with our fellowhumans and try our best to alleviate their remorse, tears, sufferings and other maladies by our Christian spirit of humility, simplicity, meekness, forgiving, patience, tolerance, and admirable hospitality with love and joy. Indeed, this is the one and only way, as the Psalmist sings, not only to receive blessings from the Lord and reward from the God who saves us; but much more to have a legitimate and ascertained entry to the House of God, and to see our God in Jesus face to face.

Prayer: *Our Father of mercies, and our God of all consolation, when we fall into the pit of sin and malice, you always offer a long rope to us and leave it to our choice to be used either to grab it, and climb up and escape from the pit, or to hang with it, as Judas, and die to hell. We earnestly pray that we make the best use of all the resources you bestow to us through Jesus and climb up from our fallen condition to a risen life which is more joyful, peaceful and fruitful in* your kingdom. Consequently, we may be privileged to stand in your holy place and receive a most incredible reward from you. And that is: to see your face forever, as our hearts are longing. Amen.

WEEK - 30

Monday

Only those, consumed by the Spirit, feel
'all humans are God's children'
(Scriptural Passages: Rom. 8: 12-17; Ps. 68; Lk. 13: 10-17)

Today's first reading shares with us how Paul esteemed the mysterious presence of God's spirit within humankind. The Holy Spirit reveals to our human spirit that we are children of God. Later he is even more pointed, *"The whole created world eagerly awaits the revelation of the children of God."* With all faith-filled disciples, like Saint Paul, we are absolutely convinced that, besides being liberated from the slavery of the sinful flesh, we are led by the Spirit of God to claim that we are the sons and daughters of God; because of the same Spirit we have been empowered to cry boldly to God as 'Abba, Father'.

This audacious holding has been implanted within us, as the Psalmist sings, because our God is the God of salvation, who, bears all our burdens. With his immense power he emerges as a victorious warrior in scattering all his enemies. Being the Father of orphans and defender of widows, God gives a home to the forsaken; he leads forth prisoners to prosperity. Therefore his just children as we are, we rejoice and exult before him all our days.

Moreover, as Jesus reveals in today's Gospel, our God, through his Son and his Spirit, takes an amazing engagement as his priority in his dealings with us. And that is, beyond the laws and regulations that may come in any form, our human life's salvific health, happiness and prosperity are to be attended to.

In Jesus' Gospel Kingdom, salvation for humans is a process, that starts in satisfying the physical needs of humanity and proceeds through the humans' proper development of emotionality and intellectuality, and ends with the climax of salvation as spiritual fullness in God. This is how Jesus looked and dealt with the needy people who were sick, crippled, physically and mentally and spiritually impaired.

In this context we find Jesus seeing one such needy woman while teaching in a synagogue one sabbath day, not minding about the traditional denial of 'any work to be done on the sabbath', he was instinctively drawn to help and to heal, whenever his help was needed. As one preacher underlines, 'as God rested on the Sabbath Day, on this particular sabbath, the creative, healing force within Jesus would not let him rest until this ailing woman was restored to what she was meant to be.'

Prayer: *Lord, we read in the Gospel the cure of the stooped woman was one small but first step of her salvation in the direction of the restored and transformed humanity. We are convinced that such an act of healing renews our faith that despite all our infirmities, you are still at work in us, to fulfil the growth of our stature as your children and as Jesus' disciples. Grant we pray, being transformed to the stature of Jesus, we may look anew with the eyes of faith upon all human beings as God's children and we* *may serve with love and wholistically heal them, especially those who are displaced, marginalized and disparaged. Amen.*

Tuesday

Despite our smallness, hope in God makes us taller and happier (Scriptural Passages: Rom. 8: 18-25; Ps. 126; Lk. 13: 18-21)

In today's Responsorial Psalm we are told how the captives of Zion, when they were liberated from their exilic life, were rejoicing by remembering and reflecting about the goodness of their God who had done marvelous deeds for them. Also they were constantly and hopefully praying for the restoration of their fortunes.

Paul's letter to the Romans today sparkles with the same magnificent hope for us, due to the tiny little and hidden grace of God, that was placed within us both in creation and redemption. He believes that every one of us, whether we are Christians or non-Christians or non-believers of God and religion, carry within us not only the physical seed of producing natural life, but also the seed or image or eternal life with God and as a result we are called to be children of God. Both kinds of seeds are hidden and they become the source of life only when those seeds grow, going through proper process.

Paul also confirms today that an amazing transformation has happened through Jesus Christ for all of humanity. Because of such miraculous impact from death and resurrection of Jesus, we know that all creation is groaning in labor pains and waiting with eager expectation the revelation of the children of God. Together with all creation, even we ourselves, who have the firstfruits of the Spirit, also groan within ourselves as we wait for adoption, the redemption of our bodies. We firmly believe, in such hope, we are saved.

Both parables of Jesus today in the Gospel, about the gardening of a man and the baking of a woman, have the same moral teaching. Each contrasts very small beginnings with the great effect they can have. The mustard seed grows large enough to shelter nesting birds. A tiny pinch of leaven ferments a basin full of flour. Jesus says that the kingdom of God works like that. In the eyes of God what starts very small can bring a rich result.

Besides, both parables talk about the 'fully grown'. When the mustard seed is fully grown, it becomes a large bush and consequently supports many people, like birds, who are like strangers and refugees, searching for their dwelling. And so with the whole batch of dough, when it is mixed with yeast, it becomes leaven which will then made into bread, food to support again the needy and hungry humans.

That is the way kingdom of God works within us and among us. Until we become grown and matured disciples, we can never understand the amazing style of God's deeds among us and through humans. What we hopefully groan for, is not visible but as we hear from Paul, still we should wait with endurance. We will be one day fully grown up, strengthened and enlightened by Jesus' Spirit and then, we will be ready to offer support to others who are struggling still in their development.

Prayer: *Father of compassion and God of all encouragement, you exhort us, through your Son, to be patient and to live our lives to the full by performing daily even small actions and initiatives, unnoticed by most people, and thus to help promote the kingdom of God spread extensively. As our experience says, our earthly life is always a difficult pathway to*

357

heaven, we hope for your help to end our groanings in your own time. And we too beg you to strengthen us in trying to accomplish many worthwhile things in our lives for your sake, and in striving to help others and to make this world a better place to live in for our future generation. Amen.

Wednesday

We can reach heaven, not by broad and cozy way, but by narrow path
(Scriptural Passages: Rom. 8: 26-30; Ps. 13; Lk. 13: 22-30)

We read in today's Gospel some asking Jesus, *Lord, will only a few people be saved?* He answered them in a subtle way: *Behold, some are last who will be first, and some are first who will be last.* He also clearly explained what his answer meant: Those who will be saved may seem to be in the eyes of the world as 'last'; but they will be first in the row of saved people, because *they are the ones who strive to enter through the narrow gate.*

Regarding this 'narrow-gate entering', Jesus has plainly educated us through his Sermon on the Mount and mainly by his very life and death. As said by him, the strategy of entering into heaven consists, not in merely calling God outwardly 'Lord, Lord' and even eat and drink in his company and seeing and hearing and allowing him to teach in their streets; but mainly *'doing the will of God willingly and sincerely'.*

And since these faithful people are already waiting obediently and faithfully for their Master's arrival, they would easily enter into the Master's House and stay with him; but others who failed their Master in fulfilling his will, will be only going on standing outside and knocking his House door for letting them in. But according to Jesus, they will hear from the Master, *'Depart from me, all you evildoers! I do not know where are you are from.'*

The most striking and frightening message Jesus uttered finally is: While strange people will come from the east and the west and from the north and the south and will recline at table in the Kingdom of God, those, who are already branded as 'God's chosen ones', will lamentably meet eternal suffering and death.

Through this message Jesus places a high value on human effort and fidelity. It is easy to enter through an ample, wide doorway. But to get through a narrow entrance, we need to be focused and pay attention to what we are doing. By this image, he teaches that staying on the way that leads to life involves struggle and effort. There is a striving involved, even though we are supported by the grace of God and the promptings of the Spirit.

However, it should not be an anxious striving, because the Lord wants us to succeed. Within this frame of reference, we should consider the teachings of Paul in his Letter. For him, not only the entire creation is groaning in labor and pains to be set free from slavery to sin and to share in the glorious freedom of the children of God, but also we ourselves, who have the firstfruits of the Holy Spirit, groan within ourselves for the redemption of our bodies. This groaning comes out of mainly our frustration and our insufficient strength to comply with the demand of Jesus, as we hear in today's Gospel.

In this critical situation, Paul consoles us and encourages us today with his beautiful reminder that the same Holy Spirit comes to the aid of our weakness, especially in our communing with God, he intercedes with inexpressible groanings. Such amazing interaction of God's Spirit within us is possible because there is an eternal truth, as Paul himself underlines today, that *all things work for good for those who love God, who are called according to his purpose.*

With this assurance of Paul, let the heart of each one of us must rise up every moment of our life in this world and not only confessing to God in Jesus with the Holy Spirit, as the Psalmist sings, *our hope, O Lord, is in your mercy,* but also singing with gladness and gratitude, for we have already received from him the salvation which we earnestly pleaded for.

Prayer: *God of power and might, we firmly believe your Spirit comes always to the aid of our weakness, especially in our inability to pray as we ought. We are also grateful to you to know that your Spirit himself intercedes on our behalf with inexpressible groanings. With the same Spirit we beg you earnestly to abide by your Son's direction in walking with him through the narrow gate that takes us to your House. We make this prayer with our firm belief and hope because of your assurance that we have been called and predestined by you to possess the glory of Christ after our death. Amen.*

Thursday

With the love of Christ we can face any challenge as it comes
(Scriptural Passages: Rom. 8: 31-39; Ps. 109; Lk. 13: 31-35)

Life in this world is very risky, precarious and win or fail-situation. In general, all of us invariably at one time or another are challenged by failure, anguish, distress, persecution, famine, nakedness, peril, or the sword. Unfortunately even for many among us their life is an unending fight.

We know from the Scriptures how Jesus, Mary's Son, went through his earthly life, which was miserable, contemptible and absurd. Today's Gospel events describe a bit about it. Most of his contemporary religious and political leaders, like Herod, behaved like foxes against him and tried to murder him as their prey. Also, Jesus demonstrates his inner hurting in his spirit because of his disappointments about his human brothers and sisters. He literally laments saying: *Jerusalem, Jerusalem, how many times I yearned to gather your children together as a hen gathers her brood under her wings, but you were unwilling!*

One surprising thing he deliberates in the midst of such critical situations is he never lost his hope-filled conviction that his life's finale would be glorious and victorious. First he says: I will continue to perform healings today and tomorrow, and on the third day I accomplish my purpose. And secondly he breathtakingly declares: *Many of you will be under the wrath of God's justice; and as for me, you will not see me until the time comes when you say, 'blessed is he who comes in the name of the Lord.'*

When we, as the disciples of Jesus, face such hurting situations in the bitter and darkened valley of tears, the Psalmist today teaches us how to relate ourselves to God. We are to always speak our thanks intently to the Lord, and never fail to praise him in the midst of the crowd for the valid reason that he stood with and for the poor people, in order to save them from those who would condemn their souls. Besides, in those critical situations the Psalmist wants us to imploring God earnestly, as he does, that God must come and save us; must deal kindly with us for his name's sake; and should help and rescue us in his generous mercy.

Likewise, Paul, a typical human as we are, becomes a rolemodel in how to handle those desperate situations. He was fully conscious of all the miserable and excruciating lifesituations, he encountered, which were worse than we experience. He portrays today his thought about them as he writes: *We are being slain all the day; we are looked upon as sheep to be slaughtered.* Nonetheless, at those moments, he was emboldened and survived victoriously and happily lived until his old age, not only by frequently raising some faith-filled questions within himself, but also by holding certain justifying convictions which we hear from him today.

He asks: "If God is for us, who can be against us? If God did not spare his own Son and gave him up to ignominious death for the salvation of humanity, how will he not also give us everything else along with him? Since we are his chosen ones, who will dare to condemn us? Since we are associated to Jesus by our wholehearted love, what evils such as death, spiritual or earthly powers and any other creatures will separate us from the love of Christ?" And the Apostle adds his most resourceful positive conviction, proclaiming: *'In all these evil situations we conquer overwhelmingly through God in Jesus who loved us.'*

Prayer: Father and Lord of all, *we do trust in your divine will. We trust in the plan you have laid out for us and try our best refusing to be influenced or intimidated by the foolishness and malice of the world. Your Son echoed your voice by uttering heartly that he wished to gather us together, as a mother hen gathering her brood under her wings and to show us the way to safety and salvation. Welcoming his help with open arms and open hearts, Father, we appeal to you to grant us courage and wisdom to keep our eyes on your Son's love and surrender ourselves to his promptings in all things and at all times. Amen.*

Friday

Mercy-steered deeds are preferred by Jesus to law-bound practices
(Scriptural Passages: Rom. 9: 1-5; Ps. 147; Lk. 14: 1-6)

The Psalmist today invites us to profess with him that our God immensely loves us with his whole heart and therefore we need to praise and glorify him wholeheartedly. He is a loving Parental God, who encloses us with his love as his children. We are reminded in that same Psalm that not only God promised Jewish people that he would never leave them; he would always love them with an everlasting love, but also he proved his faithful love by his marvelous deeds.

It is the Lord God who proclaimed his word to his people throughout their history. Thanks to him they were blessed with patriarchs, Commandments, worship, and the covenant. And even their ancestors endured exile and on their return the temple was rebuilt. Yet, there were many among them, especially their religious leaders, who stabbed their unique history by their faithless and self-centered life. Such miserable and pitiable grim situation existed in the time of Jesus too.

Disappointingly, those God's beloved people became so arrogant and hardheaded that when God sent his Son to them for sharing with them more power, wisdom, and joy, they ignored him and even threw him out of their territory and cooperated with their political and religious leaders to disown him and even plotted out his ignominious death. In that way while heathens got the salvific benefits of God, those chosen ones lost every blessings from him. They found fault with Jesus in so many of his wise sayings and compassionate deeds.

363

That sort of incident we hear in today's Gospel. On a Sabbath Day, Jesus healed a man who suffered from dropsy. By this merciful action of healing, he tried to declare the heavenly truth that compassion and mercy transcend the law and the fulfillment of it is the standard underlying the very purpose of the law. This was totally in contrast to the Pharisaic vision of subservience to it. Certainly those leaders' fake self and perverted pride were very much hurt. Instead of overcoming their sinful attitude they did a horrible act of conspiring against Jesus' life.

About these regrettable happenings Paul in today's second reading shares with us his heart-breaking sentiments. As he was arrested in Jerusalem and was taken to Rome for trial, he disclosed vividly in his Letter his steadfast faithfulness to his Master Jesus Christ as well as his true humanity that was craving for the salvific glory of his blood-plus-faith--related Jewish brethren. His love for his Jewish community was mixed with anguish. They were his kith and kins. However, he was very careful in maintaining sincerity of his words by underscoring that all his outward confession about his inward thoughts and aspirations were totally proven truthful by his inner conscience that was well-balanced and groomed by his Master's Spirit of Truth.

Prayer: *God of love and truth, all the promises, which you pronounced to the Israelites, were reiterated by our Master Jesus with us and confirmed by him that they would be fulfilled in our lives. Very sadly, we may read in the Scripture this most remarkable message of Jesus or hear it preached in homilies by our religious leaders; but sometimes though, as the ancient Israelites, we do not see or believe it. We are blinded. Hence Lord, kindly grant us the grace to make our path right in our intense listening and faithfully abiding by Jesus' message. Amen.*

Saturday

Higher our outer status, humbler must be our inner spirit
(Scriptural Passages: Rom. 11: 1-29; Ps. 94; Lk. 14: 1, 7-11)

From the self-profile that Paul presents today in his Letter, we observe clearly his mindset of being 'poor in inner spirit'. He admits he is of the least tribe of Benjamin; and we know from his life how because of his conversion in Lord Jesus, he changed himself from Saul to Paul-which means he labeled himself as 'little one'. It is from that self-liberated person we hear about an unfathomable revelatory truth on how sin was necessary for grace to be poured in. He brings his own people's sinfulness and wickedness as an occasion for God's merciful deed wrought in human history.

According to Paul, God, who can create everything out of nothing, demonstrated his enduring patience for his people by not rejecting them whom he foreknew for some greater purpose, namely, to make his Son born in their race. Also, God arranged in such a way that through his people's transgression, salvation should come to the Gentiles, so as to make them jealous. Another stunning mystery in God's dealing with Israelites was, as Paul considers, a hardening has come upon Israel in part, until the full number of the Gentiles comes in, and thus all Israel will be saved.

The above-mentioned and so many other revelatory truths came out of Paul because he was a person of humble and simple heart. As Jesus glorified such people, God shared all his truths about himself and his Son to the little one Paul. Today's Psalm plainly announces that only those upright of heart, like Paul, are instructed by the Lord in his Law and Truth. They will never be abandoned them because they are his inheritance. Above all, *when their foot is slipping, they hopefully persevere in God's mercy and indeed they experience that it sustains them.*

More than any other attitudes, the best one Jesus uniquely blessed with was, as he claimed: *I am meek and humble of heart.* The entire NT Books are crowded with this attribution to Jesus. Specifically we hear from Paul in one of his Letters that Jesus, even at the onset of his life, before he came into this world, *though he was in the form of God, he did not regard equality with God something to be grasped. Rather, he emptied himself, taking the form of a slave, coming in human likeness.*

It is from this humble and meek Jesus we hear today in the Gospel a parable that strikingly intrigues and exhorts us to follow his way of humility and meekness. He enforces his counsel by startling statement: *Everyone who exalts himself will be humbled, but the one who humbles himself will be exalted.* A common pursuit of all humans is, to covet promotion, prestige, particularly in election and selection. Jesus in his Gospel Parable warns us against such looking for celebrity and putting too high a value on titles, status and publicity.

Our human heart always crave for being 'number one' in the group or crowd; and the only winner in competing other contenders in debate or test. From our childhood we have been instilled a want or a must to be publicly known and admired, or to use ones wealth or status to become the privileged guest of honor. Jesus does not deny all this ambitious dream. He only advises us to sit in the lowest place *so that the host will say, My friend, come up higher, then you will be honored.* Interpreting these words, I heard one preacher saying: Jesus tells us: *'If you gravely seek esteem, at least go about it in a proper and civilized way'.*

Prayer: *God of all goodness and truth, today we hear the hardest advice of your Son demanding us to follow his footsteps of humility and meekness. While his demand seems to us impossible to be fulfilled, we also hear from him about the abundant outcome of its observance. As he turned out the humble way of living to be a pathway to glory, he expects us to be glorified by you, Father, because of our humility and meekness. Help us with your Spirit of Power to learn from your Son and abide by his instruction so that as he promised, our 'yoke will be easy and burden will be light'. Amen.*

WEEK - 31

---◆•◆---

Monday

Jesus is the Merciful and Truthful Way to attain our eternal Life
(Scriptural Passages: Rom. 11: 29-36; Ps. 69; Lk. 14: 12-14)

We are told by Jesus in today's Gospel Acclamation: *If you remain in my word, you will truly be my disciples, and you will know the truth.* What is his word that offers the truth? Jesus directly offers us the first answer to our question in today's Gospel passage. Through his powerful word he paves the right path for how to be blessed by God: *When you hold a banquet, invite the poor, the crippled, the lame, and the blind; blessed indeed will you be because of their inability to repay you.* He too adds his promising word of repaying us after our death. He says: *You will be repaid at the resurrection of the righteous.* Through this dynamic and practical teaching, he indicates that when we host, treat, and share happiness with the needy and the weak, we will be lavishly blessed in this world and the world to come.

Another one of his Spirit's astounding word today for us is found in the Letter of Paul, who proclaims: *The gifts and the call of God are irrevocable.* By this he means, any good things, we get in this world, are the gifts of God, which are based on his call to possessing better and greater heavenly ones than natural and material gifts. Paul also elucidates this revelatory word in his Letter: *Our disobedience, to his love command in thoughts and deeds, is simply the source of attaining God's mercy.* This merciful mindsetup of God, according to Paul, *is inscrutable, unsearchable based on the depth of the riches and wisdom and knowledge of God, from whom, and through whom and for whom are all things get their essence and existence.*

We should note well, this amazing message of Paul came out of his own profound personal experience of God's mercy. We know from Acts and from his own writings how he had persecuted God's people and how deeply he had sinned. At the same time we find how he received God's mercy as an amazing gift. Thus, we find both the unprecedented God's mercy toward him as well as the divine call for him to accomplish a new mission in God's Kingdom coming together in his life-experience.

It is such experience Jesus expected all of us, his disciples, to be shared through his Word. On our part, as God's Word demands from us, joining today and every day with his Psalmist, not only we need to praise and thank God for his mercy but also beg him to protect our continuous relationship to him, with his saving help. This is the definitive truth, which Jesus advises us to uphold and feel self-fulfilled.

Prayer: *Our compassionate Lord, since we have truly experienced your mercy in us, we too are called to be witnesses of your mercy to our fellowhumans. However, we find ourselves still far away from fulfilling your goal in our life. We request you, Lord, to offer your grace, that gratefully accepting your unconditional gift of love and mercy, we may discern and abide by your Son's clarion call for us to bear witness to it in our daily* *life so that in turn, not only our brothers and sisters receive your mercy, but also we personally find our true happiness. Amen.*

Tuesday

When God is all in all to us, our gifts
become all for all common good
(Scriptural Passages: Rom. 12: 5-16; Ps. 131; Lk. 14: 15-24)

As the most relevant introduction to the Parable of Jesus about the Great Feast, Luke shares with us today a proclamation of an unknown follower of Jesus: *Blessed is the one who will dine in the Kingdom of God.* This reminds us what John in his vision saw, heard, and wrote in his Book. The Spirit proclaims: *Blessed are those who have been called to the wedding feast of the Lamb. These words are true; they come from God.*

This unique Banquet-Proclamation is about three of the most stunning truths about God's creative and redemptive deeds of salvation for every human being: One, God esteems his every action toward us is a sort of banquet in which he shares with us his life of joy and peace in our human relationships of family and community; two, this banquet continues even after our death but it would be an unending, unbelievable, and classy one; three, a sad truth, namely though God invites warmly all humans for this banquet, many of us would be prone to reject him and his invitation.

Paul's invitation today echoes the same uncompromising and eternal invitation of God. The Apostle, in the prompting of God's Spirit, reminds us to hold on to and respond to God's unbelievable invitation to enjoy his Eternal banquet. Plus, he instructs us to rejoice always; he offers hope and love as the effective tools for truly rejoicing; and insists we should never fail in being charitable and hospitable to each other, especially when our neighbors become the needy as the requirements for entering into God's Banquet Chamber.

Speaking about how we humans deal with God's loving invitation, one of my mentors told me: There are three groups among us: First, there are people who reject God's invitation intentionally and purposefully; the second group of people accept his invitation unintentionally, with murmuring, and saying to God as a kind of routine yes but with no interest whatsoever; and third group of people who, like the saints, intentionally and willfully accept and do the right thing God wants us to do.

As the result of continuous rejection to God's invitation intentionally or unintentionally, there are many among us who experience themselves so many hurtful struggles, loss of peace and hope; and psychologically they feel empty, depressed and unfulfilled. If we sincerely stay at Jesus' feet and listen to him attentively, we will know in our life this happens far more often than we may at first think!

While the readings challenge us to live fully in Christ, the responsorial Psalm is very comforting and bringing peace of Christ to us. It makes us to focus on contentment, derived from God's words and from Jesus' intimate presence. The Psalmist encourages us to be still, to be at peace in our daily living. In this still and peaceful existence we will come to know, to discern our goal in life, our gifts specifically shared by God with us and then find an appropriate way in sharing these gifts with one another all for the common good of the community and more for the greater glory of God.

Prayer: *Lord God, our mighty King, help us to accept willfully and intentionally your challenging invitations through Jesus and his dear Apostle Paul, so that our actions and reactions in human relations may not make our life as well as others' life distasteful, laborious and burdensome but enhance every one's life very tasteful, fruitful and restful; enable us to contribute to the needs of our community members; to bless those who persecute us; to bless and not to curse them; to rejoice with those who rejoice, and to weep with those who weep. Amen.*

Wednesday

True love, detaching from peripheral,
attaches us to service and sacrifice
(Scriptural Passages: Rom. 13: 8-10; Ps. 112; Lk. 14: 25-33)

Through today's Responsorial Psalm God's Spirit declares that only those humans, who relates himself wholeheartedly to his needy neighbors, will be blessed by him. Their love-deeds towards other humans must primarily come out of the love and fear of the Lord. They must be first upright and sincere in greatly delighting in obeying his commandments; plus they too must try to be gracious and merciful and just in their relationship, especially with the needy.

To augment what the Psalmist reveals to us about the requirement of neighborly love for achieving significant blessedness from God, Apostle Paul shares with us a specific importance of that love in every Christian life. Daringly he states: We, as disciples of Jesus, *owe nothing to anyone, except to love one another.* It is because, as he adds, *for the one who loves another has fulfilled the law.* Basing his argument on Jesus' summing up of all the

Commandments, deliberated by God in the past, Paul underlines that we fulfill every command and precept we hear from Scriptures by loving our neighbors as ourselves and by doing no evil to them.

We hear from Jesus in today's Gospel making some love-based demands from his would-be disciples. Though his demands may seem to be very costly, very unrealistic, and very challenging, tough, severe, and stressful, if we dig deeper into his Gospel-value-system, we can perceive all of them are focused on the one and only new command of neighborly love he promulgated as his manifesto to all his disciples. According to him, any genuine heartfelt godly love-service requires from the doers to detach themselves from worldly and fleshly distractions as much as possible, in order to fully focus on the life of the beneficiaries and fulfill their needs in such a gracious way that they can feel the magnificent Love of God for them.

Indeed, Jesus cautions his followers, before they take the first step to say 'yes' to his call to discipleship, they should know fully its price tag and sit and count the cost they would be paying to those demands. Jesus' main reason for such demands is, that he prefers loyal and chivalrous warriors to work in his Kingdom.

Many of us are, like the early followers of Jesus, either quitters or losers. Some may have tried to back off from Jesus; but many others may have breached out of that childish behavior, after coming in contact with those, who have indeed counted the cost of discipleship of Christ; and though they might have found it too burdensome or too irksome or too much demanding, but they would have witnessed in their life a total submission to their Master's demands, and despite the struggles and hardships, they were truly swimming against the current as Jesus asked them. Thanks to them, we are what we are today.

Therefore let us today, more than speaking to Jesus in prayer, listen to him, who encourages every one of us.

Listening Prayer: Jesus says to us: *Yes, it is possible for you, my friends, to count the cost and live upto my demands: First, live closely and sincerely connected to God. Because nothing is impossible with God; secondly, love one another as I have loved you and taught you; come to me and learn from me; be meek and humble of heart; then my yoke would be easy and my burden would be light; thirdly, I want you to follow what my Apostle Paul writes in his Letter: In every step you take to fulfill my demands, keep only one thing in your mind, 'owe nothing to anyone, except to love one another'. As myself and my Father experience, my friend, you will come to know that love will always have a fragile character. It cannot be regulated or sustained by structures, rules, and committees. It can be only sustained by self-sacrifice.*

Let us all say: *Thank you Jesus. Amen.*

Thursday

*Our joy becomes true, only when our
Father rejoices in our renewal*
(Scriptural Passages: Rom. 14: 7-12; Ps. 27; Lk. 15: 1-10)

There are many innate godly elements in us because we were created by God as his image and in his likeness. One of them is the ability of judging rightly the difference between God's goodness and Satan's wickedness and living justly according to God's Spirit. But we misuse such outstanding ability in our dealings with our neighbors. We often criticize and hurt our neighbors by wrongly judging them by our biased attitude. Hence through Paul's Letter, today the Spirit asks us: *Why do you pass judgement on your brother?* This question simply echoes the eternal voice of Jesus who has advised us repeatedly to be just and careful in the matter of judging others.

Paul also writes that there is some incredible 'other side' of each one of us that is heavenly. *None of us lives for oneself, and no one dies for oneself. For if we live, we live for the Lord, and if we die, we die for the Lord; so then, whether we live or die, we are the Lord's.* Moreover, as Paul reminds us, every one of us is destined for that final day in which we shall all stand before the judgment seat of God and give an account of our personal self to God. In order to get reward and avoid punishment on that day, we should be more cautious in judging others.

And the most stunning reason to avoid judging and treating others wrongly and badly, is expressed by Jesus today: The same holy and just God we worship, has a melting heart of forgiving, seeking, and bringing back any so-called wicked and sinful person to his home; when he receives those strayed and lost persons, he behaves in a weird way like a Shepherd who lost and found one of his sheep and like a housewife who lost and found one of her coins. He rejoices overwhelmingly as Jesus portrays: *There will be more joy in heaven over one sinner who repents than over ninety-nine righteous people who have no need of repentance.*

Valid reason for this is: Every human person whom we judge wicked and sinful, is infinitely precious in God's eyes. To reach this high view of using our ability to judge needs the spirit of the Psalmist, as we hear him today, aching and yearning for dwelling in the House of the Lord, and that too, *all the days of our life.* We need also a hope-filled heart that gives us a surety to say daringly in front of God and our fellowhumans: 'I can be sure that I shall see the good things of the Lord in the land of the living'.

From all the words we hear from today's Scriptural words, we can list out some valid reasons why we should not judge others. First reason is: Only God has the exclusive right to judge humans; second, we often judge others either by their external actions and words or by our own wickedly cherished biased attitude, whereas God judges us according to our inner spirit; third, every human in God's eyes is precious as our Parental Possessor and Lover.

Prayer: *God of our life and destiny! We are informed through your Scriptures and human history, that so many of your agents have been holding their pious and devout affection towards you at all times, and thereof they were very cautious in judging their neighbors and even they are compelled to do so, they were very compassionate and just in their judgement. Gracious God, you know we are not worthy enough to be included in that amazing club of your beloved souls. Yet, trusting in your unending mercy, we beg you to help us, to think continuously that you are the only Judge who can judge your human creatures. And we too know you will never forget us; and as we wait for you hopefully that one day you will come and judge us, grant us to stand humble before you always but stand before this world with head on high to defeat Satan, the cruel liar. Amen.*

Friday

Only by the power of God's Spirit all
his stewards are empowered
(Scriptural Passages: Rom. 15: 14-21; Ps. 98; Lk. 16: 1-8)

In calling his faithful disciples, Jesus loved to use the word 'Stewards', next to 'friends'. In many of his teachings, especially in some of his parables, he used fondly this word. He was the one who said to his disciples: 'I don't call you servants but friends'. But in his teachings about his Second Coming as master of the House and about the final judgement of God in rewarding or punishing regarding his disciples' use of God's gifts, he expected his disciples in his Kingdom as faithful, good, wise, generous, kind, and surrendering stewards to their Master.

In continuation of such teachings, through a Gospel Parable today Jesus takes us back to the remarkable call of God to join him in his Kingdom through our Baptism; and he called us also to be responsible stewards to live and preach his Gospel, that brings salvation to the entire humanity. Though today's parable is a puzzling story, after digging deeper into biblical Treasure Hunt, we can find that using this undesirable Parable, Jesus admonishes us to be prudent enough in using our earthly resources for receiving blessed welcome into the heavenly blissful Home, more than making use of material good and riches, to get in this world a good name, popularity, and excellent status among our fellowhumans.

In striking link with the Gospel's message about our stewardship, we can find some valuable view point, in Apostle Paul's letter today. Though he does not use the term 'steward', that the stewardship-idea is certainly there. A steward is a manager of another person's goods. Among the qualities of a good steward, proposed in the Scriptures, the most important ones are faithfulness and honesty. Stewards must constantly remember that all the resources they oversee do not belong to them. Within this frame of reference, we hear Apostle Paul focusing entirely on what God has done in him.

He insists that he is a mere steward and that all the graceful treasures, pertaining to that call, came from God. Plus he admits his limitation: *I will not dare to speak of anything except what Christ has accomplished through me.* He lists out also some of those impressive projects Christ has accomplished through him: Preaching the Gospel and establishing churches, and writing some amazing letters for his converts. Plus, Paul does not forget to attribute all those accomplishments to the power of the Spirit of God.

Paul's main aim to speak about all his achievements as steward of the Lord is meant to instruct how all the disciples of Christ must be faithful, honest and good stewards in God's kingdom. He enforces the eternal truth that 'we are stewards; we cooperate with God in using the treasures that he gives us; we have nothing of our own to boast about. Therefore, we should spent prudently and faithfully everything we have entrusted with, be it grace, love, talents, vision and son, for God's glory and for the extension of his Kingdom in this world.'

Affirming the stewardship role of every child of God, today's Psalm inspires us to proclaim incessantly the saving power God has revealed to the nations. As a faithful steward of God, the Psalmist's proclamation about God includes the gleaming fact that through his wonderous deeds, God's right hand has won victory. With the same marvelous deeds God has revealed his justice, his kindness and faithfulness. It is only by such loud and constant proclamation of God's stewards, like the Psalmist, all the ends of the earth would see and encounter the salvation of our God.

Prayer: *God of immense Intelligence and Light, we are very much upset since the world misunderstands and mistreats most of your stewards as weaklings, because we behave like little ones exactly as your Son teaches us; therefore, Father, facilitate us to live and act as the children of light and as your prudent and genuine stewards in our words and deeds. We too plead with you to offer us enough understanding and sufficient strength to fulfill* *our call to Gospel's stewardship as our age, our gender, and our present lifesituation allow us to do. Amen.*

Saturday

*By sharing our earthly resources to the
poor we gain heavenly prosperity*
(Scriptural Passages: Rom. 16; Ps. 145; Lk. 16: 9-15)

After sharing greetings to all his coworkers in God's Kingdom, Paul closes his Letter today with the loud glorification to God whom he professes as the sole Sovereign Proprietor for everything happening in the universe, very specially in the realm of his Kingdom on earth. Finally enumerating and reminding his coworkers about the continuous divine interactions from dominion of God in all their salvific works, he writes: *Now to him who can strengthen you, to the only wise God, through Jesus Christ, be glory forever and ever.*

The Psalmist too inspires us to praise prayerfully in the same spirit of glorifying God's Name forever, explaining to us the reason for it. He says: *Great is the Lord and highly to be praised; his greatness is unsearchable.* He too motivates us to join with other whole humanity past and present, adding: *All generations praise his works and proclaim his might. They speak of the splendor of his glorious majesty and tell of his wondrous works.*

The core reason for giving such glorification to God is because, as we recited in Gospel acclamation, *Jesus Christ became poor although he was rich, so that by his poverty you might become rich.* Yes, that is indeed a marvelous deed Jesus did, when he, leaving from his rich mansion, came into this world and born poor, in order to share all his riches with us and become our Redeemer.

Paul was never stopped reflecting and contemplating in his Letters about this stunning but necessary act of God's Son for the sake of our salvation. Apostle praises Christ for his benevolent attitude of becoming poor. He writes: *Though he was in the form of God, he did not regard equality with God something to be grasped. Rather, he emptied himself.* All for what? So that we humans, poor in all factors of life, especially in spiritual dimension, might be enriched overwhelmingly.

It is this service of enriching 'poor' that Jesus talks about today and teaches how we should handle both earthly poverty and prosperity. Primarily, he rings a bell within us about our psychological problem of serving simultaneously two masters. *Either we hate one and love the other, or be devoted to one and despise the other.* The same problem can also exist in our spiritual life in serving concurrently God as well as money (mammon). The only possibility is, either we should hate one or love the other. In other words, as any intelligent human can understand and experience, God's prosperity is tremendously different from earthly prosperity. While the former is eternal and total fullness, the latter is transient, destructible and can turn out to be devilish.

Moreover, Jesus exhorts us that if we want to gain genuine and full prosperity from God, we must make friends for ourselves with dishonest wealth, so that when it fails, we will be welcomed into eternal dwellings. Specifically, he means that by all merciful deeds, such as almsgiving and selling every possession and share that earning with the poor, we can gain God's abundant prosperity more than anything else.

In addition, Jesus confirms that if we are trustworthy before God to make well use of the transient material things, entrusted to us individually, for fulfilling his plan of sharing with one another for their good, then God will be pleased very much and at the end of the day he will appreciate us saying: *'Well done, my good and faithful servant. Since you were faithful in small matters, I will give you great responsibilities. Come, share your master's joy.'*

Prayer: *Sovereign Lord, we sincerely thank you for sharing with us all your mercy, power, wisdom and the material things we need for our survival and success in this world. We regret and beg pardon for not using them according to your will and command, and many times making use of them for our own self-gratification. We also request you, as you satisfy the hungry with food from heaven, to enrich our poverty from your abundance, so that we help and enrich the poor in your name. Amen.*

WEEK - 32

———————◆———————

Monday

Guided by God's Wisdom, let our life
stride through everlasting Way
(Scriptural Passages: Wis. 1: 1-7; Ps. 139; Lk. 17: 1-6)

Today's Psalm stimulates us to be guided by the Lord in walking through everlasting way. Psalmist instructs also how to walk in everlasting way. The entire content of the lengthy Psalm, making us thrilled but pricking our hearts, forcing us feel humble and sincere, to accept our personal limitations, Also, it inspires us to recognize our Creator's immense wisdom, power, plus his ceaseless interactions with us, about us and in us.

Psalmist describes about God's breathtaking interactions with us in stating: He probes us and knows who we are and what we are; he is aware of when we sit and when we stand; he understands our thoughts from afar; even before a word we utter, he perceives the whole of it; behind and before us, he hems us in and rests his hand upon us. The Spirit also directs us through the Psalmist to perceive, not only our limited creatureliness, but much more, God's immanent presence in and around our life as guiding, watching and protecting Parent.

Furthermore, the Author of the Book of Wisdom today shares with us some practical guidelines in being guided by God during our striding earthly life in everlasting way. He advises us, it is achievable by *loving justice, by thinking of God in goodness, and by seeking him in integrity of heart.* The valid reason for such spiritual engagement is, according to the Author, because the wisdom of God does not dwell where there is deceit, evil and injustice. It is found only by those who don't test God; and he manifests himself only to those who do not disbelieve him.

God's Wisdom challenges us to seek justice and integrity. Conversely, this demand to high standards includes in it a sense of the grace available through the Spirit. We are not on our own in this task. For wisdom, as the Author claims, is a kindly Spirit of the Lord, who fills the world, is all embracing, and knows what we think, say, and do.

We know well enough about our weakness in walking with God through everlasting way. We stumble in obeying his commandments. In such pitiable situation we are encouraged by Jesus through his two remarkable statements we hear in the Gospel: One, we can rectify it, we can purify ourselves from such sins and rise up and walk by getting pardon from God with our contrite and humble heart; two, we are given the assurance that anybody whom we offend by our sins is demanded by God to forgive us seventy times seven, as a condition for getting forgiveness from him.

At the same time, when we become the reason for other people, especially his little ones, stumble and commit sin, Jesus threatens us by his tough and harsh words. We are indeed cursed by him with the worst punishment we would be indicted with: *It would be better for him if a millstone were put around his neck and he be thrown into the sea than for him to cause one of these little ones to sin.*

As God's Wisdom exhorts us, let us be convinced that all our wicked deeds, such as judging others wrongly, holding resentment and unforgiveness against others, and above all, becoming sources of scandal, are caused only by our personal separation from our holy God due to our twisted, perverted and undisciplined heart and mind.

Prayer: *All-powerful Good, we are aware of the eternal fact that you fill the entire universe with your Spirit of Wisdom; you are keen observer of our hearts; you fondly love justice and you are the one who rightly judge the earth and all humans. Hence, relentlessly holding your merciful hand, particularly in our sinful and darkened days, we call out to you. In all our steps and moments of life let your hand guide us, and let your right hand hold us fast and thereby we will boldly and consistently walk in your everlasting way. Amen.*

Tuesday

God's loving care is endlessly with his elect, the just ones
(Scriptural Passages: Wis. 2: 23-3: 9; Ps. 34; Lk. 17: 7-10)

As God is imperishable and eternal, the humans, who are created by him in his likeness and image should be also endowed with those characteristics. Therefore the Book of Wisdom today confirms that *God formed man to be imperishable; the image of his own nature he made them.* Unfortunately, because of the Devil's envy, sin entered into humans' life and so eternal death accompanied it.

Nonetheless, as the 'Wisdom' attests, the eternal death is experienced only by those, who are in devil's possession. And those just ones, who always persevere abiding in God and his Commands, are well protected in the hands of God. *By his mercy, he sees to it that death and its affliction and torment would not affect them; they would be in peace; even they are chastised a little, they shall be greatly blessed by the Creator because of their amazing hope full of immortality.*

These just ones are those who cherish perpetually in their inner spirit the hopeful prayer of the Psalmist we hear today. They are fully convinced what he sings: *The Lord has eyes for the just, and ears for their cry. The Lord confronts the evildoers, to destroy remembrance of them from the earth. The Lord is close to the brokenhearted; and those who are crushed in spirit he saves.*

This positive thought about humans energizes us to lead our earthly life, as a process of firmly upholding such inner sublime spirit, and witnessing to the divine justice, truth and love. And we will end our life by discovering the fullness of that image in Jesus Christ, when he returns in glory and welcomes us into the afterlife. Moreover, this belief enlivens us today, in this irreligious and secular environment, to hold a self-esteem that each of us, regardless of race, gender or wealth, has a trigger of godhead within us. It induces us to cherish and live upto the divine ideals of justice, love, peace and truth and even to be ready to sacrifice our lives for such ideals. We would very easily undergo any hardships and sufferings, as a magnificent tool for God, to test us like gold in the furnace, then to take us to our Home sweet Home.

In such breathtaking process of glowing life, Jesus advises us through his Gospel today, not to hold a wrong kind of pride, which pushes us to affirm our own fake ego and makes us do harm and disown others, who do not go in line with our attitude of 'my way is the only High way'. To take us to such 'paradigmshift', he brings to our inner sight, through his Parable, what would be happening when he arrives at the end of our life.

In the Parable Jesus narrates, when the Master, who returns home after his long journey, instead of ordering his servants to get up and prepare and serve him the food, surprisingly, he asks them to sit at table and he serves the food for them. After his narration, he shares with us the meaning of his Parable. When Jesus, the Master of the House, returns at the day of our life's end, we must behave faithfully like those servants, mentioned in the Parable, waiting for his arrival, not passively nor lazily, but performing actively our duties of love as he had already ordered us, and be ready to open the door immediately when he comes and knocks. Then, our Master Jesus, finding us vigilant at his arrival, will bless us; undoubtedly, we will be royally treated by our Master in the heavenly Banquet.

Through his Parable our Master also expects us to behave like humble and modest faithful servants. Hence he instructs us: *So should it be with you. When you have done all you have been commanded, say, 'We are unprofitable servants; we have done what we were obliged to do.'* In other words, no matter how well we live, no matter how much good we do, the grace of God remains a free gift. The good news is, we don't need our own merits in order to have God's favor. God loves us and shows his love by giving us his Son for oursake. In response to such amazing love, let us try to serve faithfully, by doing his will, as we discern it.

Prayer: *God of love and fidelity, we are truly blessed by keeping faithfully as your servants with the guidance of your Son's word. Through his word we are guaranteed by him to be loved*

*by him and by you, and particularly we will have the privilege
of having both of you in our inner sanctuary as our source of
power, wisdom, and love. Grant we pray that we may not lack
in our fidelity but wait and serve you until your Son arrives in
splendor to hand over to us his reward of blissful banquet as well
as eternal prosperity. Amen.*

Wednesday

*Discipled leaders never miss God, the
Alpha and Omega of their ID*
(Scriptural Passages: Wis. 6: 1-11; Ps. 82; Lk. 17: 11-19)

Today's Scriptural passages teach us how we should
esteem and handle our Christian leadership both in
religious and political dimensions of human life. The
passage from the Book of Wisdom, with good reason,
warns us to value and use our talents and high-leveled
lifesituations. It actually addresses those people, who
hold authority and power in the society; as a matter of
fact, all of us possess power over others in the area of our
giftedness or by reason of our position in family, society
or church, as parents or teachers or leaders, ordained or
elected; we may be also qualified as power-holders, if we
are well educated or eloquent speakers or physically strong
and impressive or morally sure of ourselves.

Given these elevating-backgrounds, disappointingly,
we may easily dominate others, take advantage of others
for our own selfish advancement and display unusual
forms of prejudice. This is because we often forget every
gift of leadership and authority flows from the Sovereign
Authority of God. Therefore the Book of Wisdom
admonishes us today: *For the Lord of all shows no partiality,*

nor does he fear greatness. Because he himself made the great as well as the small, and he provides for all alike; but for those in power a rigorous scrutiny impends.

Today's responsorial Psalm beautifully summarizes and firmly affirms the words we hear from the first reading. God's Spirit rouses the Psalmist soul to proclaim God's authoritative but always just and compassionate leadership. Praying for the afflicted weaklings in this world, we hear the Psalmist begging God: *Rise up, O God, bring judgment to the earth. Defend the lowly and the fatherless; render justice to the afflicted and the destitute. Rescue the lowly and the poor; from the hand of the wicked deliver them.*

World history attests, that from the start of humanity living in communities, there are good many of our fellowhumans obviously affected by lack of food, shelter and enough wealth and proper health and they are in utter poverty and lowliness. Such miserable human lifesituation exists by many causes, especially by the political and religious leaders and social elites who think wicked, speak about good ideas but do unjust things against poor and weaklings. For the sake of maintaining their superior identity they bring divisions among people by sowing the seed of hatred and violence.

When Jesus came to this world he found the same in his society. There was an open hostility between the Jews and the Samaritans. Stirred wrongly by their leaders, the Jews esteemed themselves the purest, the most righteous and the specially-chosen people of God; they held low esteem of the Samaritans, whom they judged as the most contaminated and the most sinful untouchables.

Jesus, who came to restore brotherhood, unity, and love in humanity, wanted as much as he could, to lessen this pathetic antagonism between two neighborly cultures. Through his own behavior and his miraculous deeds, specially for the downtrodden, marginalized, and outcasted people, he taught them that even those. who appeared as unworthy outsiders and strangers to evil eyes of certain sophisticated people, could have true faith and receive salvation.

One among those miracles is narrated in today's Gospel. In this incident we see Jesus meeting ten lepers. All the ten individuals were shunned by others because of their origins, homelessness, strange culture, and mainly because of their horrible illness of leprosy. We hear in this Gospel event, even though lepers were, in those days, should stand apart from others, they approached near to Jesus and cried out *Jesus, Master, have pity on us.* Jesus did not chide them but went close to them, had pity on them.

Usually he would touch them and heal such sick people. But in this event we see him immediately sending them to see the religious leaders-priests, who would verify their cure. By this, Jesus wanted to share a strong message to all of us, who hold leadership in different ways and in different lifesituations. His intention was that Christian leaders must do away with their dividing behavior and factor in all their compassionate and just services they do for the sick and the poor.

Plus, he ascertained the same serviceable leaders have to remember always to connect their undertakings to God and his statutes. Moreover, we too find Jesus expecting all those who were benefitted by our Christian leadership, as the single healed Samaritan did, must be led to focus on God and be grateful to him for his marvelous deeds in our midst.

We should remember this admirable message of our Lord in every work we accomplish as leaders of the family, church, community and nation. Otherwise anything we do becomes shear waste, sometimes poisonous and sinful and it would do nothing for the salvation of the beneficiaries and of ourselves too.

Prayer: *God of bountiful mercy and abundant richness, due to the posteffect of our fake superiority-complex, worldly-driven leadership and their product of hateful and evil-oriented attitude, we manytimes forget the ordinary human task and courtesy of appreciating and thanking you and your agents. Strangely enough, your finest gifts, our life and health, our ability to think and act creatively, and our leadership in our lifesituations are often taken for granted. Father God, we are indeed lowly and poor without you. Bless our life and the good gifts which you have bestowed upon us, so that we may always render justice to the afflicted and the destitute. Please make us as your instruments in gathering the needy around your table of salvation. Amen.*

Thursday

God's Kingdom is nowhere than within and around us
(Scriptural Passages: Wis. 7: 22-8: 1; Ps. 118; Lk. 17: 20-25)

Jesus from the start of his public life and ministry knew well many valid questions arising in the hearts of his followers about what they had already heard from their OT Prophets, particularly about the end of human life and of the universe. Almost all the Prophets foretold that the time and occasion of that end would be the Day of the Lord, in which God will pronounce the final judgement of punishing the wicked and rewarding the just. And also that would be the Day, when the glorious kingdom of God would be visible and audible and permanent.

As we hear in today's Gospel, one of those questions was raised to Jesus by the religious teachers of his time only to catch him wrong. But, to their question, 'when the Kingdom of God would come?', Jesus prudently and meaningfully responded: *The coming of the Kingdom of God cannot be observed, and no one will announce, 'Look, here it is,' or 'There it is.' For behold, the Kingdom of God is among you.*

From all his teachings and those of his Apostles, we know what he meant: In his answer, Jesus instructs us not to be preoccupied with the question of *when* the Day of the Lord will come; instead, we should be focused on *how* that Day of God's Kingdom would come. The Big Day of the arrival of God's Kingdom is not to be identified with a particular point of time, as those who try to predict the end of the world on such and such a day.

One more surprising matter Jesus insists is: We should not fix and locate the rule and reign of God to this or that place. Jesus' answer is puzzling but also consoling; he declares: *The kingdom of God is already here among you.* In other words, there is no any singular holiest place where God dwells, reigns and performs his salvific deeds. Through our union with Jesus, God's reign has already begun and established within our hearts. We too already have a foretaste of eternal life. From him we find strength to do what is right and to sense that all life is gift.

Since people were in the past taught and formed to misinterpret and abuse the term 'Kingdom of God', Jesus throughout his life tried, by his words and deeds, to make them clearly understand the true meaning, nature and content of this Kingdom.

The summary of what Jesus preached can be found in today's first reading and the Psalm. Both highlight that the kingdom of God consists of leaders and citizens, who live by the spirit of wisdom, instilled in their hearts and minds and God's words offered in the Scriptures. The most mind-blowing truth is, when the reign of God through

Jesus is established well within us by our cooperation, then we will surely encounter the same God's ruling existence in the whole universe, which had been already started existing from the day of creation. This is the lesson we hear in today's first reading. The reign and kingdom of God has been portrayed in many metaphors such as God's Word, God's Wisdom, God's Spirit, and so on.

This is exactly the Psalmist today sings. He ascertains that the mystery of God's Kingdom is 'God's Presence within us; this amazing Kingdom revealed first in the light of the words of the Lord. This God's word is permanently present within us firm, trustworthy, creative, enlightening and guiding. And to enjoy its helps we need to be simple because only to such meek and humble of heart God's mysteries are revealed.

In God's mysterious ways, the entire creations of God, mainly human creatures, are overwhelmingly endowed with reigning Presence of God, as the Word and as the Wisdom. When Christ came in our midst he reestablished and restored it and influenced us to encounter such inconceivable fact of the Presence of God's Kingdom.

Prayer: *Parental God, ever-living within us, we firmly believe, as Jesus claimed, your Kingdom is in our midst and among us. But we are aware of the fact, that your Triune Presence is in oblivion and hidden, until the Final Day, designed by you, arrives; meanwhile, we have to encounter your presence in disguise within those of us who, like your Son, take up their crosses, their hardships, their bloodshed and Brokenbody in their terminal, chronic illnesses, accidental and permanent disabilities, and much more spiritual sicknesses of sinful habit. Lord, kindly open our spiritual eyes wide to see and our spiritual ears sharp to hear your Son's excruciating outcry in those sufferers. Since our faith is not so strong and matured, we beg you as his Apostles cried to your Son: Lord, Increase our faith. Amen.*

Friday

Let's surrender in faith all our earthly things and affairs
To God our Judge before we meet him in person
(Scriptural Passages: Wis. 13: 1-9; Ps. 19; Lk. 17: 26-37)

Jesus in today's Gospel reveals one of the most inspiring context of our life in this world. When he says, "Where the body is, there also the vultures will gather," he means that until we integrate our visible body with the invisible God, our Creator, we will be pathetically and uselessly wandering in search of that body and its fulfillment in vain. Lord Jesus uses the term 'body', as a metaphor to point out the entire physical dimensions of the whole universe, mainly including our human physicality in all its circumferences.

This is why, today the Book of Wisdom conjures us not to be called by our Creator 'fools', by forgetting the intrinsic connection between the 'body' and God; instead, we should be fondly entitled by him, as his wise children, in appreciating all his creations and thank him every day for the beauty and power of his creative and redemptive interactions, and their fruits; for the gifts of every creature, the ploughing, sowing, reaping, and silent growth while we are sleeping, and for the future needs in earth's safekeeping entrusted to many of us, who are of good will. We are continuously in awe for the good all human beings inherit, for the wonders that astound us, and for the truths that still confound us.

The Psalmist too motivates us today to be of the same attitude, proposed by the Author of the Book of Wisdom. We are called to acknowledge to God with our gratitude and awe, saying: *The heavens declare the glory of God, and the firmament proclaims his handiwork. Day pours out the word to day, and night to night imparts knowledge.*

Most importantly, Jesus advises us in the Gospel to recognize gratefully and appreciate wholeheartedly the greatest love God has demonstrated in sharing his salvation with us through his beloved Son, who has already revealed to us, that the Creator of all wondrous things is our Father in heaven, who has prepared for us a Kingdom that will never end.

And Jesus also forewarns us that our entry into that Kingdom will be preceded by the Last Judgement at the second coming of Christ, the day when the son of Man is revealed. That day will come suddenly. This suddenness of his coming demands that we must be always ready, living a life ever pleasing to God. It is for such spectacular and successful finale of our life we are directed by Jesus to surrender and integrate our wholistic bodily dimension to our Creator.

Prayer: *Dear Lord, make us more and more to surrender our entire earthly life, with its care, concerns, and future, to your mercy and compassion so that the stunning thought of Last Judgement does not make us fearful. Rather, we may completely rely on your bountiful heart, hoping confidently the result of your judgement to us on that Day will be one of mercy, not of condemnation. Kindly bestow us also a bright faith and power to go beyond our creations' beauty and splendor, and find your immense mighty hands and your unending love, so that every day we may turn to you in total abasement. Amen.*

Saturday

God can be overcome only by childlike prayer
(Scriptural Passages: Wis. 18: 14-16,
19: 6-9; Ps. 105; Lk. 18: 1-8)

If there be anything we know well, as disciples of Jesus, and if anything we are quite assured beyond all doubt, it is the fact of 'praying in faith and love' is never spent in vain. In the Bible, particularly in Jesus' sayings, we read so many references about the power of human prayer. However, some merciful and most special blessings and gifts are not given to us except in answer to forceful prayer. In today's Gospel passage Jesus enlightens us about this factual truth; and through his parable he teaches us how to make our prayer powerful and fruitful. He says: If our prayer is to be productive and effective, we should *pray always without becoming weary*. That is to say, 'Pray and appeal to God not just once, but repeatedly as many times as possible until we get it'.

Many of us may be confused about the words we hear today from Jesus, when we remember, it is the same Master who advises us in his Sermon on the Mount: *Do not be like pagans. Your Father knows what you need before you ask him*. While God knows all our needs of the day or moment, valid question arises, why should Jesus order us to pray and plead to God, as the widow did to her judge, for what we need persistently to the extent of annoying him?

However, we should never forget Jesus' Gospel, which puts before us only one condition for our salvation of entering into God's Kingdom. *Be like a child*. The same condition holds good also in any effort we make to attain salvific gifts while we live in this world. As many cultures say: *Only the crying babies receive milk*. As a matter of fact, to make our prayer very productive, it should be an affectionate, filled with confidence and humility based on faith. In the mind of Jesus, our prayer is to be the childlike voice of faith in the Fatherly Love of God, the humble voice of our confidence in him, plus it must be always the manifestation of our affectionate love for him.

Being childlike means, as the Book of Wisdom today teaches, our sincere recognition of God's mightiest power, uncompromising justice, and immense compassion. In order to preserve us, his children unharmed, God designed the entire universe around us serve him flawlessly by the natural laws he instilled in them; surprisingly sometimes, according to his will of assisting us, he also makes all other creatures devoid from their regular natural courses and safely takes us to the right goal for which he leads us. For example, for the sake of his people's liberation to enjoy a prosperous future life of flowing with milk and honey, as the Book reminds us, out of what had before been water, he brought dry land emerging; and a grassy plain out of the mighty water.

Furthermore, following the advice of the Psalmist, with childlike attitude, we should remember the marvels the Lord has done to his people from the beginning of Abraham's close connection with God till this day we are blessed by him through his Son's incarnation. All those seek the Lord should rejoice and glorify God unceasingly. Remembering his holy word of promises, and reminding ourselves constantly that he is the one who can fill us with his prosperity and peace, we must also continue praying for our welfare in this world and the world to come.

Indeed it is very hard for most of us, who live in this more civilized and better rationalized Postmodern Age, to hold on to such childlike faith, hope and surely affectionate love for the heavenly Father. Knowing already our pitiable condition, Jesus has prophesized with an aching and longing heart: 'When the Son of Man comes, will he find faith on earth?'

Prayer: *God, Creative and Redemptive Father of all, we profess sincerely that you have called us through the Gospel of Jesus to possess all your promised glory, prosperity and joy. Lord, we long to be your beloved children; we desire to grow in faith, in love, and in knowledge of you. By your grace keep our faith alive in our life so that when you come to visit us, you may find in us the light of our faith burning brightly. Amen.*

WEEK - 33

Monday

Abiding in Jesus' light, we can heal the interiorly blinded people
(Scriptural Passages: 1 Macc. 1:10-
63; Ps. 119; Lk. 18: 35-43)

Difficulties in life can have one of two effects on us. Either they beat us down or they make us stronger. In the light of Scriptures, we can say, the way those difficulties make us stronger is by fostering within our souls an even greater trust in and dependence upon the mercy of God.

This is what happened in the history of the Israelites, as we hear in today's first reading. Having been sweet-talked by a new Gentile king's team, some of the God's people surrendered to the king's order, and they willingly accepted the way of living of the Gentiles. Ignoring God's law, they began sacrificing to idols and violating the Sabbath. Whereas many in Israel were determined in their hearts not to eat anything unclean; they preferred to die rather than to be defiled with unclean food or to profane the holy covenant.

As the Psalmist sings today, those God-fearing people were apprehended with outrage when they found their own kith and kin forsaking God's Law. They communicated to God in prayer their tensed feelings regarding their neighbors' wickedness and their enemies' oppression. They held repugnance against the apostates who did not keep up to their promise to God. These good-willed people were pleading for only one thing from the Lord that he must bestow 'life' so that they can fulfill faithfully his commands.

Today, Jesus places before us the blind man as a rolemodel in handling our life's difficulties, as those good-willed people did in earlier time. That blind man, being a beggar and homeless, was generally treated by the public very poorly as if he were no good and a sinner. Sadly, when he began to call out for mercy from Jesus, those around him unsympathetically ordered him to be quiet.

Yet, that needy man never bothered about the public's oppression and ridicule, rather, kept calling out to Jesus all the more loudly: *Son of David, have mercy on me!* We see him never discouraged; he persisted in his seeking and begging for the precious gift of sight. Demonstrating his strong faith and hope in Jesus, he pleaded to Jesus: *Lord, let me see again.* Jesus miraculously healed his blindness.

One more lesson we get from this visually-impaired man: After receiving back the gift of his sight, he began to follow Jesus, giving glory to God. His life now had a new focus. He could see his wife and children, his friends and surroundings, as treasured gifts.

Undoubtedly like this blind man, all of us are overwhelmed in daily life with many ailments and hardships, which make us very stressful and very difficult to deal with. Should we give in to the struggle and then retreat into a hole of self-pity? On the contrary, the Lord instructs us to hold on to our Christian faith, exactly like the healed man, to whom he said: *Have sight; your faith has saved you.* When we feel oppressed, discouraged, frustrated, misunderstood, or the like, we need to use this as an opportunity to turn to Jesus with even greater passion and courage calling upon His mercy.

Prayer: *God, the Light dividing night from day, have pity on us and through your Son, kindly bestow wholistic healing to us in body and spirit. Open our inner eyes to see your healing presence in our needs, weaknesses and struggles. Help us to turn to you with even more passion all the more in times of distress and frustration in life, so that as the healed man, in the Gospel, continued to follow your Son praising you, we too may glorify you round the clock. Amen.*

Tuesday

Faith in Jesus enables us to live and die joyfully and victoriously
(Scriptural Passages: 2 Macc. 6: 18-31; Ps. 3; Lk. 19:1-10)

Today's Gospel brings before us Zacchaeus, who was shamed as a public sinner. He plainly depicts how we have been weak in the past as sinners before God, as well as strong as winners in economic, social and religiously in search of God. Like Zacchaeus, all of us may be accomplished materially, physically and socially the most we could; also like him we may be firmly attached to our religion and its teachings in search of the invisible, holy and heavenly God through his Son and his Church. We got also his forgiveness many times and purified ourselves by hosting his Son in the poor and the needy with our available treasure, talent and time. Unquestionably many times we heard him blessing us with his material and spiritual gifts saying to us as Jesus blessed Zacchaeus:

Today salvation has come to this house. This is how we are what we are today.

In the first reading we hear about Eleazar who was a person of advanced age and noble appearance and ended his life victoriously. According to the Bible, he faced his death due to his religious fidelity. But the way he met such death is amazing and breathtaking. Primarily, he had very clear understanding of the glory and honor of his old age bestowed by God; and therefore he never allowed anything to bring shame and dishonor to his long life.

Secondly he considered the nobility of his old age consisted in recognizing fully the sovereignty of God who holds every bit of his life in his hands. Hence he declared: *Since the Lord in his holy knowledge knows full well all about my beginning and end; I shall never, whether alive or dead, escape the hands of the Almighty. Therefore, by manfully giving up my life now, I will prove myself worthy of my old age.*

Finally because of such faithful adherence to God and his commandments, he felt assured he would leave behind in his death a shining example to his young ones; a model of courage and an unforgettable example of virtue, not only for the young but also for the whole nation. Due to such conviction he uttered his final words: *I am not only enduring terrible pain in my body from this scourging, but also suffering it with joy in my soul because of my devotion to him.*

One thing is certain. These good and venerable souls, being humans, like the Psalmist, would have encountered lots of inner and outer sufferings. They too, like the Psalmist, would have cried aloud to their God of goodness to help them in their frailty, saying: *Lord, how many are my adversaries! Many rise up against me! Many are saying of me, There is no salvation for him in God.* At the same time they too would have expressed their unrelenting hope, as the Psalmist does: *But Lord, you are my shield; my glory, you lift up my head!* And this is how those elderly persons teach us how to live and die in this world.

Prayer: *God of Goodness and Gentleness, placing before us those two admirable personalities, you declare to us today that we are blessed in belonging to the group of such noble men and women. Your Son also prompts us to do the best we can to be connected to you. Being fully aware of our sufferings and trials to be faced in this life, we entreat you to give us your wisdom and strength so that, not only we may experience in this world the inner joy as the Eleazar and Zacchaeus possessed, but also we may inherit your complete joy eternally. Amen.*

Wednesday

*Chosen by Jesus, we have no other choice
except bearing choicest fruits
(Scriptural Passages: 2 Macc. 7: 1, 20-
31; Ps. 17; Lk. 19:11-28)*

In today's Gospel Acclamation Church makes us recite the Jesus' words, which he uttered to us, as our benevolent Master: *I chose you from the world, to go and bear fruit that will last.* It's a command of love from him and one he takes seriously. He chose us as his disciples for one magnificent purpose and that is: Willingly accepting from him all his gifts, we are directed by him to use them faithfully as effective instruments in our efforts of building up his Kingdom of his Gospel values. Consequently despite our limited and restricted lifesituation, if we obey his order we will reap fruits of great honor and joy that will last.

Nonetheless, he utters the most disturbing words at the end of today's Gospel: *To everyone who has, more will be given, but from the one who has not, even what he has will be taken away.* Although he admires, appreciates, and rewards copiously all those who make the maximum use of the divine gifts for right purpose of developing and widening God's Kingdom, he sadly curses, rebukes those who are careless in their using God's gifts out of their self-gratifying, twisted attitude about their Giver and his gifts; moreover, he punishes them by snatching those gifts from them and giving them to his good and faithful servants.

While we are so much troubled by this plain admonition of Jesus, the Spirit today introduces to us the Psalmist and an honorable Jewish family of Maccabees from Old Testament, portraying their superb mindset and behavior in adhering to the divine guidance as that of Jesus.

The most admirable person in that family is the mother who witnessed her seven sons being murdered in a single day. Plus, being stirred by noble spirit, she encouraged them to stand by God's Law, telling them: *It was not I who gave you the breath of life, nor was it I who set in order the elements of which each of you is composed. It is the Creator who did everything for you; he, in his mercy, will give you back both breath and life, because you now disregard yourselves for the sake of his law.* All her sons truly energized by her words as they were at the edge of death and met it willingly and courageously.

Everyone in the family of Maccabees had their heartbeats singing hopefully within them the words of the Psalmist we recite today: *Lord, when your glory appears, my joy will be full. My steps have been steadfast in your paths, my feet have not faltered. Keep me as the apple of your eye; hide me in the shadow of your wings. But I in justice shall behold your face; on waking, I shall be content in your presence.*

It is indeed hard for us to serve God wholeheartedly and to commit faithfully to building up his kingdom within ourselves as well as around us. However let us do it at least because it is a duty. Also it is a remarkable duty for which God will ultimately hold each of us accountable and when we stand before the Divine Judge's Throne we will be blessed with hearing the most extraordinary words from him: *'Well done, good servant! You have been faithful in this very small matter.* And he will surely give us a seat at his right hand with his Son.

Prayer: *Lord, Destiny of our life, may we never waste the grace you have given us. Help us to always work diligently for the up-building of your divine kingdom. And help us to see it as a source of joy and peace in this world; and we too firmly believe and hope when you come in your glory to judge us, our joy and peace will be true and complete. Amen.*

Thursday

End of our life is Eternal Rest; and way to that end is peace-driven life
(Scriptural Passages: 1 Macc. 2: 15-
29; Ps. 50; Lk. 19: 41-44)

In today's Responsorial Psalm with King David we recited as its response: *To the upright I will show the saving power of God.* Now who are those upright? David sings about the way of the upright that enables them to encounter their fulfilling salvation. According to him, these upright people begin their lifejourney through God's way with God's values and despite the hurdles they face, they win all of them and finally they achieve their goal.

However we know how most of us behave in this journey; either we lose sight of the goal or frustrated and weary to battel with hurdles or even stonyhearted not listening the way God directs us to walk through. Surely our loving Father in heaven is sad about it. And so his Son Jesus. That is what we hear in today's Gospel. Jesus knew well what is wrong with our life that is still peaceless and restless. He knew the whole human race would be misbehaving like his own Jewish brethren not walking through God's peaceful way of living.

As we hear in today's first reading, due to human fake pride, fake self-image and arrogance, even those orthodox Jewish people like Mattathias were warmongers as they took pride in killing those people who downgraded their Jewish culture and religion. Such human pathetic issue is never-ending. And this is why true peace has not settled in humanity. *Jesus knew them all, and did not need anyone to testify about human nature. He himself understood it well.*

Jesus from his conception through his entire life lived and preached only one message about the true way to attain our ultimate goal. He underlined the way of peace is alone that takes us to encounter God's salvation in this world and the world to come. However, God's people as we are, we don't listen to him nor do we follow him. Like his own people in the past, we too misbehave. Therefore Jesus wept and still weeping not only for our disobedience and hardheadedness; but also for the evils we will be crushed with as an inevitable consequence.

Today he invites us once again, to sit down with him and listen carefully what he instructs regarding how to be peaceful and become peacemakers. And we hear him say repeatedly: 'If today you hear his voice, harden not your hearts'.

Prayer: *Lord, God of Peace and Justice, we are your faithful ones, gathered as Church in this world, to witness your genuine peace through the way of justice. We are reminded today how your Son was lamenting in tears on the ignorance* and disobedience of your chosen ones in the past to your true way of peace. We feel sorry that most of us become deaf to your guidelines in maintaining your peace. As we don't want to meet the disasters, prophesied by your Son, we beg you to send your Spirit of wisdom so that we can adhere to the way of authentic peace and share it with our fellowhumans. Amen.

Friday

*Our upgraded zeal for God's Presence
can protect his earthly dwellings*
(Scriptural Passages: 1 Macc. 4: 36-
59; 1 Chro. 29; Lk. 19:45-48)

In the First Reading we see God's people, on the anniversary of the day on which the Gentiles, so-called their adversaries, had defiled their temple but later crushed in defeat, they purified the sanctuary and reconsecrated and rededicated it with songs, sung with harps, flutes, and cymbals. Indeed, it is God who had been trying his best to accomplish such purification of his sinful children by his loving words through Prophets, and by permitting trials and sufferings through their enemies. We see such incredible action of God in today's OT passage in making the Maccabees to crush the enemies of his people, in order to purify the desecrated sanctuary of his Temple and to reconsecrate it.

Surprisingly, God, who prefers sacrifice of contrite and broken heart of humans, better than their ritual sacrifices, has been very particular in maintaining the purity and sacredness of his Temple, where he had declared he was present in glory. This is why, we hear, from the passage of first Book of Chronicle that we recite as today's responsorial Psalm, the prayerful words of the Israelites, when they came in to the Temple, professed about their faith in the almighty powerful presence of God in their midst. They loudly declared: *We praise your glorious name, O mighty God. Yours, O Lord, are grandeur and power, majesty, splendor, and glory. For all in heaven and on earth is yours. You have dominion over all, In your hand are power and might; it is yours to give grandeur and strength to all.* Breathtakingly, some of them, like Jesus of Nazareth, held the zeal for God and his House burning within them.

As Jesus was burnt with that same zeal for God's House, in today's Gospel we find him entering the temple area and proceeded to drive out those who were desecrating God's sacred dwelling through their secular marketing of selling and buying things. We know well from the Gospels Jesus' primary ministry was to purify and heal his people both in their body and spirit. That is what his Father called him to do. But unfortunately, when Jesus came into this world, not only he found God's own people were desecrating the Sacred Temple, but also he foresaw they would do the same to his Body, the true dwelling Place of God. Hence, as we hear in the Gospel, he proceeded to drive out those who were degrading God's dwelling place by making use of it as a commercial environment, and said: *It is written, my house shall be a house of prayer, but you have made it a den of thieves.*

History portrays all the religious communities of the world, have been often celebrating the defeats of their enemies and the rededication of their cultural "altars" to their beliefs and purposes. They esteem they celebrate their power and strength in places they deem holy. But are Christians somehow different? Certainly. As Jesus claimed if we are faithful sheep of Jesus, our Good Shepherd, we will hear his voice. Our Lord was zealous of his Father.

So he also calls us to be so; but to be zealous of what? Primarily, he advises us to recognize wholeheartedly *the sovereignty of God over all power and might and grandeur in this world. And, riches and honor come from God and are given to all, not just a chosen few.*

Also, very importantly he expects us to go deeper into the mind of Christ, who drove out the defilers of God's Temple. As all the Gospel Writers underline, he did such violence-like deed to point out how much more the significance, beauty and greatness of his own three Bodies: One his Physical Body which he got from his Mother; two, his mystical Body the Church which is made of both him as the Head and we, as his members; three, the Body of each one of us about which he declared: *The Kingdom of God is within you*; and what all his Apostles underscored, *you are the Temple of God's Spirit.*

Prayer: *God of purity and holiness, we are aware of your perennial action purifying all the places of your Presence in this world. You have been trying your best to accomplish such purification of your sinful children by your loving words through your agents, and by their trials and sufferings and bloodshed. While so many of our fellowhumans disfigure and degrade your dwellings- your Church, the Body of Christ and your physical temples, our own bodies, either you destroy them with your powerful justice or convert them with your amazing mercy, and take them into your abode and make them your effective witnesses to your Plan of salvation. Help us, Father, to acquire the same zeal of your Son for your Dwellings, so that we can do the best we can in protecting, and safeguarding your Houses from the clutches of evils. Amen.*

Saturday

Those, who die every day a bit to sin, won't
certainly fear to meet final death
(Scriptural Passages: 1 Macc. 6: 1-13; Ps. 9; Lk. 20: 27-40)

Fear of death or of dying is quite common, and most people fear death to varying degrees. To what extent that fear occurs and what it pertains to specifically varies from one person to another. While some fear is healthy because it makes them more cautious, some people may also have an unhealthy fear of dying. In fact death is inevitable for living creatures and so with us too. As Benjamin Franklin would say in a funny way, '*In this world nothing can be said to be certain, except death and taxes*'. The act of death is neutral but it takes its various adjectives and qualities according to an individual person considers and makes it. So it is no surprise that death-related worries sometimes take us by storm.

As for us, being sincerely committed to our Master's directives and instructions, death is a breakthrough, an interval, a comma, the last but one chapter of human life by which our life is changed not taken away. In today's Gospel Jesus is very clear in his emphasis: First, it is foolishness to debate, to research about the afterlife by comparing and contrasting it to present life. God underlines in the Bible our physical body was made with clay; and therefore its end is dust unto dust, ashes into ashes. However, pointing out to the Prophetic words Jesus insists our faithful spirit will live forever because since *heavenly Father is not God of the dead, but of the living, for to him all are alive.* Jesus adds one more important reference to the life after death for us. If those of us are faithful to God till the end, Jesus prophesizes: *They can no longer die, for they are like angels; and they are the children of God because they are the ones who will rise.*

This sort of Jesus' Gospel Values on human life's birth and death, inspire many fellowhumans to be firm in their faith and hope in Jesus the truthful Way to everlasting Life. And they never fail to sing joyfully in their inner spirit, as we hear from the Psalmist today: *I will give thanks to you, Lord, with all my heart; I will declare all your wondrous deeds. I will be glad and exult in you; I will sing praise to your name, Most High.*

We should in no way be tensed with undue anxiety and fear about death. Such pathetic feelings belong only to those people who lead their life in a twisted and perverted way as we read in today's first reading about King Antiochus, who recalled in his deathbed all the evil he had done in his short tenure of leadership; he was struck with fear and very much shaken; sick with grief because all his designs had failed, he remained in bed many days, overwhelmed with sorrow, for he knew he was going to die. He died lamenting, 'I am perishing of deep grief.'

If we read attentively this king's lamentation before death, we would find the reality of life most of us lead. Like him, we would remember surely the good things we had done; but also we would be pricked by remembering clearly the wrong things we have done and the good things we had omitted. We can assure ourselves from the narration of this king's death, that while our physical eyes' brightness slowly diminishing, our inner eyes would be brightened with splendid light of God and see through in an instant our entire life's good and bad about which we had been blindfolded.

Prayer: *God of glory and power, joining with Jesus we fully accept we are made from the clay and at death, we will be dust unto dust; at the same time we also warmly accept his* *affirmation, that since you, our Creator, are the God of the living, and you infused within us at our conception your undying spirit, we would be living forever with you after our death. Grant we pray that we may persevere in our walk with Jesus so that in our final moments we may be not tensed but rejoice in the hope that we are going to be angels and as children of God we will be joyfully playing in his heavenly Mansion. Amen.*

WEEK - 34

Monday

Come what may, Christian nobility is to
stick definitely to Jesus' values
(Scriptural Passages: Dan. 1: 1-6, 8-20; Dan. 3; Lk. 21: 1-4)

The single truth, emphatically stressed by God's words today is: *With the grace of God, our human honesty and loyalty to him and his values will sustain us through life.*

We hear in today's first reading about how Daniel and his three companions had a critical choice to make as they had started their youthful life with an ambition of better future. These young men were already in birth blessed by the Creator without any defect, handsome, intelligent and wise, quick to learn, and prudent in judgment. As every human confronts in climbing up the ladder of life, these youngsters' peaceful existence was disrupted, especially they were led to make some compromises in their religious observances.

In this situation, besides being grateful to their Creator for all the gifts he had granted them, as ambitious youth, they were willing to adapt themselves to current and strange lifesituation; they learned the new language and Babylonian customs, but as loyal Jews, they never compromised their religious faith. They were seriously tested by King's team to find out how, after eating their traditional vegetarian food and drinking normal water for ten days as they demanded, they look in comparison with the other young men who eat from the royal table. Eventually their integrity and courage made them admired and loved by even pagans. And their loyalty to the will of God brought its own reward.

As the sincerity and fidelity of those youngsters were appreciated by God, we hear in today's Gospel a widow being praised by Jesus for dropping her last two copper coins into the Temple's collection box. Jesus admires at her generous giving all she could afford, and highlights that 'she gave more than the wealthiest donor'. Her integrity and loyalty to God is appreciated by Jesus.

During our precious days of earthly life, during which we are dutifully staying awake and waiting for the Lord's coming for bestowing his full salvation to us, we are exhorted by the Lord to behave like Daniel and his friends and also like the poor widow of the Gospel. We are to elevate our mind and heart like those young men, singing their canticle which we recited as responsorial Psalm, in praising and glorifying our God every moment of our life: 'Blessed are you, O Lord, the God of our fathers, praiseworthy and exalted above all forever; And blessed is your holy and glorious name. Blessed are you Lord who are enthroned above in the firmament of heaven, and look intensely into the depths of the universe. You be praiseworthy and exalted above all for all ages'.

Prayer: *Benevolent God, you invite us today to be ready when your Spirit inspires us to go beyond our comfort zone, so as to bond with Jesus who gave himself totally on the cross. You too expects from us the same fidelity and honesty even in our trials of*

413

life, as those ambitious young ones and the poor widow. Grant us Lord your abundant grace to let not those life's struggles, destroy our Christian spirit, rather to take the sufferings from your hands as the tools of actually purifying us to become worthy of reaching our heavenly kingdom. Amen.

Tuesday

Remaining faithful to God until death,
we will be given the crown of life
(Scriptural Passages: Dan. 2: 31-45; Dan. 3; Lk. 21: 5-11)

Once again making us to sing Daniel's canticle as today's responsorial Psalm, the Spirit of God enthuses us to remain faithful to God until death and we will be granted the crown of heavenly life. Besides, we should believe that God holds solely the dominion and strength, power and glory over all creations. This is the message that today's readings share with us.

In the first reading we hear Prophet Daniel interpreting the king's dream of some statue being struck down and shattered into pieces. He too includes in it the most positive point of the dream, namely the stone that is hewn from the mountain represents a 'kingdom', which God would setup after breaking into pieces all other kingdoms of bronze, clay, silver, gold or even iron. Daniel prophesied: *In the lifetime of those kings the God of heaven will set up a kingdom that shall never be destroyed or delivered up to another people; rather, it shall break in pieces all these kingdoms and put an end to them, and it shall stand forever.*

When we go deeper into the reading, we notice that God wants to share with us today some amazing truths about our life that may hurt our fake-self. God confirms to us about his sovereignty and the vulnerability of humanity. Mainly, in the interpretation of the King's dream, the Prophet uses the term 'God's Kingdom' to mean God's rule and regime. *In the lifetime of those kings the God of heaven will set up a kingdom that shall never be destroyed or delivered up to another people; rather, it shall break in pieces all these kingdoms and put an end to them, and it shall stand forever.* Through this prophecy, Daniel proclaimed the sole supremacy of God over his creatures, especially over the humans and their undertakings-in whatever way they would have completed, as religious monuments, social systems, global enterprises, and scientific inventions and so on.

Jesus too in today's Gospel thoughtfully refers to this fact. According to him, the Temple which was the pride of Jewish people of his time adorned with costly stones and votive offerings, would be completely destroyed: *"All that you see here–the days will come when there will not be left a stone upon another stone that will not be thrown down."*

Besides, all creations are not eternal at all; as the Bible says, they are all like the clouds or grasses that pass by, disappear, and fade away. There is no earthly permanence for them, including humans. We are vulnerable not only to this earthly life but also we are capable of paving the way for its destruction. This is well confirmed by Jesus' prophecies about the insurrections, infights, and wars and so on.

While accepting such bitter truths, God offers us also some sweet hopeful instruction today. He expects us to remember what the Lord Jesus said about the 'kingdom of God'. He was always reminding us *the kingdom of God is not anywhere; it is in our midst; among us; within us and within our reach.* Our relationship with him a spiritual kingdom.

We have to build it up strongly by as Jesus instructed 'remaining faithful until death.'

Prayer: *Lord, the King of all kings, you attest that any kind of human and earthly power-be it kingly, queenly or manly and womanly, comes only from you, our Creator and the King of heaven and earth. Lord, we may dream about ourselves as very large and exceedingly bright statues; or made of pure iron, gold, silver and bronze. But all that we dream about ourselves, our achievements and our personal enterprises would be crumbled instantly as we are buried or cremated. We pray humbly to grant us your grace to abide by your guidance, given through Jesus and Prophets, so that the Kingdom, which is established in us by you and restored by your Son, may never be destroyed by our selfish and unfaithful deeds until we reach our ultimate destiny of your eternal Kingdom. Amen.*

Wednesday

*Between our birth and death God is the
only help for our fruitful survival*
(Scriptural Passages: Dan. 5: 1-28; Dan. 3; Lk. 21: 12-19)

During an imminent threat about the downhill or failure in our business or in any other efforts, I am sure some of us would have heard or said the words: *The hand writing is on the wall.* That is what, as we hear in today's OT reading, the King Belshazzar literally saw the fingers of a human hand appeared, writing three unknown words on the plaster of the wall in his palace. May be, he got that vision when he was under influence. But one thing was sure. As Prophet Daniel interpreted, it was all about the king's life of supreme power that was to be going down the hill.

The king, who invited Daniel to interpret those words he saw on the wall, was the one who desecrated the Temple; he was the one who praised handmade idols; but he didn't move an inch in his life to glorify God in whose hands the king's breath and the course of his life was. Daniel through his prophetical interpretation made the king come to terms with his rebellious and abominable deeds done against the true God and straightforwardly the Prophet prophesied to the king's face how his arrogant power and leadership would come to destruction.

Going down and down is not exceptional only to the king; whether we like or not, every one of us at one time or another would experience such downhills in our life. Our Master Jesus underwent them; and he knew we too will not be exempted. Hence in today's Gospel, he advises: *By your perseverance you will secure your lives.* In this Gospel verse, the Greek word *hypomoné* is used to mean patience or endurance or consistency and dependability.

In this perseverance the Spirit of the Lord through Daniel's canticle, exhorts us to go on glorifying God in every step we take to climb up the ladder of our life's progress. Never we should forget the total sovereignty of our Creator and also his unending benevolence toward us. He it is who in our conception shared with us his image and likeness which generates from within us the power to control the evils pertaining to the society, the wisdom to act prudently in our relationship and leadership and above all, the spiritual adherence to worship the God and God alone.

There are some valid reasons for such patient and godly endurance. As Gospel Acclamation, we hear Jesus indicating a valid reason: *Remain faithful until death, and I will give you the crown of life.* And he also exhorts us that we need to live and endure all hardships patiently as the seed in the field, which bears fruit only "through patience". Paul echoing the same statement of Jesus, offers a detailed reason in one of his Letters, *affliction produces patience, and patience produces character, and character produces hope.*

Prayer: *Father in heaven and Ruler of the Universe, we pledge always stay loyal to you, particularly in our testing times. However, as we lack in the conviction that sooner or later you will justify us, we request you to assist us with your spiritual stamina in patiently endure all our sufferings in faith, hope and charity for your sake, that will enable us to secure not only our personal life but also the lives of all our loved ones in this earthly journey toward our blissful life. Amen.*

Thursday

Holding on to Godly Power we can stand
erect in every life's disaster
(Scriptural Passages: Dan. 6: 12-28; Da. 3; Lk. 21: 20-28)

Today as Responsorial Psalm we recite once more the prayer of praise from the Book of Daniel. In this prayer Daniel invites, not only his soul to praise and glorify God, but also all creations to join him in that prayer of praise, singing: *Give glory and eternal praise to God and exalt him above all forever.* We find here two important spiritual attitudes of Daniel: First, he attests to God that he is one with all creatures of God; that is, Daniel is just one among all the creations, a typical creature made by the same Creator out of clay.

Secondly, Daniel confirms that he has the responsibility to invite and lead them all to perform the sacrifice of praise and thanksgiving, since he was entrusted such power over them. On the sixth day of creation after creating human beings in his image and after his likeness, God blessed them and said to them: *Be fertile and multiply; fill the earth and subdue it. Have dominion over the fish of the sea, the birds of the air, and all the living things that crawl on the earth.* Thus, the Prophet confesses he is both a leader as well as an ordinary creature-made of clay.

The other readings of today also emphasize that those twofold attitudes are expected from all the children of God, especially from the disciples of Jesus. In the event narrated in the first reading we see two persons Prophet Daniel and King Darius contesting each other, being supported by two kinds of power. On one side, Darius is totally depending on his own human power as king, who daringly named himself as god and totally concerned about his fake self-image and glory and as its natural endresult, he becomes a cruel, inhuman, and immoral personage.

On the other side, Daniel is a young man who wholeheartedly depends on the power of his God. We see him very faithful to his God and his religious rituals that were available in his time. He was found communicating with God in ceaselessly praying and pleading before him. We know he accepted all happenings in his life were God's design such as that he and some of his friends had to be serving in the court of pagan kings like Darius.

The interesting phenomenon occurring in this tug of war is while as usual, the political, fanatic and self-serving attitude and behavior of Darius failed, because of totally trusting in his God's Power and Love, Daniel won and was delivered unhurt from the mouth of lion. Also, we see Darius, as any earthly politician and power-hungry megalomaniac would do, applied his usual diplomacy of regretting for his mistake but we can be sure within few minutes he would act more cruel and inhuman. On the contrary, we would see Prophet Daniel always stood without changing, lifting his heads and hands to High and be with his God till his death.

Exactly this winning quality of Daniel's life is what Jesus today asks us to possess. In today's Gospel he portrays the future Big-Bang events happening in our lives as his disciples. His main advice is, *don't be agitated; my Father and I together with the Holy Spirit be with you and never we leave you alone and orphans during those disasters, calamities, big-bang events'. He encourages us also with a hopeful promise, 'not a hair on your head will be destroyed.*

Prayer: *God of our safety and security, Your Son exhorts us that by our perseverance we will secure our lives. On the Day of your Son's coming, when the unthinkable signs begin to happen, not only he cautions us to be unduly anxious and fearful because such state of mind may take us to doing perverted actions but also he expects us to stand erect and raise our heads by fully hoping that our redemption would be at hand. Kindly offer us your favorable and redemptive aid, so that we may be qualified to see face to face you enthroned together with your Son and also we may be lavished with Godly peace and joy with no limit and no end. Amen.*

Friday

*The light shines in the darkness and
the darkness never puts it out*
(Scriptural Passages: Dan. 7: 2-14; Dan. 3; Lk. 21: 29-33)

In world history we hear and read millions of people's sharing how they faced their life's dark days and gloomy nights. During those hard times if they come across even a tiny little light around them or far away from them, they immediately rose up to walk smilingly; because they were liberated from any despair. For example, St. Francis of Assisi was delivered from his despair and depression, after reading an invitational word of Jesus in the Gospel: *If you wish to be perfect, go, sell what you have and give to the poor, and you will have treasure in heaven. Then come, follow me.*

In today's Gospel, Jesus ascertains the effectiveness of God's Words, saying: *Heaven and earth will pass away, but my words will not pass away.* The Word of God may at times seem unattractive, even lifeless, like a fig tree in winter. But as the same tree bursts forth into bloom with the first signs of spring, so the Word, which is always vibrantly alive, can burst giving enlightenment to a believer when he or she least expects. The Word of God will endure in its purpose. Our cultures may change; our systems may disappear; our relationships with humans and worldly things will fade and vanish. But nothing had, in the past and in the future, would affect God's Word.

Through his vibrant words God enables us with positive and inspiring message to see our self within us and our neighbors outside of us. It would be like Prophet Daniel who got an enlightening bright vision at night. He narrates about it: *One like a son of man coming, on the clouds of heaven; When he reached the Ancient One and was presented before him, He received dominion, glory, and kingship; nations and peoples of every language serve him. His dominion is an everlasting dominion that shall not be taken away, his kingship shall not be destroyed.*

As he interpreted that vision, the Church invites us to believe that the Son of man, the Prophet saw in his vision, was none other than our Lord Jesus Christ, the Messiah for whom the Prophet, together with his fellow-Jews, was earnestly waiting. Jesus in the Gospels attests also it is reference to him. With this conviction, from that moment on Daniel was continuously singing the classical canticle of glory and praise to God, that we recite today from his Book. *God comes on the clouds of heaven; with his dominion he rules the universe; his domain is an everlasting one that shall not be taken away, his kingship shall not be destroyed.*

Furthermore God's message is enlivening our inner spirit, which sometimes is so desperately craving for hope-filled thoughts, as Jesus assures us today: *The God's Kingdom you long for, is already near; and among you.* In addition, he advises us as a Parent and Lover would do when we feel lethargic and depressed: *Therefore stand erect and raise your heads because your redemption is at hand.*

Prayer: *God of Supremacy and Sovereignty, we are indeed grateful to you for one thing that your awesome grace-filled Word, though it changed even millions of natural, physical, social elements around us, never annihilated any one of your obedient children; rather, your Word indeed changed our wicked ways by inserting into our inner spirit a stunning paradigmshift and converted us and enhanced our entire life. Since sometimes we are prone to be under winter-weather of hopelessness and despair, we earnestly ask you to share the warmth of your Holy Spirit so that we can easily sprout and grow like green trees and bear good fruits of life-saving and life-sharing with our neighbors. Amen.*

Saturday

Today is the only day to make our tomorrow
the beautiful and fruitful one
(Scriptural Passages: Dan. 7: 15-27; Dan. 3; Lk. 21: 34-36)

In today's responsorial Psalm we recite the final verses of the Daniel's lengthy canticle of glory and praise to

God. After inviting all creations of the universe, as the summit, Daniel in his canticle invites sons of men, Israel, the chosen people, priests who were anointed, all other human servants of the Lord and the spirits and souls of the just and virtuous, to join him in giving the glory and praise that is due to God.

The first reading today, though it brings before us a sort of weird vision of Daniel, it refers to the ultimate end of the 'wickedness' of humans who totally forget to acknowledge his glory and power as good-willed people like Daniel hold. This has been the cause of disorderliness and conflicts and many other social evils found in this world. Also, reference is made by this vision to the final victory of the 'Goodness' that governs the heart and mind of the lowly and good-willed people. After defeating the wicked powers by final and absolute destruction through an unprecedented terrible bloody war, the kingship and dominion and majesty of all the kingdoms under the heavens shall be given to the holy people of the Most High, whose Kingdom shall be everlasting: all dominions shall serve and obey him.

We find in today's Gospel Jesus' words of caution and guidance to his disciples regarding that final hour of the world. He asks us not to be drowsy and sleepwalking under the influence of carousing and drunkenness and the overanxieties of daily life. Regrettably most of us fall prey to such excess of evil, the Lord points out today, with such regularity that we lose sight of what is good and right and holy. Additionally there are good many of us, as our Lord refers to, who may not be under influence much, but we become drained by hearing, seeing and reading daily about the persistent oppression and human suffering around our neighborhood and globally.

Positively Jesus exhorts that we should be vigilant at all times; and that too, not passively being still, but heartily praying to our Father so that we have sufficient strength to escape the tribulations that are imminent and to stand before the Son of the Living God, the Holy Judge and King.

We don't know when and where our Lord will appear before us and take up to his Abode to give judgement to us whether we are to be blessed or to be punished. Yet it is in this duration of waiting for the Lord, he expects us to pray ceaselessly, keeping his words burning in our inner spirit. This prayerful exercise will assist us to encounter and acknowledge God's will and his love, and uplift us to adore the King of kings in glorious praises and thanks.

Prayer: *Almighty God, in whom created things all come to rest, we sincerely thank you for permitting us to come to the final day of this Liturgical Year. As tomorrow is the beginning of advent, a season to strengthen our intimate relationship with Jesus our Judge and prepare for his Comings in our midst. Together with your Son's warnings about his Second Coming, today we are strengthened by the hopeful promise he shared with us that we will have a just and compassionate Judge. Grant us, Father, your Holy Spirit's power and wisdom so that we may put all our anxieties in your loving hands and we may focus on preparing for your Son's coming and appreciate the warmth of Divine Love. Amen.*

Author's Other Books

- ❖ **SONday SONrise**: Sunday Homilies for three years Readings
- ❖ **Daily Dose for Christian Survival**: Daily Scriptural meditations
- ❖ **Prayerfully Yours**: Quality-Prayer for Quality-Life
- ❖ **Catholic Christian Spirituality**: A Guide for beginners
- ❖ **My Religion-Reel or Real**: True Assessment on Catholic Faith-Journey
- ❖ **Hilltop Meditations -vol. I**: Sunday Homilies for two years Readings
- ❖ **Hilltop Meditations-vol. II**: Sunday Homilies for third year Readings
- ❖ **Blessed the Merciful**: The CHESED-Oriented Christian Life
- ❖ **Ministry in Tears**: International Priests' Missionary Life & Ministry
- ❖ **Discipled Leadership**: The nuts/bolts of being successful parish leader
- ❖ **Living Faith Daily**: Leading life in Jesus' Way of Spirit & Truth
- ❖ **The Fire-tried Golden Heartbeats of Goldenagers**

- ❖ **ON THIS DAY: Food for Spiritual Hunger-Vol. I:** Scriptural Reflections for Advent, Christmas, Lent and Easter weekdays
- ❖ **ON THIS DAY: Food for Spiritual Hunger-Vol. III:** Scriptural Reflections for weekdays of Ordinary Time-Cycle 2